Learning Conversational Indonesian

# INDONESIAN
## FOR BEGINNERS

Katherine Davidsen & Yusep Cuandani

**TUTTLE** Publishing

Tokyo | Rutland, Vermont | Singapore

# Contents

**How to Download the Audio Recordings and Answer Key for this Book.**

1. Check your Internet connection.
2. Type the URL below into your web browser.

   https://www.tuttlepublishing.com/Indonesian-for-Beginners

   For support email us at info@tuttlepublishing.com

# Selamat Datang! Welcome!

Welcome to the Indonesian language, people, culture and nation! In this course you will learn not only how to understand, speak, read, and write basic Indonesian, but you will also study important aspects of Indonesia's amazingly diverse culture, as well as its people and its 17,000 islands. This course aims to provide access to understanding the language and culture, applying it in a way that is relevant and meaningful, as well as appropriate, to the learner. At the same time, the learner will be challenged to take risks, use prior knowledge and understand that communication takes many forms, both spoken and written.

## Background to the language

Indonesian is a modern language, being a contemporary variety of Malay that came into being after Indonesian independence from the Dutch in 1945. Historically, Malay had been the lingua franca of the Indonesian archipelago (sometimes called Nusantara, literally "the islands between"), from pre-colonial times onward to when European explorers and colonizing powers such as the Portuguese and Dutch arrived. Malay continues to be one of Indonesia's major regional languages (along with Javanese and Sundanese), and is also spoken in Malaysia (as **Bahasa Malaysia**), Singapore and Brunei.

Indonesian was chosen as the national language not only for its ubiquity around the archipelago, but also as it does not have hierarchical speech levels (as do Javanese and Sundanese), and was thus thought to be more egalitarian. Like English, it has both been influenced by and borrowed from a range of other languages: basic everyday words like **sekolah** ("school") and **bendera** ("flag") are originally from Portuguese; technical words relating to vehicles and machinery are often of Dutch origin, such as **bensin** ("petrol") or **pabrik** ("factory"), while the most recent borrowings tend to be from English (**media sosial** or **medsos** for "social media"; **paket** for "packet"; **asimilasi** for "assimilation"). There are also neologisms from Sanskrit, a reminder of Indonesia's Hindu past, such as **karyawisata** ("school trip") and **tunawisma** ("homeless"), borrowings from Hokkien Chinese (especially foods) and a great deal of input from Arabic, as the holy language of Islam, the region's dominant religion. Add to this influence from regional languages, both in vocabulary and structure, and you will begin to appreciate the richness of Indonesian.

As a national language, Indonesian is known as **Bahasa Indonesia** (please avoid the foreigner's trap of referring it to "Bahasa," which just means "language") and coexists with the variety of regional languages around the country. Particularly outside the big cities, children grow up learning the regional language as their mother tongue, before starting to learn Indonesian at school. Increasingly, Indonesian is being spoken in the home, and there is a shift in some areas away from regional languages. Yet, the variety of Indonesian spoken in a particular place will reflect characteristics of that area: the Indonesian as spoken in Manado, the capital of North Sulawesi province, is very different to the Indonesian found in Medan, North Sumatra, or indeed the Jakarta dialect. Indonesian therefore acts as "the language of Indonesia," a unifying force and national standard which is compulsory to pass in any educational setting.

While this course is to some extent aimed at upper Secondary learners (such as those studying Indonesian B ab initio for the International Baccalaureate), it should also be of great use to those studying Indonesian as a modern language in other secondary school courses, such as the International General Certificate of Secondary Education, or Higher School Certificate. Ideally you as the learner should have a teacher, whether a native speaker (ideal for pronunciation and accent) or a former learner of Indonesian who is now proficient (who can empathize with learning it as a second language). However, if you do not have access to an educator of the language, you should still be able to make use of this course, particularly through the ability you will develop to transfer skills and language beyond the contexts given in this book. Today's interconnected world, where information and resources in hundreds of languages are only a click away, facilitates integrating various forms of communicative interaction in ways not thought possible when language learners relied solely on black and white textbooks and cassette recordings.

This course involves reading and writing, as well as some listening and speaking tasks, incorporating readings, various text types and dialogues. These are adapted from or inspired by a variety of sources and media (online, print, electronic, visual, etc.) from across the archipelago, demonstrating different social strata and various ethnic settings. This should provide the learner with a broad overview of contemporary Indonesia, its people and language.

The format of this course is structured around the concept of a year in Indonesia, with 12 units covering different events, seasons and happenings taking the learner on a journey through time. It has been proven that if we can relate our learning to a particular context, we are far more likely to embed our knowledge and develop our skills for future use. In this way, culture and background information become key to the learner's understanding of the language, and help her or him to place what they have learned in context as part of a wider narrative.

We strongly advise mastering structures and vocabulary in each unit before proceeding further, as language skills are built on vocabulary and mastery of grammar. However, it is important to remember that you do not have to understand every word when learning a new language. The course will challenge you to think, guess from context and use your prior knowledge, as well as the glossary. The hope is that you can use the book (and your teacher) to help you become more independent in your learning of Indonesian.

Units are based on the following format, and contain:

- An introduction, with images and captions
- Key grammar points
- New vocabulary and phrases lists
- Sample conversations
- Listening practice
- "Indonesian and me"—using Indonesian about ourselves
- Key questions and statements
- Reading texts

A brief outline of pronunciation and basic facts about the structure of the language can be found in the Quick Reference Grammar.

# Quick Reference Grammar

## Pronunciation and Sounds

Indonesian is a phonetic language and is therefore relatively simple to pronounce. There are six vowel sounds:

| | | | |
|---|---|---|---|
| **a** | long *a* as in "c<u>a</u>r" | **e** | shwa or unstressed *e* as in "fast<u>e</u>r" |
| **é** | *e* as in "r<u>e</u>d" | **i** | *i* as the second "i" in "min<u>i</u>" |
| **o** | *o* as in "ph<u>o</u>to" | **u** | *u* as in "bl<u>ue</u>" |

There are also three diphthongs:

| | | | |
|---|---|---|---|
| **ai** | as in "Haw<u>aii</u>" | **au** | as in "s<u>au</u>erkr<u>au</u>t" |
| **oi** | as in "j<u>oi</u>n" | | |

| Consonants pronounced as in English | | | |
|---|---|---|---|
| **b** | as in "<u>b</u>ravo" | **m** | as in "<u>M</u>ike" |
| **d** | as in "<u>d</u>elta" | **n** | as in "<u>N</u>ovember" |
| **f** | as in "<u>f</u>oxtrot" | **p** | as in "<u>P</u>apa" |
| **g** | as in "<u>g</u>olf" | **s** | as in "<u>s</u>ierra" |
| **h** | as in "<u>h</u>otel" | **t** | as in "<u>t</u>ango" |
| **j** | as in "<u>J</u>uliet" | **w** | as in "<u>w</u>hisky" |
| **k** | as in "<u>k</u>ilo" | **y** | as in "<u>Y</u>ankee" |
| **l** | as in "<u>L</u>ima" | **z** | as in "<u>Z</u>ulu" (pronounced *j* in some parts of Indonesia) |
| **Consonants with a special pronunciation** | | | |
| **c** | like "ch" in "cello" | **r** | a trilled or rolled "r," using the tip of the tongue |
| **k** | at the end of words the **k** is cut off, almost like a glottal stop. For example, **Bapak** sounds like **bapa**. | **sy** | like "sh" in "sheep." This sound is found mainly in loanwords of Arabic origin. |
| **kh** | as in "lo<u>ch</u>", a guttural sound. This sound is found in loanwords of Arabic origin. | **-t** | at the end of words this is almost cut off (i.e., the final puff of air is not aspirated) |
| **ny** | like the Spanish **ñ** | **v** | the **f** sound. This sound is found in loanwords of Dutch origin. |
| **ng** | as in "sing." This sound sometimes starts a word, which can be difficult to learn, e.g., **ngeri**. It can also be found in the middle of a word—e.g., **tinggal**, **tunggu**—where it is spelt "**ngg**." | | |

The English words given in the left column of the above table are taken from the NATO phonetic alphabet. This is widely known in Indonesia and can be useful when spelling out names (e.g. London Echo Echo spells 'Lee').

The complete Indonesian alphabet is given below

| | | | | | | | |
|---|---|---|---|---|---|---|---|
| **a** | *ah* | **b** | *bé* | **c** | *sé* | **d** | *dé* |
| **e** | *é* | **f** | *éf* | **g** | *gé* | **h** | *ha* |
| **i** | *ee* | **j** | *jé* | **k** | *ka* | **l** | *él* |
| **m** | *ém* | **n** | *én* | **o** | *oh* | **p** | *pé* |
| **q** | *kee* | **r** | *érr* | **s** | *és* | **t** | *té* |
| **u** | *oo* | **v** | *fé* | **w** | *wé* | **x** | *éx* |
| **y** | *yé* | **z** | *zéd* | | | | |

Word stress normally falls on the second-last or penultimate syllable. However, you can never stress an unstressed **e** sound, so when an **e** is the penultimate syllable, the last syllable is stressed instead. The accents below indicate the stressed syllable:

**ká-ta    me-nga-tá-kan    be-nár    se-ben-tár**

## Indonesian spelling

Indonesian, known as **Bahasa Indonesia** in Indonesian, being a relatively young language (officially proclaimed and developed from the nation's independence in 1945) uses the Latin alphabet. Its spelling is very similar to Malay—not a surprise, considering that it was based on a regional language, Malay, used in Sumatra.

There are five vowels, with two variants of **e. É** is much less common than **e**, and for that reason, Indonesian does not use accents in writing. In this book, **é** will be marked in the glossary, but not in general text. This is to make your reading as authentic as possible, but allow you to check pronunciation if you are unsure.

## Sentence word order

Indonesian word order is much like that in English. The subject comes first, then the verb, and then the rest of the sentence:

| **Saya** | **tinggal** | **di** | **Indonesia.** |
|---|---|---|---|
| *I* | *live* | *in* | *Indonesia.* |

One important difference in word order, however, is that the noun comes first, followed by the modifier:

| **Nama** | **saya** | | **Danny.** |
|---|---|---|---|
| *name* | *my* | *(is)* | *Danny.* |

**Adalah** is used for the "to be"-verb:

| **Ini** | **adalah** | **bola** | **besar.** |
|---|---|---|---|
| *This* | *is* | *ball* | *big.* |

However, **adalah** is often left out:

| **Ini** | | **bola** | **besar.** |
|---|---|---|---|
| *This* | *is* | *ball* | *big.* |

## Singular and plural forms

Indonesian often does not use singular and plural forms. **Buku** can mean "a book," or "several books." Whether there is one or many can often be worked out from context:

| **Dia** | **beli** | **mobil** | **baru.** | |
|---|---|---|---|---|
| *She* | *buy* | *car* | *new.* | = *She bought a new car.* |

| **Banyak** | **mobil** | **di sana.** | |
|---|---|---|---|
| *Many* | *car* | *there.* | = *There are many cars there.* |

However, there are some words which can be used to indicate plurality. For example, when referring to people, **para** is used before the noun to show that there are a large number:

| **penumpang** *passenger* | **para penumpang** *passengers* |
|---|---|

## Reduplication of words

Reduplicating words, or doubling them, can also indicate plurality or variety of things or actions.

| **buku** | *book* | **buku-buku** | *books* |
|---|---|---|---|
| **putar** | *turn* | **putar-putar** | *turning around, driving around* |

Sometimes the doubled form can take on a whole new meaning:

| **kalau** | *if* | **kalau-kalau** | *in case of* |
|---|---|---|---|
| **rata** | *flat* | **rata-rata** | *average* |
| **laki** | *man* | **laki-laki** | *male* |

Some words are reduplicated as a set form, where the reduplication gives the words no special meaning:

| **gado-gado** | *Indonesian salad with peanut sauce* |
|---|---|

## Gender

There are generally no masculine, feminine, or neutral nouns or pronouns in Indonesian. For example, the word for "he," "she," or "it" is **dia**.

There are a small handful of nouns that are gender specific (most of these are given gender by the addition of Sanskrit suffixes):

| **karyawan** *male employee* | **karyawati** *female employee* |
|---|---|

## Pronouns

As stated above, Indonesian pronouns do not show gender, nor do they differ according to subject and object. However, they do have their own singular and plural forms:

| Singular | | Plural | |
|---|---|---|---|
| **aku, saya** | *I, me, my* | **kita** | *we (including person addressed)* |
| | | **kami** | *we (excluding person addressed)* |
| **kamu** | *you (familiar)* | | |
| **engkau** | *you (formal)* | **kalian** | *you, your, yours* |
| **Anda** | *you (neutral)* | | |
| **saudara** | *you (for someone the same age, lit., "brother, sister")* | | |
| **dia** | *he, she, it* | **mereka** | *they, them, their, theirs* |
| | *him, her, his, its, hers* | | |

These pronouns are sometimes shortened and used as affixes. For example, **aku** is sometimes shortened to **-ku** (**bukuku** "my book," **kujalan** "I walk"), **kamu** can become **-mu** (**mobilmu** "your car"), and **engkau** can become **kau** (**mobil kau** "your car"). Meanwhile, **dia** on the end of a word usually becomes **-nya** (**bukunya** "her book," **dibuatnya** "made by him").

Demonstrative pronouns follow the pattern below:

| | | | |
|---|---|---|---|
| **ini** | *this, these* | **di sini** | *here* |
| **itu** | *that, those* | **di situ** | *there* |
| | | **di sana** | *over there, yonder* |

## Comparatives and superlatives

To make a comparative in Indonesian, simply add the word **lebih** ("more") before the adjective, and to make a superlative simply add **paling** ("most"):

| | | | | | |
|---|---|---|---|---|---|
| **baik** | *good* | **lebih baik** | *better* | **paling baik** | *best* |
| **lucu** | *funny, cute* | **lebih lucu** | *funnier, cuter* | **paling lucu** | *funniest, cutest* |

The **ter-** prefix can be used with various adjectives to show the superlative:

| | | | |
|---|---|---|---|
| **muda** | *young* | **termuda** | *youngest* |
| **miskin** | *poor* | **termiskin** | *poorest* |
| **baik** | *good* | **terbaik** | *best* |

Conversely, use the word **kurang** ("less") if you want a negative focus:

**kurang lucu** *not so funny*     **kurang baik** *worse*

# Word Forms and Affixes

Many new words in Indonesian are created by adding prefixes, suffixes or both (affixes) to other words.

## The prefix *ber-*

**Ber-** usually shows that a word is an intransitive verb. You can usually translate a **ber-** verb as meaning to have something, or to have a certain characteristic. As a result, **ber-** verbs can often be translated as adjectives:

| | | | |
|---|---|---|---|
| **nama** | *name* | **bernama** | *to have a name, be named* |
| **beda** | *different* | **berbeda** | *(to be) different* |

**Ber-** very occasionally appears as **be-** (e.g., **belajar** "to study").

## The *ber-an* form

**Ber-** sometimes appears with an **-an** suffix. This shows that something is being done between two subjects (reciprocity), or plurality:

| | | | |
|---|---|---|---|
| **salam** | *to greet; greeting* | **bersalaman** | *to greet each other* |
| **pergi** | *to go* | **bepergian** | *to go (out, of many people)* |

## The prefix *meN-*

Adding the prefix **meN-** signifies that a verb is transitive which means it can take a direct object. The last letter of this prefix varies, depending upon the first letter of the word it is added to, as shown in the table below:

| *meN-* form | For words beginning with letter | Examples |
|---|---|---|
| me- | l, m, n, r, w, y | melihat, memulai, menikah, merasa, mewajibkan |
| mem- | b, f, v | membuka |
| men- | c, d, j, z | mencari, mendapat, menjadi |
| meng- | a, e, i, o, u, g, h | mengangkat, mengekspor, menginap, mengobrol, mengubah |

When the prefix **meN-** prefix is added to verbs starting with **t, k, s,** or **p** the following **meN-** forms are used and the first letter of the verbs is dropped off:

| *meN-* form | For words beginning with letter | Examples |
|---|---|---|
| me- | t (the t disappears) | **tangis** becomes **menangis** |
| mem- | p (the p disappears) | **pukul** becomes **memukul** |
| meng- | k (the k disappears) | **kunjung** becomes **mengunjungi** |
| meny- | s (the s disappears) | **senang** becomes **menyenangkan** |

Nearly all these verbs take an object:

| | |
|---|---|
| **Saya melihat taman.** | *I look at the park.* |
| **Saya membuka buku.** | *I open the book.* |
| **Saya memukul bola.** | *I hit the ball.* |
| **Dia mencari buku.** | *She looks for books.* |
| **Indonesia mengekspor beras.** | *Indonesia exports rice.* |

A few of them do not:

| | |
|---|---|
| **Dia menangis.** | *He cries.* |
| **Kita mengobrol.** | *We chat.* |

## The verb suffix *-kan*

MeN- verbs can also take suffixes. One of the most common is **-kan**. This shows that there is a direct object that the verb is affecting:

| | |
|---|---|
| **Mereka memaafkan kami.** | *They forgave us.* |
| **Guru membagikan kue.** | *The teacher handed out cakes.* |

Sometimes **-kan** may mean "to do something for someone":

| | |
|---|---|
| **Ibu membangunkan anaknya.** | *The mother awakened her son.* |

The **-kan** suffix can also change the verb into an adjective:

| | |
|---|---|
| **menyenangkan** | *pleasant* |
| **membosankan** | *boring* |

## The verb suffix *-i*

MeN- verbs can also take the **-i** suffix, which can imply any of the following:

| Implication | Example |
|---|---|
| the direct object is a person | **Murid menghormati guru.** *The students respect the teacher.* |
| the object is a physical place | **Kita mengunjungi taman.** *We visited the park.* |
| the action was problematic | **Ada orang memasuki rumah.** *Someone entered the house (illegally).* |

## The verb prefix *memper-*

This prefix is a variant of the **meN-** prefix. **Memper-** is used in the same way as **meN-**, but with a sense of someone specifically causing an action.

| | |
|---|---|
| **panjang** | *long* |
| **memanjang** | *(something) grows longer* |
| **memperpanjang** | *extends (something), makes (something) longer* |

## The verb prefix *di-*

While the addition of **meN-** makes a verb active, the addition of **di-** makes a verb passive. **Di-** is attached to the base form of the verb, but unlike the **meN-** prefix it never changes:

| Active form | | Passive form | |
|---|---|---|---|
| melakukan | *to do something* | dilakukan | *to be done* |
| mengatakan | *to say something* | dikatakan | *to be said* |
| menunggu | *to wait* | ditunggu | *to be awaited* |

With a **di-** verb, the doer of the action can be mentioned using the word **oleh** ("by"), though since word order alone is enough to show who performed the action, **oleh** is not always used:

**Dia ditunggu (oleh) temannya.**    *He was waited for by his friend.*

There are other more complex passive forms using **di-** which are not included in this book.

## The noun form *ke-an*

**Ke-an** usually indicates a noun form. Generally speaking, **ke-an** nouns have general, abstract meanings:

| raja | *king* | → | kerajaan | *kingdom* |
|---|---|---|---|---|
| laut | *sea* | → | kelautan | *maritime* |

Some **ke-an** words suggest a condition of suffering:

| dingin | *cold* | → | kedinginan | *suffering from cold* |
|---|---|---|---|---|
| hujan | *rain* | → | kehujanan | *caught in the rain* |

**Ke-an** can also indicate something accidental:

| tidur | *sleep* | → | ketiduran | *to fall asleep (unintentionally)* |
|---|---|---|---|---|

## The prefix *pe-*

The **pe-** prefix indicates a noun or doer:

**pemain**  *player*      **pemarah**  *angry person*      **peserta**  *participant*

## The prefix *peN-*

This prefix is similar to **pe-**, but tends to have verbs or actions as its base word. Where the base word is a verb, the word may mutate as the verb does:

| pandu, memandu | *to guide* | → | pemandu | *guide* |
|---|---|---|---|---|
| pimpin, memimpin | *to lead* | → | pemimpin | *leader* |
| menerjemahkan | *to translate* | → | penerjemah | *translator* |

## The *peN-an* form

These words usually refer to a noun (often a process, or a gerund) related to corresponding **meN-** nouns.

| | | | | |
|---|---|---|---|---|
| **memanaskan** | *to warm up* | → | **pemanasan** | *warming up* |
| **membagikan** | *to share, divide up* | → | **pembagian** | *sharing, dividing up, division* |
| **memotong** | *to cut* | → | **pemotongan** | *cutting* |

## The *per-an* form

This prefix-suffix pair usually creates a noun from a **ber-** verb:

| | | | | |
|---|---|---|---|---|
| **bekerja** | *to work* | → | **pekerjaan** | *work* |
| **bersatu** | *to unite* | → | **persatuan** | *unity* |

## The noun prefix *se-*

This very common prefix can refer to:

- a, one (**seékor** "an animal," **seorang** "a person")
- as (**setinggi gunung** "as high as a mountain")
- all (**seIndonesia** "across Indonesia")

## The prefix *ter-*

The **ter-** prefix has two key meanings. First, it can show that a verb is passive and refers to a completed action, often accidental or independent of a doer:

| | | | | | | | |
|---|---|---|---|---|---|---|---|
| **kenal** | *to know* | → | **dikenal** | *to be known* | → | **terkenal** | *famous (known by many)* |
| **tulis** | *to write* | → | **ditulis** | *to be written* | → | **tertulis** | *written (anonymously)* |

**Ter-** can also be used to make an adjective a superlative, as a synonym for **paling**. Most (but not all) adjectives can use **ter-** to show the superlative.

| | |
|---|---|
| **paling tinggi, tertinggi** | *highest, tallest* |
| **paling kecil, terkecil** | *smallest* |

## The suffix *-an*

This suffix usually refers to a noun or an extension in meaning from a base word.

| | | | | |
|---|---|---|---|---|
| **catat** | *to take notes, note* | → | **catatan** | *notes* |
| **makan** | *eat* | → | **makanan** | *food* |

## The suffix *-asi/-isasi*

This suffix was borrowed from Dutch. It roughly corresponds to *-ation* or *-tion* in English:

| | | | |
|---|---|---|---|
| **organisasi** *organization* | | → | **proklamasi** *proclamation* |

### The suffix *-lah*

**-Lah** softens whatever you are saying, to reduce impact and increase politeness:

**baiklah**   *fine, then*          **tidaklah**   *no, it isn't*          **begitulah**   *well, it's like that*

### The suffix *-kah*

This is a slightly literary suffix which creates a question, usually from short utterances: **Sudahkah?** *Already?*

**Inikah bukunya?**  *Is this the book?*

It can also be used to ask rhetorical questions.

### Question words

Questions are generally created by starting a sentence with **Apakah** (literally, "whether"), or **Apa** for short. The question is then asked with a rising intonation, just as in English.

| | |
|---|---|
| **Dia sudah pulang.** | *He has gone home.* |
| **Apa dia sudah pulang?** | *Has he gone home?* |
| **Sri belum makan.** | *Sri hasn't eaten.* |
| **Apakah Sri belum makan?** | *Hasn't Sri eaten?* |

Other important question words are:

| | | | |
|---|---|---|---|
| **apa** | *what* | **siapa** | *who* |
| **kapan** | *when* | **berapa** | *how many, how much* |
| **di mana** | *where* | **mengapa** | *why* |
| **bagaimana** | *how* | **(yang) mana** | *which* |

### Time markers

Indonesian does not have any verb tenses as such, but shows the tense through various words that can be described as time markers. The most important of these are:

| | | | |
|---|---|---|---|
| **sudah** | *already* | **Saya sudah belajar.** | *I have studied.* |
| **sedang** | *-ing, in the process of* | **Saya sedang belajar.** | *I am studying (right now).* |
| **pernah** | *once, ever* | **Saya pernah belajar.** | *I studied, once.* |
| **akan** | *will* | **Saya akan belajar.** | *I will study.* |
| **mau** | *want to* | **Saya mau belajar.** | *I want to study.* |
| **belum** | *not yet* | **Saya belum belajar.** | *I haven't studied yet.* |

It should be noted that as tense is not explicitly stated, but is made clear from the context, the same phrase could be translated into different tenses in English, according to the situation: **Dan dia datang** could be "And she came" when talking about an event last week, but present ("And she's coming") if we are talking about a party tonight.

## Adverbs

Adverbs that describe action use the word **dengan** ("with") or **secara** ("in the way of").

| | |
|---|---|
| **Usain lari dengan cepat.** | *Usain ran quickly.* |
| **Makanan dimasak secara tradisional.** | *The food is cooked in a traditional way.* |

## Prepositions

Important prepositions include:

| | | | |
|---|---|---|---|
| **depan** | *front* | **belakang** | *back* |
| **dari** | *from* | **ke** | *to* |
| **dekat** | *close* | **jauh** | *far* |
| **sebelum** | *before* | **sesudah, setelah** | *after* |
| **luar** | *outside* | **dalam** | *inside* |
| **atas** | *above* | **bawah** | *below* |
| **dengan** | *with* | **di** | *at* |
| **kepada** | *to (a person)* | **oleh** | *by* |
| **pada** | *on* | **sebelah** | *beside* |
| **samping** | *next to* | **untuk** | *for, to* |

## Negation

To negate a noun, you use **bukan** ("no"):

| | |
|---|---|
| **Dia bukan adik saya.** | *She is not my younger sister.* |
| **Bukan, bukan buku itu.** | *No, not that book.* |

To negate a verb, you use **tidak** ("not"):

| | |
|---|---|
| **Anda tidak bisa datang.** | *You cannot come.* |
| **Tidak, dia tidak mau datang.** | *No, he doesn't want to come.* |

To negate an adjective, you also use **tidak** ("not"):

| | |
|---|---|
| **Tidak jauh.** | *Not far.* |
| **Sari tidak tinggi.** | *Sari is not tall.* |
| **Dia bukan orang yang tinggi.** | *She is not a tall person.* |

# Acknowledgments

We would like to thank the following for their invaluable assistance in producing the recordings: Johansjah Sugianto, Suriadi Johansjah, Prawira Pikanto, Dong Min Lee, Aurelia Elimin, Shania Herman, Rini Yefrida, and Elizabeth Alwi. Thanks also to Ian Peirson, Pua Masykur, and Dani Johansjah.

For Paman Rob and Bibi Narelle. Selamat belajar! – K.D.

For Ica Wulansari – Y.C.

# Cast of Characters

The following appear in the book:

Danny    Adi    Johan    Ibu Maya

Sena    Hari    Nina    Riri

Ayu    Nyoman

This dialogue appears on page 21.

# 1

# Selamat Tahun Baru Imlek!

## Happy Chinese New Year!

In this unit, we will:

- Learn some basic facts about the Indonesian language, such as word order,
- Learn the numbers,
- Talk about arrivals,
- Introduce yourself briefly,
- Learn about Chinese New Year,
- Use simple descriptive adjectives.

## 1.1 Tiba di Jakarta  Arriving in Jakarta

### Basic Sentences

1. **Danny tiba di Jakarta naik GA700.**
   *Danny is arriving in Jakarta on flight GA700.*
2. **Dia akan tinggal bersama Adi dan keluarganya selama setahun.**
   *He will be staying with Adi and his family for a year.*
3. **Adi tinggal di Bintaro.**
   *Adi lives in Bintaro.*
4. **Bintaro di Jakarta Selatan.**
   *Bintaro is in South Jakarta.*

Contoh rumah, di mana keluarga besar umumnya tinggal.
*A typical house where an extended family may live.*

Bintaro di Jakarta Selatan.
*Bintaro is in South Jakarta.*

## ▌ New Words and Phrases

| | | |
|---|---|---|
| **tiba** *arrive* | **akan** *will* | **keluarganya** *family* |
| **di** *at, in* | **tinggal** *live* | **selama** *during* |
| **naik** *ride, go on* | **bersama** *together* | **setahun** *a year* |
| **dia** *he, she, it* | **dan** *and* | |

## ▌ Grammar note: Indonesian word order

Indonesian sentence order is much like that in English. The subject (person, thing) comes first, then the verb (action word), then the rest of the sentence (predicate). For example,

| **Saya** | **tinggal** | **di** | **Indonesia.** |
|---|---|---|---|
| *I* | *live* | *in* | *Indonesia.* |

| **Saya** | **berasal** | **dari** | **Lombok.** |
|---|---|---|---|
| *I* | *come* | *from* | *Lombok.* |

However, unlike in English, if you are describing something the noun will come first, followed by the adjective or modifying word

| **Nama** | **saya** | **Danny.** | |
|---|---|---|---|
| *name* | *my* | *Danny. (= My name is Danny.)* | |

| **Umur** | **saya** | **18** | **tahun.** |
|---|---|---|---|
| *age* | *my* | *18* | *years. (= I am 18 years old.)* |

We will look at how noun modifiers work more closely in Unit 2.

From the word-by-word translation above, you should notice that **adalah** (the "to be"-verb) is often left out. Most of the time you will not need this word, though it may take you a while to become attuned to when it should be used and when it should be left out.

There are a number of questions in the dialogue above. When speaking, questions may be formed simply by using a rising intonation at the end of the utterance. You can use question words (**siapa**, **apa**, **berapa**) when speaking or writing, either at the beginning or elsewhere in the utterance.

As you can see from the above, Indonesian follows the same sentence structure as that in English (subject, verb, predicate). However, adjectives go after the noun (**Jakarta Selatan**) rather than before it (South Jakarta). There are no articles (a / the), and you will also see in the last box that the verb corresponding to "is" (to be) can be left out.

## 1.2 Tiba di rumah Adi    Arriving at Adi's house

Danny arrives at Adi's house and introduces himself to his host family. He will be staying with them for one year, to attend Indonesian high school and improve his command of the language.

## Basic Sentences

1. **Nama saya <u>Danny</u>.**                                  *My name is Danny.*
2. **Umur saya delapan belas tahun.**              *I am 18 years old.*
3. **Saya berasal dari <u>Australia</u>.**                *I come from Australia.*
4. **Saya tinggal di <u>Perth</u>.**                          *I live in Perth.*
5. **Saya tiga bersaudara.**                              *I am one of three children.*
6. **Saya mahasiswa. Saya kuliah di Universitas Curtin.** *I am a university student at Curtin University.*
7. **Dulu saya pelajar di SMA Perth.**              *I used to be a student at Perth High School.*

## New Words and Phrases

**nama** *name*
**saya** *my (also "I," "me")*
**umur** *age*
**delapan belas** *18*
**tahun** *year*
**berasal** *to come from*
**dari** *from*

**tiga** *three*
**bersaudara** *to have brothers and sisters*
**mahasiswa** *university student*
**kuliah** *go to university, take lectures*
**universitas** *university*

**dulu** *before, once, first*
**pelajar** *(high school) student*
**SMA (Sekolah Menengah Atas)** *senior high school*

Can you introduce yourself, by replacing the underlined words in Danny's introduction above, with your own details?

## Dialogue: Nina dan Danny

NINA:   **Halo, siapa namanya?** *Hello, what's your name?*
DANNY:  **Nama saya Danny.** *My name is Danny.*
NINA:   **Apa kabar?** *How are you?*
DANNY:  **Baik-baik saja.** *Just fine.*
NINA:   **Danny berasal dari mana?** *Where do you come from, Danny?*
DANNY:  **Saya berasal dari Australia.** *I come from Australia.*
NINA:   **Bersaudara berapa?** *How many siblings do you have?*
DANNY:  **Tiga bersaudara.** *Three siblings.*
         **Nina kelas berapa?** *What class are you in, Nina?*
NINA:   **Saya di kelas III SMP.** *I'm in third grade, junior high school.*
DANNY:  **Nina belajar apa?** *What do you study, Nina?*
NINA:   **Saya belajar Bahasa Inggris.** *I study English.*
DANNY:  **Ayo, belajar bersama!** *Let's study together!*

## New Words and Phrases

**halo** *hello*
**siapa** *who*
**-nya** *his, her, its, the*
**apa kabar?** *how are you?*
**baik-baik saja** *just fine*

**mana** *where*
**berapa** *how many?*
**kelas** *class, year, grade*
**apa** *what*
**belajar** *to study, learn*

**bahasa** *language*
**Inggris** *English*
**ayo** *come on, let's*

## Grammar note: -nya (1)

In spoken Indonesian, we often just attach **-nya** (meaning "his," "her," or "their") to the end of **nama**, **judul**, and other nouns to show possession. This is an alternate, less formal way of saying "to be named" or "to be titled":

| | |
|---|---|
| **Namanya Danny.** | *His name is Danny.* |
| **Judul buku itu "Matematika SMA."** | *The book's title is* High School Maths. |
| **Judulnya "Matematika SMA."** | *Its title is* High School Maths. |
| **Saudaranya banyak.** | *She has lots of brothers and sisters.* |
| **Siapa namanya?** | *What's your (lit., the) name?* |

## Grammar note: Numbers 1–10

Danny has just stated his age, and how many siblings he has. Indonesian numbers are simple and easy to learn. All of the numbers from 11 to 100 are logically built on the numbers 1–10.

| | | | | |
|---|---|---|---|---|
| *1* **satu** | *2* **dua** | *3* **tiga** | *4* **empat** | *5* **lima** |
| *6* **enam** | *7* **tujuh** | *8* **delapan** | *9* **sembilan** | *10* **sepuluh** |

To make numbers ending in "-teen," just add the word **belas** after the Indonesian number.

| | |
|---|---|
| **Danny delapan belas tahun.** | *Danny is eighteen years old.* |

### Exercise 1

Make true statements about yourself using the phrases below.

1. **Nama saya** _____.

2. **Umur saya** _____ **tahun.**

3. **Saya berasal dari** _____.

4. **Saya tinggal di** _____.

5. **Saya** _____ **bersaudara.**

6. **Saya mahasiswa di** _____.

7. **Dulu saya pelajar di** _____.

### Exercise 2

Match the questions to their answers.

1. **Siapa namanya?**
2. **Berapa umurnya?**
3. **Berasal dari mana?**
4. **Tinggal di mana?**
5. **Berapa bersaudara?**
6. **Kuliah di mana?**
7. **Dulu sekolah di mana?**

a. **Dulu saya pelajar di SMA Perth.**
b. **Nama saya Danny.**
c. **Saya berasal dari Australia.**
d. **Saya tiga bersaudara.**
e. **Saya tinggal di Perth.**
f. **Saya mahasiswa di Universitas Curtin.**
g. **Umur saya 18 tahun.**

## Exercise 3

Ask your friend or teacher these questions. Write down their answers.

1. **Siapa namanya?** _____

2. **Berapa umurnya?** _____

3. **Berasal dari mana?** _____

4. **Tinggal di mana?** _____

5. **Berapa bersaudara?** _____

6. **Kuliah di mana?** _____

7. **Dulu sekolah di mana?** _____

## Exercise 4

Danny still has his boarding pass from the flight. Look at it, and then try to answer the questions. You will not know all the Indonesian words on the boarding pass.

| GARUDA INDONESIA | | | NAMA Danny Lee |
|---|---|---|---|
| NAMA Danny Lee | | | PENERBANGAN GA700 |
| | | | TGL 5 Januari 2016 |
| PENERBANGAN GA700 | TANGGAL 5 Jan | | DARI Perth |
| DARI Perth | TUJUAN Jakarta | | TUJUAN Jakarta |
| JAM 6:00 | JAM 10:00 | | JAM 6:00 s/d 10:00 |
| PINTU E4 | | | PINTU E4 |
| PINTU E4 | KELAS Ekonomi | NO. TEMPAT DUDUK 2K | KELAS Ekonomi |
| | | | TEMPAT DUDUK 2K |

1. What is his seat number?

2. What time did his flight leave?

3. What time did he arrive in Jakarta?

4. What gate did Danny leave from?

5. What date in January did he fly?

## Exercise 5

Write down the following numbers, then say them in Indonesian.

1. What year are you in at school?

2. How old are you?

3. How many sisters and brothers do you have?

4. How many subjects do you study?

5. What is your favorite number?

## 1.3 Keluarga Adi   Adi's family

| | |
|---|---|
| 1. **Suriadi Wulandaru berumur 17 tahun.** | *Suriadi Wulandaru (Adi for short) is 17 years old.* |
| 2. **Dia lahir di Jakarta dan tinggal di Bintaro.** | *He was born in Jakarta and lives in Bintaro.* |
| 3. **Adi empat bersaudara: kakaknya dua, Hari dan Sena, dan adiknya satu, Nina.** | *Adi is one of four children: he has two older brothers, Hari and Sena, and a younger sister, Nina.* |
| 4. **Adi mahasiswa di Universitas Indonesia.** | *Adi is a student at the University of Indonesia.* |
| 5. **Dulu dia pelajar di Sekolah Al-Azhar.** | *He used to study at Al-Azhar (High) School.* |
| 6. **Ibunya Adi orang Sunda.** | *Adi's mother is Sundanese.* |
| 7. **Ayahnya orang keturunan Tionghoa.** | *His father is of Chinese descent.* |

### Meet Adi's family.

Maya
ibu saya

Johan
ayah saya

Nina
adik saya

Hari
kakak nomor satu

Sena
kakak nomor dua

Adi
saya

## New Words and Phrases

ibu *mother*
ayah *father*

kakak *older brother or sister*
adik *younger brother or sister*

# 1.4 Imlek, Tahun Baru Tionghoa  Chinese New Year

## ▌Basic Sentences

1. **sepuluh ...**   *ten ...*
2. **sembilan ...**   *nine ...*
3. **delapan ...**   *eight ...*
4. **tujuh ...**   *seven ...*
5. **enam ...**   *six ...*
6. **lima ...**   *five ...*

7. **empat ...**   *four ...*
8. **tiga ...**   *three ...*
9. **dua ...**   *two ...*
10. **satu ...**   *one ...*
11. **Selamat tahun baru!** *Happy New Year!*

New Year's Eve is celebrated across Indonesia just as it is elsewhere in the world. However, the Chinese New Year is also an important event that arrives early in the year, usually late January to early February. This year, Chinese New Year falls not long after Danny arrives in Jakarta.

1.  **Imlek jatuh pada bulan Januari atau Februari.**
*Chinese New Year falls in January or February.*

2.  **Ada tari barongsai.**
*There is a lion dance.*

3.  **Ada juga tari liong.**
*There is also a dragon dance.*

4.  **Orang Indonesia keturunan Tionghoa makan bersama.**
*Chinese Indonesians eat together.*

5.  **Anak-anak terima uang hong pau.**
*Children receive lucky money in red packets.*

6.  **Orang pakai baju merah.**
*People wear red clothing.*

7. **Banyak orang bersembahyang di kelenteng.**
*Many people pray at the temple.*

8.  **'Gong Xi Fa Cai!' Selamat Tahun Baru!**
*Gong Xi Fa Cai!, "Happy New Year!"*

## New Words and Phrases

**Imlék** *Chinese New Year*
**jatuh** *fall, falls*
**bulan** *month*
**atau** *or*
**tari barongsai** *Chinese lion dance*
**tari liong** *Chinese dragon dance*

**makan** *eat*
**bersama** *together*
**anak-anak** *children*
**terima** *get, accept*
**uang** *money*
**hong pau** *lucky money (for Chinese New Year)*

**pakai, memakai** *wear, use*
**orang** *person, people*
**baju** *clothes*
**mérah** *red*
**juga** *also, too*
**bersembahyang** *to pray*
**kelénténg** *Chinese temple*

## Grammar note: the verb 'ada'

You will see the verb **ada** used in the second and third pictures above, to describe Chinese New Year in Indonesia.

**Ada** is a very useful verb, meaning "there is" or "there are." (It can also be an informal way of saying "to have").

**Ada tari barongsai.**                 *There is a lion dance.*
**Ada juga tari liong.**                 *There is also a dragon dance.*

At the start of a sentence, **ada** means "there is" or "there are."

## Cultural Note

Chinese New Year is now widely celebrated across Indonesia. Numbering only around 3% of the population, Chinese Indonesians generally have a good standard of living. Many are involved in business and trade. By mid-January, shopping centers and public places across Indonesia are decorated with lanterns, banners, and other red and gold decorations to celebrate Chinese New Year.

For many years this was not possible. Under the New Order government (1966–1998), ethnic Chinese suffered many restrictions. They were encouraged to change their names so that they sounded "more Indonesian." The use of Chinese characters and the Chinese language was discouraged and there were no public celebrations of Chinese New Year. This culminated in the 1998 riots when Chinese Indonesians became targets for various crimes.

In the year 2000, Indonesia's fourth president, Abdurrahman Wahid (Gus Dur) recognized Confucianism as an official religion, and *barongsai* lions once again started appearing in public to celebrate Chinese New Year. Mandarin is now one of the most popular foreign languages studied in Indonesia and is taught in many schools.

One area of Indonesia with a relatively large ethnic Chinese population is Pontianak, in West Kalimantan, where approximately 8% of people identify themselves as Chinese. West Kalimantan's strategic location along the South China Sea shipping route resulted in early contact with Chinese traders and miners who came to tap Kalimantan's rich resources. Most Chinese in West Kalimantan live in the cities and towns such as Pontianak and Singkawang. Interestingly, the Chinese in this province tend to intermarry more with other ethnic groups, and are often of a lower socioeconomic status. Most West Kalimantan Chinese are either Buddhist or Christian.

# 1.5 **Shio Tionghoa** Chinese Zodiac

The Chinese zodiac or **shio** signs are well known in Indonesia. Many non-Chinese Indonesians know the animal representing the year that they were born.

This year will be the Year of the Pig. Adi and Danny are talking about their Chinese zodiac signs. Listen to their conversation.

ADI: **Saya shio kelinci. Kelinci baik dan menyenangkan. Danny shio apa?**
*My Chinese zodiac is the rabbit. Rabbits are kind and pleasant. What's your Chinese zodiac?*

DANNY: **Saya shio macan. Sensitif dan keras kepala.** *I'm a tiger. Sensitive and stubborn.*

ADI: **Ayah saya juga macan. Ibu saya naga.** *My father is also a tiger. My mother is a dragon.*

DANNY: **Ibu saya juga naga! Pandai dan keras kepala.**
*My mother is also a dragon! Clever and stubborn.*

Tikus—menyenangkan, pemarah
*Rats are pleasant but bad-tempered.*

Kuda—pandai, ramah
*Horses are clever and friendly.*

Kerbau—sabar, keras kepala
*Buffalos are patient and stubborn.*

Kambing—menyenangkan, cengeng
*Goats are pleasant but complaining.*

Macan—sénsitif, keras kepala
*Tigers are sensitive and stubborn.*

Monyét—pandai, lucu
*Monkeys are clever and funny.*

Kelinci—baik, menyenangkan
*Rabbits are kind and pleasant.*

Ayam—rajin, pandai
*Roosters are diligent and clever.*

Ular—ramah, romantis
*Snakes are friendly and romantic.*

Anjing—setia, curiga
*Dogs are faithful but suspicious.*

Naga—pandai, keras kepala
*Dragons are clever and stubborn.*

Babi—pandai, jujur
*Pigs are clever and honest.*

## New Words and Phrases

**pandai** *clever*
**baik** *kind, nice, good*
**ramah** *friendly*
**rajin** *diligent, hardworking*
**setia** *faithful*

**curiga** *suspicious*
**jujur** *honest*
**keras kepala** *stubborn*
**menyenangkan** *fun, pleasant*
**sabar** *patient*

**pemarah** *angry person; bad-tempered*
**lucu** *funny, cute*
**céngéng** *complaining*
**romantis** *romantic*
**sénsitif** *sensitive*

## Grammar note

We have learnt that Indonesian adjectives follow the noun they describe. In sentences, we can describe how something is by stating the noun, then the relevant adjective. There is no need to use **adalah** or the copula verb ("is/are/to be").

| | |
|---|---|
| **Danny keras kepala.** | *Danny (is) stubborn.* |
| **Adi baik.** | *Adi (is) kind.* |
| **Saya ramah.** | *I (am) friendly.* |

### Exercise 6

1. What is your Chinese zodiac?

2. What adjectives describe you? Do they match your Chinese animal sign?

3. Choose someone you know who has a different Chinese zodiac sign. Do the adjectives for that animal sign apply to that person?

### Exercise 7

Look at the new words and phrases for this section. Which adjectives do you think can be used for positive traits? Which ones for negative traits?

| Adjectives for positive traits | Adjectives for negative traits |
|---|---|
| e.g., **pandai** | e.g., **keras kepala** |

## Exercise 8

1. What characteristics would you look for in a friend (**kawan**)?

2. What characteristics would you look for in a boyfriend or girlfriend (**pacar**)?

3. Look at the list of adjectives in Exercise 7. Write down what you think are the five most important characteristics for a person to have.

1. _____          4. _____

2. _____          5. _____

3. _____

## Unit review

Review the words you have learned in this unit.

**ACROSS**

  3. nice, kind, good
  5. live
  6. funny, cute
  7. ten
  8. friendly
11. four
12. dragon
13. one
14. person, people

**DOWN**

  1. Chinese
  2. rat, mouse
  4. eat
  9. chicken, rooster
10. name
13. I, me

## Unit 1 End-of-unit vocabulary list

**ada** *(there) is/are*
**adalah** *is/are*
**adik** *younger sibling*
**akan** *will*
**anak-anak** *children*
**anjing** *dog*
**apa** *what*
**apa kabar?** *how are you?*
**atau** *or*
**ayah** *father*
**ayam** *rooster, chicken*
**ayo** *come on, let's*
**babi** *pig*
**bahasa** *language*
**baik** *well, good; kind, nice, good*
**baik-baik saja** *just fine*
**baju** *clothes*
**banyak** *many*
**baru** *new*
**belajar** *to study, learn*
**belasan** *dozens; teens*
**berapa** *how many*
**berasal** *to come from*
**bersama** *together*
**bersaudara** *to have siblings*
**bersembahyang** *to pray*
**berumur** *aged*
**bulan** *month, moon*
**céngéng** *complaining*
**curiga** *suspicious*
**dan** *and*
**dari** *from*
**delapan** *eight*
**di** *at, in*
**di mana** *where*
**dia** *he, she, it*
**dua** *two*
**dulu** *before*
**empat** *four*
**enam** *six*
**Fébruari** *February*
**halo** *hello*
**ibu** *mother; woman*
**Imlék** *Chinese New Year*
**Inggris** *English, England*
**Januari** *January*

**jatuh** *fall, falls*
**juga** *also, too*
**jujur** *honest*
**juta** *million*
**kakak** *older sibling*
**kambing** *goat*
**kawan** *friend*
**ke** *to (a place)*
**kelas** *class*
**kelénténg** *Chinese temple*
**kelinci** *rabbit*
**keluarga** *family*
**kembang api** *fireworks*
**keras kepala** *stubborn*
**kerbau** *buffalo*
**keturunan** *descent*
**kota** *city, town*
**kuda** *horse*
**kuliah** *to go to university, take lectures*
**lahir** *born*
**lima** *five*
**lucu** *funny, cute*
**macan** *tiger*
**mahasiswa** *university student*
**makan** *eat*
**malam** *evening, night*
**mana** *which; where*
**Melayu** *Malay*
**menyenangkan** *pleasant*
**mérah** *red*
**monyét** *monkey*
**naga** *dragon*
**naik** *ride, go on*
**nama** *name*
**-nya** *possessive; the*
**orang** *person*
**pacar** *boyfriend/girlfriend*
**pada** *on, at, in (time)*
**pakai** *wear; use*
**pandai** *clever*
**pelajar** *(school) student*
**pemarah** *angry person; bad-tempered*
**pergi** *to go*
**pintu** *door, gate*

**puluh** *multiple of ten*
**pura** *Hindu temple*
**rajin** *diligent*
**ramah** *friendly*
**ribu** *thousand*
**romantis** *romantic*
**rumah** *house*
**sabar** *patient*
**satu** *one*
**saya** *I, me, my*
**sebelas** *eleven*
**sekolah** *school*
**selama** *during, while*
**selamat** *good, happy, safe; congratulations*
**selatan** *south*
**sembilan** *nine*
**senang** *happy*
**sénsitif** *sensitive*
**sepuluh** *ten*
**setahun** *a year*
**setia** *faithful*
**shio** *Chinese zodiac*
**siapa** *who*
**SMA (Sekolah Menengah Atas)** *senior high school*
**tadi** *just now, last ...*
**tahun** *year*
**tanggal** *date*
**tari** *(traditional) dance*
**tempat duduk** *seat*
**terima** *get, accept*
**tiba** *to arrive*
**tiga** *three*
**tikus** *rat*
**tinggal** *to live; to remain*
**Tionghoa** *Chinese*
**tujuh** *seven*
**uang** *money*
**ular** *snake*
**umur** *age*

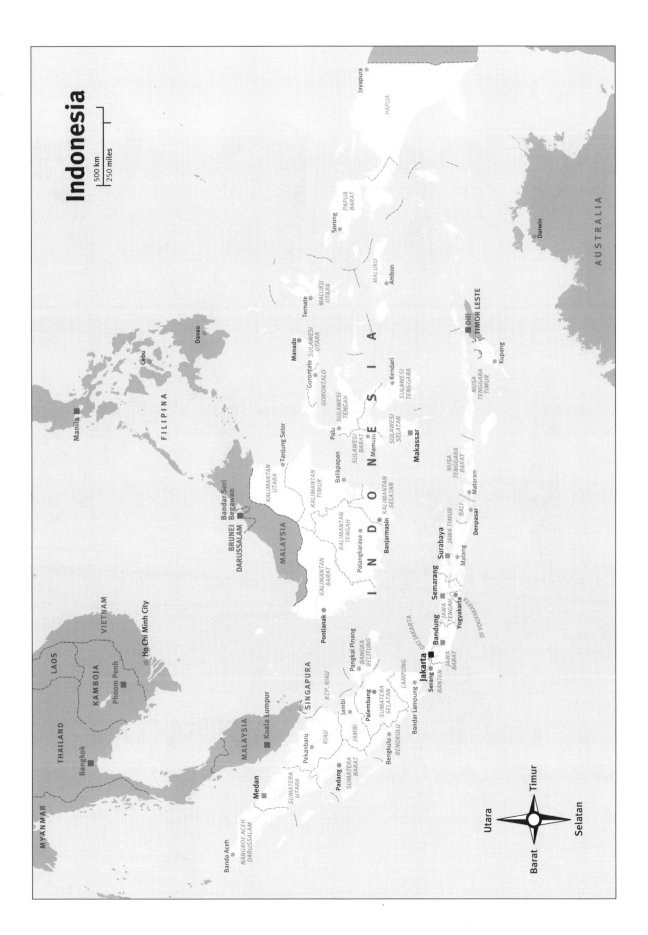

# Indonesia

500 km
250 miles

MYANMAR
THAILAND
Bangkok
LAOS
KAMBOJA
Phnom Penh
VIETNAM
Ho Chi Minh City

FILIPINA
Manila
Cebu
Davao

MALAYSIA
Kuala Lumpur
SINGAPURA

Banda Aceh
NANGROE ACEH DARUSSALAM
Medan
SUMATERA UTARA
Pekanbaru
RIAU
SUMATERA BARAT
Padang
JAMBI
Jambi
BENGKULU
Bengkulu
KEP. RIAU
BANGKA BELITUNG
Pangkal Pinang
SUMATERA SELATAN
Palembang
LAMPUNG
Bandar Lampung

BRUNEI DARUSSALAM
Bandar Seri Begawan
MALAYSIA

KALIMANTAN BARAT
Pontianak
KALIMANTAN UTARA
Tanjung Selor
KALIMANTAN TIMUR
Balikpapan
KALIMANTAN TENGAH
Palangkaraya
KALIMANTAN SELATAN
Banjarmasin

I N D O N E S I A

SULAWESI UTARA
Manado
GORONTALO
Gorontalo
SULAWESI TENGAH
Palu
SULAWESI BARAT
Mamuju
SULAWESI SELATAN
Makassar
SULAWESI TENGGARA
Kendari

Ternate
MALUKU UTARA
MALUKU
Ambon

Sorong
PAPUA BARAT
PAPUA
Jayapura

DKI JAKARTA
Jakarta
BANTEN
Serang
JAWA BARAT
Bandung
JAWA TENGAH
Semarang
DI YOGYAKARTA
Yogyakarta
JAWA TIMUR
Surabaya
Malang
BALI
Denpasar
NUSA TENGGARA BARAT
Mataram
NUSA TENGGARA TIMUR
Kupang

TIMOR LESTE
Dili

AUSTRALIA
Darwin

Utara
Barat
Timur
Selatan

This dialogue appears on page 35.

# UNIT

# 2

# Di Kampung dan Di Kota
## In the Country and the City

In this unit, we will:
- Listen and talk about being a school student,
- Learn about **ber-** verbs and how to use them,
- Talk about possession using **-nya**,
- Learn numbers 11–20,
- Understand the role of the connector **yang** in Indonesian sentences,
- Learn about a folk story from Lombok,
- Learn some basic pronouns ("you" and "me"),
- Write a short greetings card.

## 2.1 Bermain sandiwara  Acting in a play

### Basic Sentences

1. **Adi belajar di SMA3.**

   *Adi studies at SMA3.*

2. **Danny juga belajar di SMA3. Danny juga belajar di sana.**

   *Danny also studies at SMA3. Danny also studies there.*

3. **Adi di kelas III B 1. Dia belajar Matematika, IPA, Bahasa Indonesia dan bahasa Inggris.**

   *Adi is in class III B 1. He studies Mathematics, Science, Indonesian and English.*

4. **Danny di kelas III B 2. Dia belajar IPS, Ekonomi, dan Bahasa Indonesia.**

   *Danny is in class III B 2. He studies Social Science, Economics and Indonesian.*

5. **Adi berkawan banyak.**

   *Adi has many friends.*

6. **Adi dan Danny bersama kawan-kawannya ikut bermain sandiwara.**

   *Adi and Danny and their friends are acting in a play together.*

7. **Sandiwaranya berjudul "Putri Mandalika".**

   *The play's title is "Princess Mandalika."*

8. **Ceritanya berasal dari Lombok.**

   *The story comes from Lombok.*

## New Words and Phrases

**Matématika** *Mathematics*
**IPA (Ilmu Pengetahuan Alam)**
  *Science (lit., natural sciences)*
**Bahasa Indonésia** *Indonesian*
  *(language)*
**IPS (Ilmu Pengetahuan Sosial)**
  *Social Studies, Humanities*

**ékonomi** *Economics*
**berkawan** *to have a friend*
**banyak** *many*
**kawan-kawannya** *(his/her)*
  *friends*
**ikut** *join, go along with*
**bermain** *to play; to act*

**sandiwara** *play, drama*
**berjudul** *have the title, be*
  *titled or called*
**putri** *princess; daughter*
**cerita** *story*

## Grammar note: *Ber-*

You will find that Indonesian is a very logical language, based around affixes (parts attached to a word). Prefixes come at the beginning of a word, while suffixes come at the end. Understanding the affixes helps you to work out what an unknown word means.

The first prefix we will look at is **ber-**, which usually shows that a word is a verb. This verb will always be intransitive, i.e. it will not have an object. You could roughly translate it as meaning "to have" something, or to be a certain characteristic. Examples:

**belajar** *to study, to be a student*
**berkawan** *to have friends*
**berikut** *to follow, following*
**bersama** *(to be) together*
**berubah** *to change*
**bermain** *to play; to act*

**berjudul** *to have a title, to be entitled*
**berasal** *to come from, originate from*
**bersaudara** *to have brothers and sisters, to*
  *have a sibling*
**berapa** *how many?*

Which is the odd word out?

**Belajar** is the exception. Instead of "**ber-ajar**," Indonesian uses **belajar** instead, probably because it is easier to pronounce. You will see later that words derived from **belajar**, like **pelajar** ("student") and **pelajaran** ("lesson, subject") also use this exceptional spelling.

### Exercise 1

Reread the text above and decide whether the following statements are true or false.

1. Adi has lots of friends.                    (T / F)
2. Danny and Adi study at the same school.     (T / F)
3. Danny and Adi are in the same class.        (T / F)
4. Danny and Adi study different subjects.     (T / F)
5. Adi is not taking part in a play.           (T / F)
6. The story comes from Lombok.                (T / F)

## Listening and conversation: *Ber-*

What do you think **bernama** means?

**Bernama** means "to have a name," or "be named." However, we don't use this for ourselves. When asked our name, we would answer "**Nama saya ...**" rather than "**Saya bernama ...**" **Bernama**

is used in more formal contexts, such as a newspaper article, or referring to someone older such as a teacher or a famous person.

**President Indonesia itu bernama Joko Widodo.** *The Indonesian President is named Joko Widodo.*

However, for books and films, we would say **berjudul** ("titled").

| | |
|---|---|
| **Film ini berjudul "Laskar Pelangi."** | *This film is titled* The Rainbow Troops. |
| **Buku Adi berjudul "Matematika SMA."** | *Adi's book is titled* High School Mathematics. |

 ## Dialogue

One student in Adi's class, Riri, has not met Danny yet. Listen to Riri's and Danny's conversation when they meet. You will notice that it is similar to the dialogue in Unit 1.

RIRI:     **Halo, siapa namanya?** *Hello, what's your name?*

DANNY:  **Nama saya Danny.** *My name is Danny.*

RIRI:     **Apa kabar?** *How are you?*

DANNY:  **Baik-baik saja.** *Just fine.*

RIRI:     **Danny berasal dari mana?** *Where are you from?*

DANNY:  **Saya berasal dari Australia.** *I come from Australia.*
          **Riri berasal dari mana?** *Where are you from?*

RIRI:     **Saya berasal dari Lombok.** *I come from Lombok.*

DANNY:  **Riri bersaudara berapa?** *How many brothers and sisters do you have?*

RIRI:     **Saya dua bersaudara. Saya ada kakak. Danny belajar apa?**
          *I am one of two children. I have an older sibling. What do you study?*

DANNY:  **Saya belajar Bahasa Indonesia dan IPS.** *I study Indonesian and Social Studies.*

RIRI:     **Sama, saya juga belajar bahasa dan IPS!**
          *Same, I also study language and Social Studies!*

## New Words and Phrases

| | | |
|---|---|---|
| **halo** *hello* | **ada** *have (colloquial)* | **ayo** *come on, let's* |
| **apa kabar?** *how are you?* | **apa** *what* | |
| **baik-baik saja** *just fine* | **sama** *same* | |

**Exercise 2**

Read out the conversation with a partner. Then swap roles.

a.  Use the example given as a model and make sentences that apply to yourselves.
b.  Survey the other students in your class, and fill out the table below. Use Riri's questions.

| Name<br>Nama | Origin<br>Asal | No. siblings<br>(Jumlah) Saudara | Class<br>Kelas | Subjects<br>Pelajaran |
|---|---|---|---|---|
| e.g., **Danny** | Australia | 3 | III B 2 | IPS, Bahasa Indonesia |
| | | | | |
| | | | | |
| | | | | |

## Grammar note: -nya (1)

We have just learned how to use **bernama** and **berjudul**. However, in spoken Indonesian, we often just attach -**nya** to the end of **nama**, **judul** and other nouns to show possession. This is an alternative, less formal way of saying "to be named" or "to be titled." You have seen this already with **nama**.

| | |
|---|---|
| **Namanya Danny.** | *His name is Danny.* |
| **Judul buku itu "Matematika SMA."** | *The book's title is High School Mathematics.* |
| **Judulnya "Matematika SMA."** | *Its title is High School Maths.* |
| **Saudaranya banyak.** | *She has lots of brothers and sisters.* |
| **Siapa namanya?** | *What's the (= your) name?* |

Here, -**nya** shows possession, and means "his, her, their."

### Exercise 3

Match the Indonesian and English.

1. **Namanya Riri.**
2. **Judulnya "Bahasa Indonesia."**
3. **Apa namanya?**

a. What's its name?
b. The title is *Bahasa Indonesia.*
c. Her name is Riri.

## Grammar note: -nya (2)

We have learned about -**nya** as a way of showing possession, or replacing "his," "her," "their," "its." But -**nya** can also mean "the."

Indonesians learning English often forget to use "a" or "the." Some learners might say things like "I have brother" or "Give me apple." This is because Indonesian does not use these words, which we call articles. Many European languages use articles (e.g. French, German, Italian, Spanish, Norwegian). But Indonesian, like some other Asian languages (Korean, Japanese, Chinese) does not. In these languages, whether something is general ("a") or specific ("the") is usually clear from the context, or other information.

However, it is helpful for English speakers to know that -**nya** sometimes means "the" in English.

### Exercise 4

Go back to the conversation between Riri and Danny, and highlight an example of -**nya** that shows possession.

## Cultural Point: *Sekolah di Indonesia*/Indonesian schools

There are five levels of education in Indonesia:

| TK | Taman Kanak-Kanak (4-5 tahun) | *kindergarten (4-5 years)* |
|---|---|---|
| SD | Sekolah Dasar (6-12 tahun) | *elementary/primary school (6–12 years)* |
| SMP | Sekolah Menengah Pertama (13-15 tahun) | *junior high school (13–15 years)* |
| SMA | Sekolah Menengah Atas (16-18 tahun) | *senior high school (16–18 years)* |
| kuliah | Universitas (19+ tahun) | *university (19+ years)* |

In big cities, there are also **PAUD (Pendidikan Anak Usia Dini)** or preschools. This is for children younger than kindergarten age.

Most city children would study at least until graduating from **SMA**. However, in the village, many children can only afford to complete primary school, or junior high. Then they either need to help their parents in the field or business, or earn money elsewhere to help out with the family income.

It is very hard in Indonesia to get a good job without a senior high school certificate. Even university graduates struggle to find work, especially if their degree is not from overseas, and some Masters graduates work in fairly menial jobs. Competition is fierce. This is why many wealthier Indonesians send their children to study abroad, in the hope that they will later have an advantage in the job market.

## ▌Indonesian and me

### Exercise 5

Can you fill in the blanks for yourself? State where you went to kindergarten, primary and high school, and where you (want to) study afterwards.

**Waktu TK, saya belajar di** _____

**Waktu SD, saya belajar di** _____

**Waktu SMP, saya belajar di** _____

**Waktu SMA, saya belajar di** _____

**Saya mau kuliah di** _____

## ▌New Words and Phrases

**waktu**  *time, (colloquially) when*   |   **mau**  *want to, will (informal future tense)*

## ▌Grammar note: Numbers 11–20

Nowadays, most Indonesians attend school well into their teenage years. Indonesian numbers from 11–20 follow exactly the same pattern as 1–10, only that 11–19 end with the word **belas**, or "-teen."

| | | | | | |
|---|---|---|---|---|---|
| *1* | satu, se- | *9* | sembilan | *17* | tujuh belas, tujuhbelas |
| *2* | dua | *10* | sepuluh ("satu puluh") | *18* | delapan belas, delapanbelas |
| *3* | tiga | *11* | sebelas | *19* | sembilan belas, sembilanbelas |
| *4* | empat | *12* | dua belas, duabelas | *20* | dua puluh, duapuluh |
| *5* | lima | *13* | tiga belas, tigabelas | | |
| *6* | enam | *14* | empat belas, empatbelas | | |
| *7* | tujuh | *15* | lima belas, limabelas | | |
| *8* | delapan | *16* | enam belas, enambelas | | |

**Exercise 6**

When saying dates, we say the word **tanggal** first before the number. Can you read the following dates aloud in Indonesian?

1. **Tanggal 14 Februari itu Hari Kasih Sayang.**
   *The fourteenth of February is Valentine's Day.*

2. **Tanggal 17 Agustus itu Hari Kemerdekaan Indonesia.**
   *The seventeenth of August is the Indonesian Independence Day.*

3. **Tanggal 11 Maret itu Hari Supersemar.**
   *The eleventh of March is Supersemar Day (important during the New Order government).*

4. What do you think **hari** means in English?

## 2.2 Kawan-kawan di SMA3   Friends at SMA3

**Adi ada banyak kawan di SMA3 di kota Jakarta. Berikut lima kawan baiknya.**
*Adi has lots of friends at SMA3 in Jakarta. The following are five good friends.*

| Nama | Asal | (Jumlah) saudara | Kelas | Pelajaran |
|---|---|---|---|---|
| Ayu | Jakarta | | III B 2 | IPS Bahasa Indonesia |
| | Bali | 3 | III B 1 | IPA |
| Iis | Jawa Barat | 3 | III B 3 | |
| Riri | Lombok | 2 | | IPA |
| Akbar | | 4 | III B 2 | IPS Bahasa Indonesia, Bahasa Inggris |

**Exercise 7**

1. Can you fill in the gaps in the table above, using the following information?

   **Akbar berasal dari Jakarta.** *Akbar comes from Jakarta.*
   **Ayu bersaudara dua.** *Ayu is one of two children.*
   **Kampung Nyoman di Bali.** *Nyoman's village is in Bali.*
   **Nyoman dan Riri di kelas yang sama.** *Nyoman and Riri are in the same class.*
   **Iis belajar IPA.** *Iis studies Science.*

2. Who among Adi's friends would also know Danny? Remember that Danny studies Humanities, Indonesian and English.

## 2.3 Hari Kasih Sayang   Valentine's Day

Valentine's Day is an increasingly popular event in Indonesian cities. Also known as **Hari Kasih Sayang**, many young people and students exchange gifts, take a special friend out for dinner, or send and receive gifts from a secret admirer. Teddy bears and hearts are popular, as are chocolates.

In other parts of Indonesia, especially the countryside, **Hari Kasih Sayang** is seen as a Western import in a conservative, Muslim-majority nation.

Adi writes a card for Ayu to go with a bunch of flowers. Danny also receives a card and box of chocolates!

**Untuk Ayu tersayang,**
**Kamu baik, sabar dan cantik.**
**Aku sayang kamu.**
**Adi**

*For dear Ayu,*
*You are kind, patient*
*and beautiful.*
*I love you.*
*Adi*

## Exercise 8

Can you translate what the card says? (Refer to **New Words and Phrases** below to help you.)

**Untuk Danny yang**
**ganteng dan lucu,**
**Selamat Hari Kasih Sayang!**
**Sampai nanti,**
**Seorang penggemar**

_____

_____

_____

_____

## ▌ New Words and Phrases

| | | |
|---|---|---|
| **kasih sayang** *love* | **kamu** *you (singular, familiar)* | **sampai** *until* |
| **sayang** *love, fond of* | **cantik** *pretty, beautiful* | **nanti** *later* |
| **untuk** *for, to* | **yang** *which, who* | **seorang** *a (person)* |
| **tersayang** *beloved, dear* | **ganteng** *handsome* | **penggemar** *fan, admirer* |

## Exercise 9

Danny wants to send a message to Riri. Can you fill in the missing words?

**Untuk Riri _____ ,**

**_____ ramah dan baik.**

**Selamat _____ Kasih Sayang!**

**Danny**

To dear Riri,

You are friendly and kind.

Happy Valentine's Day!

Danny

## Grammar note: *Kata ganti* / Pronouns

Personal pronouns are what we call words like "I," "you," "he," "she," "it," "we," and "they." Indonesian has many personal pronouns, sometimes using people's names, and sometimes using local words from regional languages. So far in Unit 1 we have learned **saya**. In this unit we also mention that **dia** means "he" or "she" (or "it").

You will notice in the Valentine's cards that **kamu** is introduced as "you," and **aku** as an alternative for "I." These are familiar terms used between close friends.

As a rule, **saya** and **Anda** (or the person's name: these all mean "you") is the safest choice to use if you are not sure. It is better to be over-polite, than to presume familiarity and possibly appear rude. However, if someone uses **aku** or **kamu** with you, it is fairly safe to use the same words back, if you are of the same status or level.

Avoid using **kamu** with people who are older than you. Indonesia is a very hierarchical society and you should be careful to show respect. You will hear some people use **kamu** with those who are older than them, such as waiters, or in shops, or people of a lower socioeconomic status. While it is not wrong, it does suggest a lack of respect.

## Exercise 10

1. **Saya** or **aku**? Which would you choose? Tick (√).

|  | Saya | Aku |
|---|---|---|
| When talking to a teacher |  |  |
| When talking to a child |  |  |
| When talking to a close friend |  |  |
| When speaking to someone in a shop |  |  |

2. How would you say …?

    a. I study Indonesian _____ (to an elderly neighbour)

    b. I'm from America _____ (to a classmate)

    c. I love Indonesia _____ (to someone on a train)

    d. I love you _____ (to your girlfriend/boyfriend)

## Listening practice: *Betapa kucinta padamu*

This song by Siti Nurhaliza uses various words (pronouns) for "I" and "you." (Find it on YouTube and listen.)

## Exercise 11

1. Listen to the chorus and tick each time you hear these words.

    **aku / -ku / ku-**      ____ ____ ____ ____ ____

    **Anda**      ____ ____ ____ ____ ____

    **engkau / kau** (similar usage to **kamu**)      ____ ____ ____ ____ ____

    **kamu / -mu**      ____ ____ ____ ____ ____

    **saya**      ____ ____ ____ ____ ____

2. Can you explain why some words were used more than others?

# 2.4 Putri Mandalika, the play

As elsewhere in the world, Indonesia has plenty of legends. One of these is the legend of Putri Mandalika from Lombok. Adi, Danny and their friends are involved in the production of a play based on this legend.

## ▌Basic Sentences

1. **Mandalika adalah putri cantik dari kerajaan di Lombok.**
   *Mandalika was a beautiful princess from a kingdom in Lombok.*

2. **Ada banyak pangeran muda yang cinta Mandalika. Pangeran Adi juga cinta pada dia.**
   *There were lots of young princes who loved Mandalika. Prince Adi also loved her.*

3. **Mandalika bingung, mau nikah dengan pangeran yang mana?**
   *Mandalika was confused about which prince she should marry.*

4. **Akhirnya Mandalika berubah menjadi nyalé, jadi semua orang bisa sayang padanya.**
   *Finally, Mandalika turned into a sea-worm, so everyone could love her.*

## ▌New Words and Phrases

| | | |
|---|---|---|
| **kerajaan** *kingdom* | **dengan** *with* | **jadi** *so* |
| **pangéran** *prince* | **akhirnya** *finally* | **semua** *all* |
| **muda** *young* | **berubah** *to change* | **orang** *person, people* |
| **bingung** *confused* | **menjadi** *to become* | **bisa** *can* |
| **nikah** *marry (polite)* | **nyalé** *sea-worm* | |

## ▌Grammar note: *Yang*

**Yang** is a very useful conjunction in Indonesian. It means "which" or "that," and can be used to link phrases and clauses, i.e. give a longer explanation about something.

> **Ada banyak pangeran muda yang cinta Mandalika.**
> *There were lots of young princes who loved Mandalika.*

You could say:

> **Banyak pangeran muda cinta Mandalika.**
> *Many young princes loved Mandalika.*

But using **yang** makes it sound more natural in Indonesian, and keeps the nominal group (**banyak pangeran muda**) together.

> **Mau nikah dengan pangeran yang mana?**
> *Which prince did she want to marry?*

Here, the **yang** is showing that there is a choice ("which" one?) You will hear **Mana?** or **Yang mana?** quite a lot when people are choosing or identifying something from a large number.

### Exercise 12

Try to answer in Indonesian.

1. Q. **Mandalika berasal dari mana?** *Where did Mandalika come from?*

   A. **Mandalika berasal dari _____.**

2. Q. **Pangeran mana yang jatuh cinta padanya?** *What kind of prince fell in love with her?*

   A. **Banyak pangeran _____ yang jatuh cinta padanya. Pangeran Adi juga jatuh cinta padanya.**

## Reading Comprehension: Fan mail

Read the greetings card below, sent by an audience member who was impressed by Riri's performance in the Putri Mandalika play. Answer the questions in English. (There is a translation of the card in the Answer Key, available online.)

> **24 Februari**
>
> **Halo Riri,**
> **Selamat, ya! Kamu jadi Putri Mandalika yang baik. Kamu seperti seorang putri cantik yang bijaksana. Saya suka waktu kamu berubah menjadi nyale.**
>
> **Salam,**
> **Agus Suyitno**

## New Words and Phrases

**seperti** *like, as*    |  **bijaksana** *wise*    |  **suka** *like*

### Exercise 13

1. What did Agus say Riri act like?
2. Which part did Agus like?

## 2.5 Makan di pantai  Eating on the beach

Eating on the beach is very popular in Lombok. Here is a sample menu from Warung Mama:

| | | |
|---|---|---|
| 🍚 **Nasi goreng** | Rp.19.000 | |
| | (sembilan belas ribu rupiah) | |
| 🍝 **Mi goreng** | Rp.15.000 | |
| 🍗 **Ayam goreng** | Rp.18.000 | |
| 🍞 **Roti bakar** | Rp.10.000 | |
| ☕ **Teh** | Rp.5.000 | |
| ☕ **Kopi** | Rp.5.000 | |

## New Words and Phrases

| | | |
|---|---|---|
| **nasi** *rice* | **goréng** *fried* | **téh** *tea* |
| **mi** *noodles* | **roti** *bread* | **kopi** *coffee* |
| **ayam** *chicken* | **bakar** *baked, grilled, toasted* | |

The prices seem very expensive! But in actual fact, Rp.10.000 is roughly equivalent to one U.S. dollar. So, it is quite easy to read prices—just say the numbers before the dot (used instead of a comma, as in English) then **ribu rupiah** ("thousand rupiah").

## Grammar note: Numbers 20–100

In the last unit, we learned the numbers 1–10, and this unit, we have learnt to count to nineteen.

Numbers between 20 and 100 are simply put together by inserting the word **puluh** ("ten," or "multiple of ten") between the numbers. So

*40* **empat puluh**                     *70* **tujuh puluh**

For numbers not ending in ten, just add the final digit after the **puluh**. So

*43* **empat puluh tiga**                *68* **enam puluh delapan**

| | | | |
|---|---|---|---|
| *11* | **sebelas** ("satu belas") | *21* | **dua puluh satu** |
| *12* | **dua belas** | *22* | **dua puluh dua** |
| *13* | **tiga belas** | *30* | **tiga puluh** |
| *14* | **empat belas** | *40* | **empat puluh** |
| *15* | **lima belas** | *50* | **lima puluh** |
| *16* | **enam belas** | *60* | **enam puluh** |
| *17* | **tujuh belas** | *70* | **tujuh puluh** |
| *18* | **delapan belas** | *80* | **delapan puluh** |
| *19* | **sembilan belas** | *90* | **sembilan puluh** |
| *20* | **dua puluh** (lit. "two tens") | *100* | **seratus** |

### Exercise 14

How would you say …

1. **17 Agustus** (Indonesian Independence Day)?
2. **'45** (year of independence)?
3. **Densus 88** (anti-terror squad)?
4. Your own age? **…. tahun** (years)
5. Your friend has red eyes from the sea and sun in Lombok and can't read. Read the menu from Warung Mama (at the start of section 2.5) aloud to your friend.

## Listening Practice

Some beachside eateries try to cater to the foreign tourist market. To simplify the prices, they replace the .000 or "thousand" with the letter **K** (again, "kilo-" standing for 1 000).

## Exercise 15

Now listen to the following menu from Hotel Glamor. The K here means "thousands," or **ribu**. Write in the prices (in number form if you can).

1. **Nasi goreng**  _____

2. **Mi goreng**  _____

3. **Ayam goreng**  _____

4. **Roti bakar**  _____

5. **Teh**  _____

6. **Kopi cappuccino**  _____

7. Which menu is more expensive? Can you think of a reason why?

## Unit review

Read about the Putri Mandalika legend below.

*Most inhabitants of Lombok are from the Sasak ethnic group, which is Muslim, and speak a language related to Javanese and Sundanese. Prior to the 16th century, before it became part of the Dutch East Indies and Indonesia, Lombok had various kingdoms of its own, such as Tunjung Bitu. The daughter of the king of Tunjung Bitu, Putri Mandalika was famed for her beauty and wisdom. Whoever she married would forge great links between their kingdom and Tunjung Bitu. But Mandalika was confused as there were so many potential suitors, and felt she could not refuse any of them. Finally, Mandalika had a vision in which she invited a number of suitors and their people to Lombok to compete for her hand in marriage. So many princes came, who were all good, brave and handsome, that she could not decide which one to marry. Rather than war breaking out between the princes fighting for her hand, Mandalika instead gathered everyone together on the southern coast, then threw herself into the sea off a rock so that no single prince could marry her. "I will turn myself into a sea-worm so that everyone can love me," she cried as she threw herself into the water. Nyalé is a kind of sea-worm that appears in the waters south of Lombok once a year. The Sasak people of Lombok hold a Bau Nyalé (Sasak for "catching sea-worms") festival on the south coast of Lombok every February to recall the legend of Putri Mandalika, and to give thanks for these nutritious worms. Festivities include making food from sea-worms, giving presents to sweethearts and making ceremonial voyages out to sea in boats.*

After reading and understanding the story, choose which **ber-** verb fits for each statement. Refer to section 2.1 in this unit, or the glossary, if necessary.

| | | | | | | | |
|---|---|---|---|---|---|---|---|
| **berasal** | **berikut** | **berjudul** | **berkawan** | **bermain** | **bersama** | **berubah** | **berapa** |

EXAMPLE: **Cerita ini berjudul Putri Mandalika.**
*This story is called "Princess Mandalika."*

1. **Cerita ini _____ dari Lombok.**
*This story comes from Lombok.*

2. _____ ceritanya.
   *This is how the story goes.*

3. **Banyak pangeran ikut _____ kawan-kawannya.**
   *Lots of princes came along with their friends.*

4. **Ada _____ banyak pangeran?**
   *How many princes were there?*

5. **Putri Mandalika _____ menjadi nyale.**
   *Princess Mandalika changed into a sea-worm.*

## ▌Unit 2 End-of-unit vocabulary list

**akhirnya** *finally, in the end*
**aku** *I, me (familiar)*
**Anda** *you (singular, neutral)*
**asal** *origin*
**ayo** *come on, let's*
**belajar** *to study, learn*
**berikut** *following, to follow*
**berjudul** *entitled, titled*
**berkawan** *to have a friend*
**bermain** *to play*
**bernama** *to be named*
**bersama** *together*
**berteman** *to have a friend*
**berubah** *to change*
**bijaksana** *wise*
**bingung** *confused*
**bisa** *can, be able to*
**buku** *book*
**cantik** *beautiful*
**cerita** *story*
**cinta** *(romantic) love*
**dengan** *with, by*
**ékonomi** *economics*
**engkau, kau** *you (familiar)*
**ganteng** *handsome*
**halo** *hello*
**hari** *day*

**ikut** *to join (in), follow*
**Inggris** *England, English*
**IPA (Ilmu Pengetahuan Alam)**
  *Natural Sciences*
**IPS (Ilmu Pengetahuan Sosial)**
  *Social Sciences*
**jadi** *become*
**jumlah** *number, total*
**kampung** *(urban) village*
**kamu** *you (singular, familiar)*
**kasih** *love*
**kata** *word*
**kau, engkau** *you (familiar)*
**kerajaan** *kingdom*
**kota** *city, town*
**kuliah** *(university) lecture*
**matematika** *mathematics*
**mau** *want; will*
**menjadi** *to become*
**muda** *young*
**nanti** *later*
**nikah, menikah** *to marry*
**nyalé** *sea-worm (Lombok)*
**orang** *(counter for) person*
**pangéran** *prince*
**pelajar** *student, learner*
**pelajaran** *lesson, subject*

**penggemar** *fan, supporter*
**putri** *princess*
**salam** *greetings, regards*
**sama** *same*
**sampai** *until, to*
**sandiwara** *play*
**saudara** *family member*
**sayang** *love, tender feeling*
**SD (Sekolah Dasar)** *Primary*
  *School*
**semua** *all*
**seorang** *a (person)*
**seperti** *like*
**seratus** *one hundred*
**siapa** *who*
**SMP (Sekolah Menengah**
  **Pertama)** *Junior High School*
**suka** *like; tend to*
**taman kanak-kanak (TK)**
  *kindergarten*
**tanggal** *date*
**tersayang** *dear, beloved*
**univérsitas** *university*
**untuk** *for, to*
**waktu** *time; (inf.) when*
**yang** *which, that*

This dialogue appears on page 52.

# 3

# Hari Nyepi di Bali

## The Balinese Day of Silence

In this unit, we will:

- Learn how to say "this" and "that,"
- Learn how to use maps and give directions,
- Learn how to use more formal **meN-** verbs,
- Discuss going on a train journey,
- Talk about Bali as a tourist destination and Indonesian cultural phenomenon,
- Tell the time, using the 12-hour and 24-hour clocks,
- Greet people appropriately for different times of day.

## 3.1 Jalan ke Bali  Travelling to Bali

### Dialogue

Adi's friend Nyoman is going home to Bali for the Nyepi holiday. He has invited Adi and Danny to come along with him. The boys are looking at a map of Bali and discussing their trip.

| | |
|---|---|
| NYOMAN: | **Ini desa saya.** *This is my village.* |
| ADI: | **Di sini?** *Here?* |
| NYOMAN: | **Bukan, di situ, di selatan.** *(he points) No, there, in the south. (he points)* |
| DANNY: | **Desa ini? Sanur?** *This village? Sanur?* |
| NYOMAN: | **Ya, itu desa saya.** *Yes, that's my village.* |
| ADI: | **Kita naik apa ke sana?** *How will we get there? (lit., what will we travel by?)* |
| NYOMAN: | **Dari Gilimanuk, kita naik bis.** *From Gilimanuk, we'll go by bus.* |
| DANNY: | **Bis itu sampai mana?** *Where does the bus go to?* |
| NYOMAN: | **Sampai di Denpasar. Di sana dijemput kakak saya.** |
| | *To Denpasar. There, my brother will pick us up.* |

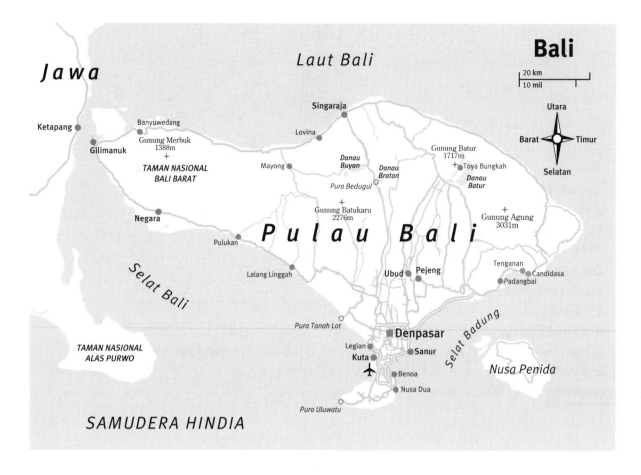

## New Words and Phrases

| | | |
|---|---|---|
| **ini** *this* | **ya** *yes* | **pulau** *island* |
| **désa** *village* | **jemput** *pick (someone) up* | **pura** *temple* |
| **bukan** *no, not* | **gunung** *mountain* | **timur** *east* |
| **situ** *there (where the listener is)* | **danau** *lake* | **laut** *sea* |
| **sana** *over there, yonder (far from both speakers)* | **utara** *north* | **samudera** *ocean* |
| **selatan** *south* | **barat** *west* | **selat** *strait* |

## Grammar note: *Ini, itu* / "This" and "that"

The Indonesian words for "this" and "that" are **ini** and **itu**. Unlike in English, simple sentences in Indonesian usually do not need the "to be" verb (**adalah**). So, we can say:

| **Ini** | **gunung.** | |
|---|---|---|
| *This* | *(is a)* | *mountain.* |

| **Itu** | **pura .** | |
|---|---|---|
| *That* | *(is a)* | *Hindu temple.* |

In more complex sentences where more information is added about the noun that **ini** or **itu** modifies, these words are placed after the noun instead of before it. Thus, we have:

| **Pelajar** | **ini** | **bernama** | **Adi.** |
|---|---|---|---|
| *Student* | *this* | *is called* | *Adi.* |
| **Pelajar** | **ini** | | **lucu.** |
| *Student* | *this* | *(is)* | *funny.* |

Here are some other examples of how the word order is changed in more complex sentences:

1. **Ini pelajar.**                            *This is a student.*
   **Pelajar ini bernama Adi.**       *This student is called Adi.*

2. **Itu buku.**                                 *That is a book.*
   **Buku itu berjudul "Pulau Bali."**   *That book is titled* The Island of Bali.

3. **Di buku itu ada peta.**            *In that book there is a map.*
   **Peta itu peta Bali.**                  *That map is of Bali.*

4. **Ini pulau.**                               *This is an island.*
   **Pulau ini Bali.**                         *This island is Bali.*

5. **Itu gunung.**                            *That is a mountain.*
   **Gunung itu Gunung Agung.**    *That mountain is Mt. Agung.*

## ▌Grammar Practice

### Exercise 1

Translate the following sentences into English.

1. **Cerita ini lucu.**

   _____

2. **Ini cerita tentang** *(about)* **Bali.**

   _____

3. **Pelajar itu Danny.**

   _____

4. **Itu pelajar dari Australia.**

   _____

### Exercise 2

Translate the following sentences into Indonesian.

1. This is my book.

   _____

2. That is a school.

   _____

3. This friend is called Riri.

   _____

4. Where is that village?

   _____

## 3.2 Naik Kereta Api I Going by train

Nyoman, Adi and Danny travel from Jakarta to Denpasar by train, bus and ferry. Adi sends his mother text messages along the way to let her know where they are.

| Time | Message |
|---|---|
| 22 Maret 08:30 | **Kami sudah sampai di setasiun Gambir. Sekarang tunggu KA ke kota Surabaya.** *We have arrived at Gambir station. Now waiting for the train to Surabaya.* |
| 22 Maret 19:00 | **Sudah sampai Surabaya, Bu! Kami ke setasiun Gubeng untuk naik KA ke Banyu-wangi.** *We've reached Surabaya, Mum! We're going to Gubeng station to get the train to Banyuwangi.* |
| 23 Maret 03:30 | **Baru sampai Banyuwangi. Dari sini naik feri ke pulau Bali.** *Just arrived in Banyuwangi. From here we get the ferry to Bali.* |
| 23 Maret 05:00 | **Selamat pagi dari Gilimanuk, Bu! Kami sudah di bis menuju kota Denpasar.** *Good morning from Gilimanuk, Mum! We're in the bus heading for Denpasar.* |
| 23 Maret 08:00 | **Kakaknya Nyoman sudah jemput kami di Denpasar.** *Nyoman's brother has picked us up in Denpasar.* |

### New Words and Phrases

| | | |
|---|---|---|
| **kami** *we (exclusive of listener)* | **tunggu, menunggu** *to wait* | **pagi** *morning* |
| **sudah** *already* | **keréta api** *train* | **jemput, menjemput** *to pick up,* |
| **baru** *just* | **naik, menaiki** *to ride, travel on* | *collect* |
| **setasiun** *station* | **feri** *ferry* | **menuju** *to approach, head for* |

### Grammar note: *meN-* verbs

In Unit 2, we learned the **ber-** verb prefix, which is used for intransitive verbs, or actions that don't require an object, e.g., **bermain** ("to play") and **berubah** ("to change"):

    **Riri bermain.**     *Riri is playing.*
    **Adi berubah.**     *Adi has changed.*

So far, other verbs we have seen (apart from **ber-** verbs) are simple verbs such as **naik**, **ikut**, **sayang**. These simple or base forms do not have a prefix. They are often transitive (i.e. taking an object) as seen below, and are most commonly found in everyday speech. However, importantly, sometimes the object can be left out.

| | | | |
|---|---|---|---|
| **Kami naik bis.** | *We got the bus.* | **Akbar ikut Riri.** | *Akbar is going with Riri.* |
| **Kami naik.** | *We got on (the bus).* | **Akbar ikut.** | *Akbar is coming too.* |

However, from these base verbs (or any base word in general), more formal verbs can be made using the **meN-** prefix. The prefix **meN-** indicates a transitive verb (with rare exceptions), which <u>must</u> be followed by a direct object. For example, for our previous statements, a more formal written version might be

| | |
|---|---|
| **Kami menaiki bis.** | *We ride the bus.* |
| **Akbar mengikuti Riri.** | *Akbar is going with Riri.* |
| **Adi menyayangi Ayu.** | *Adi loves Ayu.* |

The **meN-** prefix has a capital **N** to indicate that the first letter of the base word may change. You can see this in **sayang**, from which **menyayangi** is derived.

**meN-** verbs often take a suffix (**-i** or **-kan**, which will be discussed in later units). This may give the **meN-** verb a particular meaning that differs from its base word.

Let's compare the different verb types.

| Subject | Verb | Object | Translation |
|---|---|---|---|
| Riri | bermain. | | *Riri plays.* |
| Adi | berubah. | | *Adi changes/Adi has changed.* |
| Kami | tunggu. | | *We wait.* |
| Kami | menunggu | [not stated.] | *We wait (for something).* |
| Kami | menunggu | Nyoman. | *We wait for Nyoman.* |
| Kami | menaiki | feri. | *We ride the ferry.* |
| Kami | menuju | kota Denpasar. | *We head for Denpasar.* |
| Kakaknya Nyoman | menjemput | kami. | *Nyoman's brother picks us up.* |

As you can see, the **ber-** verbs have no direct object, while the **meN-** verbs all do.

You will have noticed that the **meN-** prefix actually consists of **meng-**, **men-**, **me-** and **meny-**, among other forms. The letters after **me-** sometimes change, depending on the base or root word of the verb:

| *Men-* Prefix | Base Word | Suffix/Ending | Translation |
|---|---|---|---|
| men- | jemput | | *to pick up* |
| men- | jadi | | *to become* |
| me- | nyenang (senang) | -kan | *to make happy; pleasant* |
| meng- | ada | -kan | *to hold, run* |

## ▌Grammar note: Missing subject

Indonesian is what we call a subject-verb-object language, much like English. However, one important difference is that in Indonesian the subject is often left out, as in some of Adi's texts to his mother. This is particularly common in spoken or informal Indonesian. Usually the subject is already made clear (or understood) from the context or existing information. If Adi were writing a longer, more formal letter or email, he would probably include the subject, for example, **Kami menunggu KA** and **Kami menaiki feri**.

Let's reread some of Adi's messages to Ibu Maya:

| | | | | | |
|---|---|---|---|---|---|
| **Sekarang** | **tunggu** | **KA** | **ke** | **kota** | **Surabaya.** |
| *Now* | *waiting for* | *the train* | *to* | *city of* | *Surabaya.* |

| | | | | | | |
|---|---|---|---|---|---|---|
| **Dari** | **sini** | **naik** | **feri** | **ke** | **pulau** | **Bali.** |
| *From* | *here (we)* | *go by* | *ferry* | *to* | *island of* | *Bali.* |

| Kami | sudah | di | bis | menuju | kota | Denpasar. |
|------|-------|-----|-----|--------|------|-----------|
| *We* | *(are)* | *already in* | *(the) bus* | *going to* | *city of* | *Denpasar.* |

| Kakaknya | Nyoman | sudah | jemput | kami | di | Terminal Ubung. |
|----------|--------|-------|--------|------|-----|-----------------|
| *Brother of* | *Nyoman* | *already* | *picked up* | *us* | *at* | *Ubung Terminal.* |

Adi is sending short, simple text messages, so he uses the short, simple version of each verb. If he was writing an email or letter, or texting someone he didn't know well, he might use the longer **meN-** versions (i.e., **menunggu, menaiki, menjemput**).

However, be careful! You can only use words that already exist. You cannot just create words randomly. As we saw in the **meN-** verb section, not all verbs have short forms, e.g. **menuju** = "to approach, head for." There is no such word as *tuju or *menujui.

Still, knowing the short and longer forms of verbs helps you to understand how Indonesian works (especially in Unit 9 when we study the **-i** and **-kan** endings.)

## 3.3 Naik Kereta Api II Taking the train

Nyoman is at the station, looking at train timetables. Listen to his conversation with a member of the railway station staff.

NYOMAN:    **Selamat pagi.** *Good morning.*

*PETUGAS:   **Selamat pagi. Bisa saya bantu?** *Good morning. Can I help you?*

NYOMAN:    **Saya mau memesan tiket.** *I would like to order tickets.*

PETUGAS:   **Sudah isi formulir?** *Have you filled in a form?*

NYOMAN:    **Ini, Pak.** *Here.*

PETUGAS:   **Terima kasih. Untuk satu orang?** *Thank you. For one person?*

NYOMAN:    **Tidak, untuk tiga orang. Dua kawan dan saya sendiri.**
           *No, for three people. Two friends and myself.*

PETUGAS:   **Untuk Kereta Api Argo Bromo Pagi, atau Malam?**
           *For the Argo Bromo morning or evening train?*

NYOMAN:    **Argo Bromo Pagi, dan Mutiara Malam.** *Argo Bromo morning, and Mutiara evening.*

PETUGAS:   **Baik. Mau duduk bersama?** *Right. Would you like to sit together?*

NYOMAN:    **Ya, kami duduk bersama.** *Yes, we are sitting together.*

PETUGAS:   **Baik. Tiga orang, naik Argo Bromo Pagi, dari setasiun Gambir jam 9.00, hari Sabtu tanggal 22 Maret.**
           *Fine. Three adults, on the Argo Bromo morning train, from Gambir station at 9 a.m., Saturday 22 March.*
           **Tiba di setasiun Surabaya Pasar Turi jam 18.00.**
           *Arriving at Surabaya's Pasar Turi station at 6 p.m.*

NYOMAN:    **Betul.** *Correct.*

PETUGAS:   **Dan tiga orang, naik Mutiara Malam, dari setasiun Surabaya Gubeng jam 22.00, hari Sabtu tanggal 22 Maret.**
           *And three adults, on the Mutiara night train, from Surabaya's Gubeng station at 10 p.m., Saturday 22 March.*

*Petugas = attendant

**Tiba di setasiun Banyuwangi Baru jam 4.00 hari Minggu tanggal 23 Maret.**
*Arriving at Banyuwangi Baru station at 4.00 a.m. on Sunday 23 March.*
**Pulang pergi?** *Return ticket?*

NYOMAN: **Kami akan pulang naik pesawat.** *We will come home by plane.*

PETUGAS: **Baik. Semuanya Rp. 2 juta. Selamat jalan.**
*Fine. That comes to Rp.2 million. Have a good trip!*

NYOMAN: **Terima kasih banyak.** *Thank you very much.*

## New Words and Phrases

| | | |
|---|---|---|
| **bantu, membantu** *to help* | **formulir** *form* | **pulang** *go home* |
| **pesan, memesan** *to order* | **sendiri** *self* | **pulang pergi** *return* |
| **tikét** *ticket* | **Maret** *March* | **pesawat** *plane, airplane* |
| **isi, mengisi** *to fill (in)* | **jam** *hour, o'clock* | |

## Language note 1: Greetings

There are four basic greetings for different times of the day in Indonesian:

| | |
|---|---|
| **Selamat pagi** | *Good morning (until around 10 a.m.)* |
| **Selamat siang** | *Good day/afternoon (between 10 a.m. and 3 p.m.)* |
| **Selamat sore** | *Good afternoon/evening (between 3 p.m. and 7 p.m.)* |
| **Selamat malam** | *Good evening (after dark)* |

You may take a while to get used to the different ways of dividing up the day. Indonesians get mixed up, too, and you might hear people saying **Selamat siang** when it is mid-afternoon, for example, particularly from people working indoors. Between midnight and dawn, it is up to you whether you want to say **Selamat malam** or **Selamat pagi**.

## Grammar note 1: *Sudah*

Indonesian does not have tenses like many other languages. Instead, where necessary, time is indicated by words like **sudah**, **mau** and **akan**. They work a little like auxiliary verbs, and can be used on their own, to indicate when something happens.

| Time marker | Example | Meaning |
|---|---|---|
| sudah | **Sudah isi formulir?** *Have you filled out the form?* | *already* |
| sedang* | **Nyoman sedang menunggu.** *Nyoman is waiting.* | *in the process of, -ing* |
| akan | **Kami akan pulang naik pesawat.** *We will go home by plane.* | *will, is going to* |
| mau | **Mau duduk bersama** *Do you want to sit together?* | *want to; will (informal)* |

* introduced in Unit 4.

## Grammar note 2: *Ya dan tidak* / "yes" and "no"

In Nyoman's conversation at the station, the words **ya** and **tidak** are both used. This is how you say "yes" and "no" in Indonesian.

Specifically, **tidak** is used to negate adjectives and verbs, while **bukan** is used to negate nouns. But **ya** and **tidak** are sufficient in everyday conversation.

There is a related word for saying "not yet" (**belum**) which will be covered in Unit 5.

### Exercise 3

1. Use the information about times from the conversation (on page 52) between Nyoman and the ticket office attendant, to help you answer which greeting the boys would use in the following situations.

| Siapa? | Di mana? | Selamat ... ? |
|---|---|---|
| Adi shows his train ticket | at Gambir station in Jakarta | |
| Nyoman asks directions | at Pasar Turi station in Surabaya | |
| Danny finds someone else sitting in his seat | at Gubeng station in Surabaya | |
| Adi is buying lunch | on board the Argo Bromo train | |

2. Practice reading the train times aloud in Indonesian.
   e.g. **18.30 = jam delapan belas tiga puluh**

| Nama KA<br>Name of train | Berangkat dari Jakarta<br>(setasiun Gambir)<br>Departs Jakarta<br>(Gambir railway station) | Tiba di Surabaya (setasiun Turi)<br>Arrives Surabaya<br>(Turi railway station) |
|---|---|---|
| Argo Bromo **Pagi** | 09:00 | 18:00 |
| Argo Bromo **Malam** | 21:00 | 06:00 |

| Nama KA<br>Name of train | Berangkat Surabaya<br>(setasiun Gubeng)<br>Departs Surabaya<br>(Gubeng railway station) | Tiba di Banyuwangi<br>(setasiun Banyuwangi Baru)<br>Arrives Banyuwangi<br>(Banyuwangi Baru railway station) |
|---|---|---|
| Mutiara **Pagi** | 22:00 | 04:00 (**besok**) |
| Mutiara **Malam** | 09:00 | 15:00 |

a. The boys want to leave Jakarta in the morning. Which trains should they book?

b. Nyoman has already filled out the contact details for the train to Surabaya on 22 March. He has brought along sticky notes from his friends with their details. Use the sticky notes from Danny and Adi to help him fill out the three passengers' details in the form on page 55.

**Suriadi Wulandaru**
**Jl Kolibri I no.5**
**Bintaro Sektor VIII**
**Nomor ID.: 34482005993149**

**Danny Lee**
**Jl Kolibri I no.5**
**Bintaro Sektor VIII**
**Nomor ID: N3046880**

Make sure you also fill out the booking details, using the trains you identified in Task a.  (Nyoman's section is already filled out, as an example.)

## FORMULIR PEMESANAN TIKET KERETA API
### ticket reservation form

KERETA API

**DATA PEMESAN / *data of person making the reservation***

| | |
|---|---|
| NAMA / *name* | NYOMAN |
| ALAMAT / *address* | Jl Kampung no. 24, Pondok Pinang |
| TELEPON / *telephone* | 0813 1234 5678 |

**DATA PENUMPANG / *passenger details***

| | PENUMPANG 1 / *passenger 1* | PENUMPANG 3 / *passenger 3* |
|---|---|---|
| NAMA / *name* | | |
| NO IDENTITAS / *ID No* | | |
| TIPE PNP / *type* | DEWASA (adult) / Bayi (infant) non seat | DEWASA (adult) / Bayi (infant) non seat |
| | **PENUMPANG 2 / *passenger 2*** | **PENUMPANG 4 / *passenger 4*** |
| NAMA / *name* | | |
| NO IDENTITAS / *ID* | | |
| TIPE PNP / *type* | DEWASA (adult) / Bayi (infant) non seat | DEWASA (adult) / Bayi (infant) non seat |

**Tipe penumpang**
bayi yaitu usia dibawah tiga tahun.
dewasa yaitu usia tiga tahun atau lebih.
**Nama dan nomor identitas harus sesuai dengan yang tertera pada Kartu Identitas yang dimiliki Penumpang (KTP/SIM/Paspor/Railcard dll), apabila usia penumpang dibawah 17 tahun dapat diisi dengan tanggal lahir penumpang bersangkutan dengan format ddmmyyyy**

**Passenger type**
*passenger under three years old is categorized as an infant, aged three years old or more are adult*
*Ensure your Name and ID number match your identity card (KTP / SIM / Passport / Railcard etc).*
*For passengers under 17 years old, ID column may be filled by their date of birth with format ddmmyyyy*

**DATA PEJALANAN / *booking details***

| | PERGI / *depart* | | PULANG / *return* | |
|---|---|---|---|---|
| NAMA KERETA API *train name* | | | | |
| KELAS / *class* | eksekutif / bisnis / ekonomi / eko AC | | eksekutif / bisnis / ekonomi / eko AC | |
| ASAL / *origin* | | | | |
| TUJUAN / *destination* | | | | |
| JADWAL BERANGKAT *departure* | TANGGAL *date* | JAM *time* | TANGGAL *date* | JAM *time* |

Tanggal keberangkatan mengacu pada waktu setempat di mana penumpang akan berangkat, Contoh:
Tanggal 1 Januari 2015, KA, Argo Bromo Anggrek Malam, rute Gambir ke Surabaya Turi, berangkat dari Gambir jam 21:30 WIB, tiba di Semarang Tawang jam 02:57 WIB, dan berangkat kembali jam 03:04 WIB dan tiba di Surabaya Turi jam 06:30 WIB.

**Formulir harus ditulis:**
a. Berangkat dari Gambir, tanggal kolom diisi dangan 1 Januari 2015.
b. Berangkat dari Semarang Tawang, tanggal kolom diisi dengan 2 Januari 2015.

*Departure date refers to the local time where the passengers will depart.*
*Example:*
*Date January 1, 2015, KA Argo Bromo Anggrek Malam, route Gambir to Surabaya Turi, departing from Gambir at 09:30 p.m., arriving in Semarang Tawang at 02:57 a.m., then departing from Semerang Tawang at 03:04 a.m. and arriving in Surabaya Turi at 06:30 a.m.*
*Then the form must be written :*
*a. Departing from Gambir, date column filled with 1 January 2015.*
*b. Departing from Semarang Tawang, date column filled with 2 Januari 2015.*

Dengan ini menyatakan bahwa keterangan yang telah diberikan pada formulir ini telah benar, dan mengerti serta menerima persyaratan dan ketentuan angkutan penumpang kereta api sebagaimana tertera di bagian belakang formulir ini.
*I hereby certify that information filled in this form are correct, and I have understood and accepted all terms and conditions defined on the back of this form.*

tanggal/date....................

**Nikmat Kemudahan Reservasi :**
http://tiket.kereta-api.co.id
Contact Center 121 / 021-121
Mobile Application (Blackberry, Android, IOS, Windows Phone)
Agen dan Channel Resmi KAI

tandatangan / *signature*

## 3.4 Hari Raya Nyepi   The Balinese Day of Silence

### ▎Cultural note

The Balinese Day of Silence (**Hari Raya Nyepi**) commemorates the Balinese new year, according to the Saka calendar. It usually falls in the month of March. As Bali is the only Indonesian province with a Hindu majority population, the Day of Silence is synonymous with Bali.

A few days before the New Year, Balinese Hindus preform a **melasti** ceremony, which is a ritual cleansing at the sea and lakes. On the night before **Tahun Baru Saka** (the Balinese New Year), villagers make monsters called **ogoh-ogoh** and parade them around, making lots of noise, to drive out bad spirits.

**Hari Raya Nyepi** begins at 6 a.m. the next day. The word **nyepi** is related to the Indonesian word **sepi** and means "to be quiet or silent." All public places, such as malls, shops, restaurants, and even the Ngurah Rai Airport are shut. Four ritual prohibitions, no working, no fire, no going out, and no having fun, are observed by the Balinese on the Day of Silence. The roads are free of cars, motorbikes and pedestrians. A silence falls across Bali, only broken by

Orang Bali merayakan Hari Raya Nyepi pada tahun baru Saka.
*The Balinese celebrate the Day of Silence at Balinese New Year.*

roosters crowing, and the sound of weather and other natural phenomena. Even tourists, so important to Bali's economy, must stay in their hotels and make minimal noise. If tourists try to go out onto the roads, they will be sent home by the **pecalang**, or traditional police.

After 24 hours of silence, Balinese then celebrate the New Year by visiting neighbors and family, to wish them well and ask forgiveness.

Sebelum Hari Raya Nyepi, orang melakukan upacara melasti.
*Before the Day of Silence, people hold a **melasti** ceremony.*

Pada malam Hari Raya Nyepi, semua orang di desa mengadakan upacara ogoh-ogoh.
*On the eve of the Day of Silence, everyone in the village holds an **ogoh-ogoh** ceremony.*

Mulai jam 6 pagi pada Hari Raya Nyepi, orang tidak boleh bepergian.
*From 6 o'clock in the morning on the Day of Silence, people are not allowed to go out.*

Mereka juga tidak boleh bersenang-senang, menyalakan api atau bekerja.
*They also may not have fun, light a flame or work.*

Sesudah 24 jam, orang Bali kembali menyalakan lampu dan mengunjungi keluarga dan kawan-kawan.
*After 24 hours, the Balinese turn their lights back on and visit family and friends.*

Mereka mengucapkan Selamat Tahun Baru dan saling memaafkan.
*They say "Happy New Year" and forgive each other.*

## New Words and Phrases

**merayakan** *to celebrate*
**raya** *great*
**hari raya** *holiday*
**Tahun Baru Saka** *Balinese New Year*
**sebelum** *before*
**melakukan** *to do, carry out something*
**upacara** *ceremony*

**mengadakan** *to hold, run something*
**mulai** *start, begin*
**boléh** *allowed, may, permitted*
**bepergian** *to go out (of many people/to many places)*
**meréka** *they, them*
**bersenang-senang** *to have fun*
**menyalakan** *to light, switch on*

**api** *fire, flame*
**bekerja** *to work*
**sesudah** *after (time)*
**kembali** *return, again*
**lampu** *light*
**mengunjungi** *to visit*
**mengucapkan** *to express, say*
**memaafkan** *to forgive*
**saling** *each other*

## Grammar note 1: *Sebelum, sesudah*

These two words, meaning "before" and "after," respectively, are related to **belum** and **sudah** which were discussed in Grammar Note 1 in section 3.3.

| | | | | |
|---|---|---|---|---|
| **belum** | *not yet* | | **sudah** | *already* |
| **sebelum** | *before* | | **sesudah** | *after* |

These are generally used when discussing time, but can also be used in other contexts (such as discussing directions. i.e. "after the roundabout").

## Grammar note 2: *Jam*

We have already learned to express simple time and 24-hour time in Indonesian, using **jam** + a number.

| | | | |
|---|---|---|---|
| **jam 4** | *four o'clock* | **jam 22** | *10 p.m.* |

To express a number of hours, or length of time, simply reverse the order, putting the number before the word for hours (**jam**).

| | | | |
|---|---|---|---|
| **4 jam** | *4 hours* | **22 jam** | *22 hours* |

## Exercise 4

Use information from the pictures and captions in the **Culture Note** above to choose the correct order of words.

1. **Orang Bali mengadakan upacara ogoh-ogoh sesudah / sebelum upacara melasti.**
   *The Balinese hold an* **ogoh-ogoh** *ceremony after / before the* **melasti** *ceremony.*

2. **Orang melakukan upacara ogoh-ogoh sebelum / sesudah Hari Raya Nyepi.**
   *People hold the* **ogoh-ogoh** *ceremony before / after the Balinese Day of Silence.*

3. **Orang tidak boleh bepergian pada 6 jam / jam 6 pagi pada Hari Raya Nyepi.**
   *People may not go out at 6 hours / o'clock on the Balinese Day of Silence.*

4. **Sesudah 24 jam / jam 24, orang boleh kembali menyalakan lampu.**
   *After 24 hours / 24.00, people may turn the lights back on.*

## 3.5 Keluarga Nyoman  Nyoman's family

Look at Nyoman's family tree.

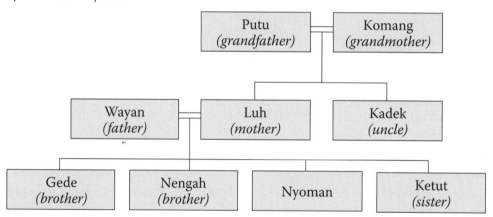

## ▍New Words and Phrases

**nomor** *number, no. (on a list or when counting)*      **kakék** *grandfather*
**nénék** *grandmother*

## ▍Cultural note: Balinese names

Nyoman's family is a typical Balinese family. In Balinese tradition, children are often given names that reflect their birth order.

The first-born child is usually **Wayan**, **Putu**, **Gede**, or **Luh** for girls
The second-born child is **Made**, **Nengah** or **Kadek**
The third-born child is **Nyoman**, or **Komang** for a girl
The fourth-born child is **Ketut**
The fifth-born child is usually **Wayan** and so on as the name cycle repeats itself.

## Exercise 5

1. What number child is Nyoman?
2. Can you guess what number child his parents and grandparents are?
3. What does the name cycle suggest about traditional Balinese families?
4. What might your name be if your family was Balinese?

## ▌ Cultural note: *Kakak & adik* / "siblings"

You will notice that Indonesian terms for siblings refer to older or younger siblings. This is different to English, where siblings are distinguished by gender ("brother" or "sister").

In Unit 1, we learned to say how many siblings you had (**Saya** [*number*] **bersaudara.**) **Saudara** is the word for "sibling" (as well as for family members in general).

| **Nyoman** | **empat** | **bersaudara:** | **dua** | | **orang kakak** | **dan** | **seorang** | | **adik.** |
|---|---|---|---|---|---|---|---|---|---|
| *Nyoman* | *four* | *has siblings:* | *two* | [counter] | *older* | *and* | *one* | [counter] | *younger.* |

## Exercise 6

1. Use the information in Unit 1 to complete the data for Adi.

   **Adi _____ bersaudara: _____ orang kakak dan _____ orang adik.**

2. Now do it for yourself.

   **Saya _____ bersaudara: _____ orang kakak dan _____ orang adik.**

   If you are an only child, you can say **Saya anak tunggal**. ("I am an only child.")
   If you are the eldest, you can say **Saya anak sulung**. ("I am the eldest.")
   If you are the youngest, you can say **Saya anak bungsu**. ("I am the youngest.")
   If you are a middle child, you can say **Saya anak nomor __**. ("I am the no. __ child.")

3. What do all these terms suggest about Indonesian social relationships?
4. Why do you think it is important to show respect for seniority (age)?
5. Can you draw your own family tree, labelled like Nyoman's?

# 3.6 Agama Hindu Hinduism

Nyoman, being Balinese, is Hindu. Adi is Muslim and Danny is Christian.

If you look at the map on page 60, you will see that most Indonesians are Muslim. Around one in ten are Christian, with minorities of the population being Hindu, Buddhist, Confucian or other religions. To understand this variety, you need to know a little about Indonesia's history.

A thousand years ago, people in Indonesia followed local tribal religions. Then Buddhism spread to the archipelago, and the great temple of Borobudur was built. However, the Buddhist kingdoms were eventually replaced by Hindu ones, such as Majapahit, which controlled an area from peninsular Malaysia, through Sumatra and Java, right across to Lombok, Ambon and beyond.

Majapahit eventually fell to Mataram, one of the first Muslim sultanates. Many of Java's Hindu population refused to accept the arrival of Islam and fled east. A few Hindus remain in the Tengger region of East Java, but most crossed the strait further east and populated the island of Bali, which

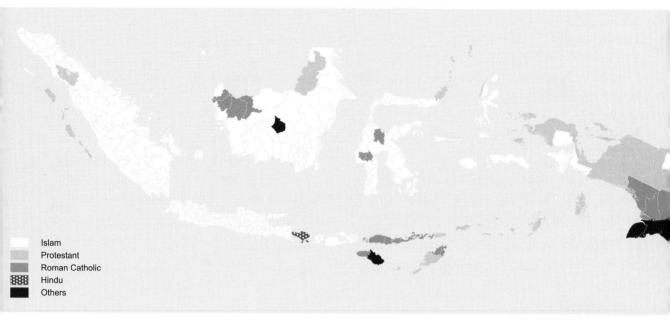

Islam
Protestant
Roman Catholic
Hindu
Others

only had very few indigenous inhabitants (Aga). This is why there are cultural and linguistic similarities between Java and Bali, even though the latter remains Hindu.

**Orang Hindu membangun candi Borobudur.**
*The Hindus built the temple of Borobudur.*

**Kerajaan itu bernama  Sancaka.**
*The kingdom was called Sancaka.*

**Pada tahun 1200, kerajaan berubah menjadi Kerajaan Majapahit.**
*In the year 1200, the kingdom changed into the Majapahit Kingdom.*

**Banyak orang memutuskan tidak menjadi orang Islam.**
*Many people decided not to become Muslim.*

**Mereka menaiki perahu pergi ke pulau Bali.**
*They took boats and went to the island of Bali.*

**Penduduk asli Bali bernama orang Bali Aga.**
*The original inhabitants of Bali were called the Bali Aga.*

## New Words and Phrases

| | | |
|---|---|---|
| **membangun** *to build* | **kerajaan** *kingdom* | **penduduk** *inhabitant, population* |
| **candi** *Buddhist temple* | **perahu** *boat* | **asli** *original* |

## Cultural note: Hinduism in Bali

Due to a long physical separation, Hinduism in Bali is rather different from the Hindu religion in India. The Balinese pray at temples called **pura**, whereas Hindu temples for Indians are called **kuil** in Indonesian, and look quite different. Beef is not a staple food in Bali, though you can still buy it. The caste system is less complex in Bali, and three main gods are worshipped: Brahma, Wisnu and Siwa. The Balinese put out daily offerings, or **sesajen**, of flowers, leaves and fruit in small worship areas of their homes. You can also see **sesajen** in the street or near larger public **pura**.

On religious occasions such as **Hari Raya Nyepi** or **Kuningan**, the Balinese worship (**bersembahyang**) at the **pura**. When they do, they wear traditional dress as shown here.

## New Words and Phrases

**ikat kepala** *tied head-cloth*
**baju** *shirt, top (also generic word for "clothes")*
**sarung** *sarong*
**kebaya** *women's traditional blouse*

**kain** *long cloth like a sarong, worn by women*
**pakai, memakai** *to wear; to use*
**kepala** *head*
**putih** *white*

The **sarung** and **kain** are usually made out of traditional woven cloth, although nowadays mass-produced cloth with gold or silver print on top is also common.

## Exercise 7

Look at the illustration above. Complete the sentence to explain what Nyoman will wear on the Balinese Day of Silence.

1. **Nyoman memakai _____ di kepala, _____ putih dan _____.**

   *Nyoman wears _____on his head, a white _____ and _____.*

2. **Adiknya, Ketut, memakai _____ dan kebaya.**

   *His younger sister, Ketut, wears _____ and a traditional blouse.*

3. **Kakaknya memakai _____**

   *His older brother wears _____*

4. **Ibunya _____**

   *His mother _____*

## 3.7 **Bagian Tubuh**  Parts of the body

We have just read a description of traditional Balinese clothing, and learned the word for "head." Look again at the picture of the two people wearing Balinese costume. Using the table below, can you label the following parts of the body on the picture?

### ▌ New Words and Phrases

| | | |
|---|---|---|
| **mata** *eye(s)* | **sepatu** *shoe(s)* | **kanan** *right* |
| **hidung** *nose* | **kuping, telinga** *ear(s)* | **mulut** *mouth* |
| **kaki** *leg, foot* | **kiri** *left* | **tangan** *arm, hand* |

 ▌ Listening practice: Song "Dua Mata Saya"

Listen to this children's song that teaches about body parts.

| | |
|---|---|
| **Dua mata saya,** | *I have two eyes,* |
| **Hidung saya satu,** | *I have one nose,* |
| **Dua kaki saya** | *I have two feet* |
| **pakai sepatu baru.** | *wearing new shoes.* |
| **Dua kuping saya** | *I have two ears* |
| **yang kiri dan kanan,** | *left and right,* |
| **Satu mulut saya** | *I have one mouth* |
| **tidak berhenti makan** | *(which) never stops eating* |

### Exercise 8

Listen again, and point to the body parts as you hear them in the song:

1. on the picture of the Balinese couple on page 61
2. on your own body

### ▌ Unit review

Put the following words in the correct order to make sentences. Each sentence is taken from a section of this unit.

1. **ada / buku / di / itu / peta** *(In that book there is a map.)*

   _____

2. **di / kami / sampai / setasiun / sudah** *(We have arrived at the station.)*

   _____

3. **api / kereta / mau / memesan / saya / tiket** *(I want to order train tickets.)*

   _____

4. **Borobudur / Budha / candi / membangun / orang** *(Buddhists built the Borobudur temple.)*

   _____

5. **dua / adik / dan / bersaudara / seorang / empat / kakak / Nyoman / orang**
   *(Nyoman has three siblings: two older ones and a younger one.)*

## ▍Unit 3 End-of-unit vocabulary list

**api** *fire, flame*
**asli** *original*
**atau** *or*
**baju** *clothes; top*
**bantu, membantu** *to help*
**barat** *west*
**baru** *just now, newly*
**bekerja** *to work*
**belas** *-teen*
**bepergian** *to go out (many people/places)*
**bersembahyang** *to perform prayers*
**bersenang-senang** *to have fun*
**bis** *bus*
**boléh** *may, permitted, allowed*
**Bu, Ibu** *Mum, mother*
**bukan** *no, not (noun)*
**bungsu** *youngest (in family)*
**candi** *(Buddhist) temple*
**danau** *lake*
**désa** *village*
**duduk** *sit*
**féri** *ferry*
**formulir** *form (to be completed)*
**gunung** *mountain, mount*
**hari raya** *festival, holiday*
**hidung** *nose*
**ikat** *tie*
**ini** *this*
**isi, mengisi** *to fill*
**itu** *that*
**jam** *hour, o'clock*
**jemput, menjemput** *to pick up, collect*
**kain** *women's sarong*
**kakék** *grandfather*
**kaki** *foot, leg*
**kami** *us (exclusive)*
**kanan** *right*

**kebaya** *traditional blouse*
**kembali** *return, again, back*
**kepala** *head*
**kerajaan** *kingdom*
**keréta api, KA** *train*
**kiri** *left*
**kita** *we (inclusive)*
**kuil** *(Indian Hindu) temple*
**kuping** *ear, ears*
**lampu** *light*
**laut** *sea*
**Maret** *March*
**mata** *eye, eyes*
**melakukan** *to do, carry out*
**memaafkan** *to forgive*
**memakai** *to wear; to use*
**membangun** *to build, create*
**membantu** *to help*
**memesan** *to order*
**menaiki** *to travel by, climb onto*
**mengadakan** *to hold, run*
**mengisi** *to fill (in)*
**mengucapkan** *to express*
**mengunjungi** *to visit*
**menjemput** *to pick up, collect*
**menuju** *to move towards*
**menyalakan** *to light, switch on*
**merayakan** *to celebrate*
**meréka** *they, them, their*
**mulai** *start, begin*
**mulut** *mouth*
**naik, menaiki** *to ride, travel on*
**nénék** *grandmother*
**nomor** *number, no. (in a list)*
**pagi** *morning*
**penduduk** *inhabitant, resident*
**perahu** *boat*
**pesan** *message*
**pesan, memesan** *to order*
**pesawat (terbang)** *airplane, aircraft*

**peta** *map*
**pulang** *go home*
**pulau** *island*
**pura** *(Hindu) temple*
**putih** *white*
**raya** *great*
**saling** *each other*
**samudera** *ocean*
**sana** *over there, yonder*
**sarung** *sarong*
**saudara** *relation, family*
**sebelum** *before (time)*
**sekarang** *now*
**selat** *strait*
**selatan** *south*
**sendiri** *self, oneself*
**sepatu** *shoe(s)*
**sesudah** *after (time)*
**setasiun** *station*
**siang** *middle of the day*
**sini** *here*
**situ** *there*
**soré** *(late) afternoon*
**sudah** *already*
**sulung** *eldest (in family)*
**taman** *park, garden*
**tangan** *hand, arm*
**telinga** *ear, ears*
**tentang** *about*
**terima kasih** *thank you*
**tidak** *no; not (for adjectives)*
**tikét** *ticket*
**timur** *east*
**tunggal** *only, single, sole*
**tunggu, menunggu** *to wait*
**upacara** *ceremony*
**utara** *north*
**waktu** *when; time*
**ya** *yes*

This dialogue appears on page 71.

# Ibu Kita Kartini
## Our Mother Kartini

In this unit, we will:

- Learn about well-known Indonesian women, including national hero Raden Ajeng Kartini,
- Learn different ways to make plurals,
- Give a physical description of someone in your family and how they are dressed,
- Compare different ways of constructing sentences,
- Learn how to use **sini**, **situ** and **sana**,
- Learn about a traditional Indonesian wedding,
- Be able to state the hour and time of day,
- Use the passive form of the verb (**di-**) as well as the active form **meN-**.

## 4.1 Hari Kartini  Kartini Day

### Basic Sentences

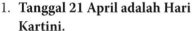

On 21 April, Indonesians celebrate Kartini Day, on the anniversary of her birth. Kartini was an early fighter for women's rights and established a school for Javanese girls at the turn of the 19th century.

1. **Tanggal 21 April adalah Hari Kartini.**    *21 April is Kartini Day.*

2. **Kartini adalah pahlawan nasional Indonesia.**    *Kartini is an Indonesian national hero.*

3. **Anak-anak merayakan Hari Kartini dengan memakai baju adat.**    *Children celebrate Kartini Day by wearing traditional dress.*

4. **Di SD 3, para guru ikut memakai kain kebaya dan pakaian adat.**    *At SD 3, teachers also wear traditional dress.*

5. **Di SMA 3, Adi dan Danny ikut acaranya sambil bernyanyi.**    *At SMA 3, Adi and Danny join in the proceedings by singing.*

## New Words and Phrases

**pahlawan** *hero*
**nasional** *national*
**anak-anak** *children*
**adat** *tradition, traditional*

**para** *more than one (shows plural)*
**guru** *teacher*
**acara** *event, proceedings*

**sambil** *at the same time as, while (doing something)*
**bernyanyi** *to sing*

## Grammar note: Plurals

Unlike in English, the Indonesian language sometimes shows that a noun is plural, and sometimes it does not, depending on the situation. There are two ways in Indonesian to show that a word is plural.

The first is by doubling. For example, the word for "child" is **anak**, while the word for "children" is **anak-anak**; and the word for "a house" is **rumah**, while the word for "houses" is **rumah-rumah**.

The second is by using the word **para** before a noun. This word is usually used in more formal situations. In the opening narrative, **para guru** signifies that the teachers are respected.

Sometimes, however, an Indonesian word should be translated and understood as plural, despite taking the singular form. For example, in Unit 3 there is the sentence:

> **Penduduk asli Bali bernama orang Bali Aga.**

This doesn't mean there is only one Bali Aga inhabitant. In English we would say: "The original inhabitants of Bali are called the Bali Aga."

CAUTION: Not all Indonesian words that are doubled are plurals. For example, **hati-hati** means "be careful," not "livers" or "hearts." And **cita-cita** means "dream" or "ambition." **Cita** is not usually used by itself, but in other combinations (e.g., **cita rasa** "taste").

### Exercise 1

Translate the following sentences into English, focusing on whether the nouns are singular or plural.

1. **Kami sudah di bis menuju kota Denpasar.**

   _____

2. **Nyoman empat bersaudara: dua orang kakak dan seorang adik.**

   _____

3. **Orang Budha membangun candi Borobudur.**

   _____

4. **Kerajaan itu bernama Kerajaan Sancaka.**

   _____

5. **Mereka menaiki perahu pergi ke pulau Bali.**

   _____

6. **Banyak orang memutuskan tidak menjadi orang Islam.**

   _____

## Exercise 2

Fill in the missing words.

1. **Nyoman bersaudara _____.**
   *Nyoman is one of four siblings.*

2. **_____ orang ke Surabaya.**
   *Three fares for Surabaya.*

3. **_____bersaudara banyak.**
   *She has lots of brothers and sisters.*

4. **_____ memakai baju merah.**
   *People wear red clothing.*

## Cultural note: *Siapa itu Kartini?* Who is Kartini?

Raden Ajeng Kartini is one of Indonesia's many national heroes. She was born into an aristocratic Javanese family on 21 April 1879. At that time, Indonesia was ruled by the Dutch and known as the Dutch East Indies (**Hindia Belanda**). Unlike most Javanese children (especially girls), she was lucky enough to be able to attend a school for Dutch students, as her father was a government official. There she learned to read and write Dutch.

However, after the age of 12, she had to remain at home according to the tradition of **pingitan**, where girls were kept inside the home until the time they were married. Kartini and her sisters, encouraged by a penfriend and local Dutch women they knew, set up a local school for girls. Eventually, Kartini was married off to a local official as his fourth wife. She tragically died in childbirth at the age of 24. Kartini's letters to her Dutch friends were eventually published and her work became more widely known.

## 4.2 Ibu Kita Kartini  Our Mother Kartini

## Listening

## Exercise 3

**Ibu Kita Kartini** is a famous song sung on 21 April to commemorate Kartini Day. Read the New Words and Phrases section, then listen to the song and fill in the missing words.

### Ibu Kita Kartini
#### By W. R. Supratman

| | |
|---|---|
| **Ibu kita Kartini** | *Our mother Kartini* |
| **Putri sejati** | *A real princess* |
| **Putri Indonesia** | *A daughter of Indonesia* |
| *(1)_____* **namanya** | *Fragrant is her name* |
| | |
| **Ibu kita Kartini** | *Our mother Kartini* |
| **Pendekar** *(2)_____* | *Fighter for her nation* |
| **Pendekar kaumnya** | *Fighter for her people* |
| **Untuk** *(3)_____* | *(Fighting) to be free* |
| | |
| **Wahai ibu kita Kartini** | *O, our mother Kartini* |
| **Putri yang mulia** | *Such a pure woman* |
| **Sungguh besar** *(4)_____***nya** | *Such big dreams she had* |
| **Bagi Indonesia** | *for Indonesia* |

## New Words and Phrases

**sejati** *real, true*
**harum** *fragrant, smells good*
**pendékar** *fighter*
**bangsa** *people, nation*

**kaum** *tribe, community*
**merdéka** *free, independent*
**wahai** *O!, Oh!*
**mulia** *lofty; pure*

**sungguh** *truly*
**besar** *big, great*
**cita-cita** *dreams, ambitions*

## 4.3 Tentang keluarga Adi  More about Adi's family

## Basic Sentences

1. **Ini foto keluarga Adi.**  
   *This is a photo of Adi's family.*

2. **Ibunya Adi kurus. Dia berkulit terang dan be-rambut hitam.**  
   *Adi's mother is thin. She has light skin and black hair.*

3. **Ayahnya Adi tinggi besar. Dia berkulit gelap.**  
   *Adi's father is big and tall. He has dark skin.*

4. **Hari, kakaknya Adi, juga tinggi tapi kurus. Dia berkulit terang.**  
   *Hari, Adi's older brother, is also tall but thin. He has light skin.*

5. **Sena, kakaknya Adi yang satu lagi, juga tinggi dan kurus dan berkulit terang.**  
   *Sena, Adi's other older brother, is also tall and thin and light-skinned.*

6. **Hari dan Sena itu kembar.**  
   *Hari and Sena are twins.*

7. **Adi juga tinggi dan kurus, tapi berkulit gelap. Rambutnya berwarna hitam.**  
   *Adi is also tall and thin, but dark-skinned. His hair is dark.*

8. **Adiknya Adi, Nina, berbadan kecil dan berkulit gelap.**  
   *Adi's younger sister, Nina, is small and dark-skinned.*

9. **Rambutnya berwarna cokelat.**  
   *Her hair is brown.*

## ▌New Words and Phrases

**foto** *photo*
**kurus** *thin*
**gemuk** *fat*
**berkulit** *to have skin, -skinned*
**terang** *light*
**berambut** *to have hair; -haired*

**hitam** *black*
**tinggi** *tall, high*
**besar** *big, large*
**gelap** *dark*
**badan** *body*
**berbadan** *to have a body, -bodied*

**kecil** *small, little*
**péndék** *short*
**lagi** *again, more*
**kembar** *twin(s)*

## ▌Language note 1

The opposite of **tinggi** is **péndék**, but this word can sometimes have a negative connotation. In the description above, Nina is described as **kecil** instead.

## ▌Language note 2: *Rambut di Indonesia* / Indonesian hair

Nearly all Indonesians have black hair (**berambut hitam**), while a few might have brownish (**cokelat**) hair. When it comes to describing the variety of colors in hair, apart from **hitam** and **cokelat**, we also use **pirang** ("blond," "blonde") and **mérah** ("red"). Some Indonesians would consider anyone who does not have black hair to be **pirang**. Hair can also be long (**panjang**), medium (**sedang**) or short; straight (**lurus**), wavy (**berombak**) or curly (**keriting**). Having no hair or a shaved head is called **botak** ("bald").

## ▌Grammar: Sentence construction

There are several sentence patterns that can be used for a description. In Unit 1, we learned the following structure:

| | |
|---|---|
| **Badan Danny** | **tinggi.** |
| *Danny's body [is]* | *tall.* |

In this unit, the following structures have also been introduced:

| | | | | |
|---|---|---|---|---|
| **Danny** | **itu** | **badannya** | | **tinggi.** |
| *Danny* | | *his body* | *[is]* | *tall.* |
| **Danny** | **itu** | **berbadan** | | **tinggi.** |
| *Danny* | | *has a body* | | *tall.* |

All of these are grammatically correct, and can be used in appropriate contexts. Sometimes we tend to use one more than the other. The first example above is perhaps the best way of showing the Indonesian word order (noun + adjective + verb). The second example is more colloquial, or typical of spoken Indonesian.

The third example shows a **ber-** verb being used.

Look at the sentences below to see how these structures are used:

**Kulit Sena terang.**
**Sena kulitnya terang / Kulitnya Sena terang.**
**Sena berkulit terang.**
*Sena's skin is light.*

**Badan Adi kurus.**
**Adi badannya kurus / Badannya Adi kurus.**
**Adi berbadan kurus.**
*Adi's body is thin.*

**Rambut Nina hitam.**
**Nina rambutnya hitam / Rambutnya Nina hitam.**
**Nina berambut hitam.**
*Nina's hair is black.*

## Exercise 4

Write about your own family using any of the three constructions above.

1. **Ayah saya** _____ .

2. **Ibu saya** _____ .

3. **Kakak / Adik saya,** _____ .

## Exercise 5

What do you think Danny looks like? Circle the correct words below.

**Danny itu badannya tinggi / péndék dan kurus / gemuk.**

**Dia berkulit gelap / terang dan berambut hitam / cokelat / pirang / mérah.**

## Exercise 6

Match the descriptions to the pictures below.

                                                              *Answer*

1. **Rambut yang berombak, panjang dan berwarna hitam.**    _____

2. **Rambut yang lurus, péndék dan berwarna cokelat.**    _____

3. **Rambut yang ikal, keriting, sedang dan berwarna pirang.**    _____

A            B            C

# 4.4 Pernikahan keluarga  A family wedding

The day after Hari Kartini, Adi and his parents have been invited to a family wedding in Bandung. It is quite common to bring friends along to weddings, so Danny will go with them. They will drive up to Bandung the night before, then drive home again the day after. The whole family is packing their bags in preparation for the trip. Adi is talking to his mother (Ibu Maya) who is standing in the doorway. She is looking for her mobile phone (**HP** [ha pé], short for *handphone, an "Indonesian English" word). Listen to their conversation.

## Listening to a Dialogue

IBU:  **Di mana HP Ibu?**  *Where's my mobile?*

ADI:  **Di sini tidak ada.**  *It's not here.*

IBU:  **Tidak ada di meja?**  *Not on the table?*

ADI:  (*looking*) **Tidak ada.**  *It's not here.*
   **Di sini hanya ada buku, HP Adi dan tempat pensil.**
   *Here there's only a book, my mobile and a pencil case.*

IBU:  **Ya, tapi Ibu melihat HP Ibu di situ tadi malam.**  *Yes, but I saw my mobile there last night.*

ADI:  **Tapi sekarang tidak ada, Bu.**  *But it's not there now, Mum.*
   **Apakah HP Ibu ada di mobil?**  *Is your mobile in the car?*

IBU:  **Tidak. Ibu sudah lihat di sana. Tidak ada.**  *No. I've already looked there. It's not there.*

ADI:  **Adi telepon ke Ibu, ya.**  *I'll ring you, okay?*

IBU:  (sound of phone ringing) **Oh, itu HP Ibu! Di kamar sana!**
   *Oh, that's my mobile! In the room over there!*

## New Words and Phrases

**HP [hapé]** *mobile phone, cell phone*
**méja** *table*
**tidak** *not, no (for adjectives)*
**hanya** *only*
**tempat pénsil** *pencil case* (lit., place for pencils)

**tapi** *but*
**lihat, melihat** *to see*
**sekarang** *now*
**Bu** *Mum, Madam, Ma'am* (term of address to married or older women)

**apakah** *whether;* (way of forming a question)
**mobil** *car*
**télépon, menélépon** *to ring, call*
**ya** *yes; okay?* (at the end of a sentence)
**kamar** *room*

## Grammar note 1: *Sini situ sana*

The **ini-itu** pattern you learned in Unit 3 also works for describing location:

**Buku Adi di sini.**   *Adi's book is here.*
**Pintu di situ.**    *The door is there.*
**Pulau Bali di sana.**   *Bali is far away, over there.*

**Di sini** = *here (in this place), i.e. where I am*
**Di situ** = *there (in that place), i.e. where you are*
**Di sana** = *over there (in that place, yonder), i.e. where neither of us are*

## ▌Grammar note 2: Names as pronouns

You will see from the conversation between Adi and his mother that they do not use **saya** or **kamu** when speaking to each other. Some families do, but Adi's family is one of the many who prefer to use their name as a personal pronoun instead. You will hear this throughout Indonesia, particularly between family members.

1. Adi: **Di mana HP Ibu?**      *Where is your mobile?*
   Adi uses "Mother" as the word for "your." This can be done to show respect to any married or older woman, not just your own mother.

2. **Di sini hanya ada HP Adi.**    *Here, there is only my mobile.*
   Here, Adi uses his own name to refer to himself, instead of **saya**.

3. **Ibu melihat HP Ibu di situ.**  *I saw my mobile there.*
   Adi's mother uses the name that Adi calls her to refer to herself.

4. **Adi telepon ke Ibu.**      *I will ring you.*
   Adi uses his name, and the word "Mother," here.

Generally speaking, if names are used as personal pronouns, both parties take the perspective of the younger or inferior speaker. You do not need to be able to use names as pronouns yourself, but you should be able to recognize when others do.

## ▌Grammar note 3: *Ya* tag

We have learned that **ya** means "yes." In the sentence **Adi telepon ke Ibu, ya** this word is used slightly differently, as a tag meaning "okay?" or "right?"

### Exercise 7

Match the following sentences using **ya** to the correct translation.

1. **Di mana, ya?**              a. *I wonder where it is?*
2. **Ya, ada di situ.**          b. *Ring me, okay?*
3. **Telepon ke saya, ya.**      c. *Yes, it's there.*

For Indonesian weddings an invitation is usually sent out a week before the event. Close family members will attend a religious ceremony at a mosque, church, or temple, while the extended family and friends will attend the reception. Most of the guests will be friends or colleagues of the couple's parents. Weddings in Indonesia are a chance to show off a family's wealth. Smaller receptions will be held at the bride's home, but in big cities, reception halls and hotels are often completely booked for over a year in advance for weddings. A total of 500 guests is not uncommon, while big society weddings may have as many as 3,000 guests.

## Reading: *Undangan pernikahan* Wedding invitations

*Akad Nikah*

**Indah Rustika, ST**

**Putri dari Bapak Tatang Erlangga dan Ibu Eulis Nurlaela**

**dengan**

**Guntur Halilintar Rasyid**

**Putra dari Bapak Zulkarnaen dan Ibu Sri Lestari Suriadinata**

**Sabtu 22 April**
**Pukul 09.00 WIB**
**Bertempat di Jalan Subang no.5, Antapani**
**Bandung**

**Resepsi**
**Sabtu 22 April**
**Pukul 11.00 - 14.00 WIB**
**Bertempat di Balai Pertemuan Bumi Sangkuriang**
**Jl Kiputih 12, Ciumbuleuit, Bandung 40142**

**Kel. H. Tatang Erlangga**          **Kel. Zulkarnaen, SH**
**Hj. Eulis Nurlaela Suriadinata**          **Sri Lestari**
**Indah dan Guntur**

## Language note: Formal vocabulary

As in any language, for certain items Indonesian has a set of words which are used on formal occasions, as opposed to everyday usage. You will see in the invitation that the word for "child" is **putra**, instead of **anak**; while "hour" is written as **pukul**; previously we had seen that the everyday word is **jam**.

Putra is a generic, polite term for "child" or "children." You sometimes see the word **putra-putri** ("son and daughter"; "children"): here, the word **putri** has a similar, elevated meaning as the word for "princess" as studied in Unit 2. **Pukul** (literally meaning "hit" or "stroke of the clock") when used for time derives from Malay, and is often used in print and more formal documents (such as wedding invitations), instead of **jam**.

## New Words and Phrases

**akad nikah** *Muslim wedding ceremony*
**putra** *son, child*
**(hari) Sabtu** *Saturday*

**pukul** *o'clock. :00*
**bertempat** *to take place*
**resépsi** *reception*
**dilaksanakan** *to be conducted*

**balai** *hall*
**pertemuan** *meeting*
**jalan** *road, street*

## *Busana pernikahan* Wedding dress: new words

**kain kebaya** *traditional women's costume of blouse and sarong*
**seléndang** *shawl, sash*

**sepatu selop** *slip-on shoes*
**batik** *traditional Indonesian wax-dyed cloth*
**celana panjang** *trousers*

**keméja** *shirt (with collar)*
**jas** *suit jacket, blazer*
**péci** *velvet cap*

The bride-to-be is actually Ibu Maya's niece, Indah. For this reason, Adi's father (Pak Johan) will wear formal dress (a suit) while Ibu Maya will wear a **kain kebaya** outfit matching her sisters' and sisters'-in-law, to show that they are close relatives of the bride, with a shawl and high-heeled shoes. Adi, Danny, Sena and Hari will wear a **batik** shirt, which most Indonesian men and boys would wear to a wedding. Nina will dress in a Sundanese costume as she is one of the bridal attendants.

You can see what they look like in the pictures below.

### Exercise 8

Write in the names of Adi's family members to describe what they are wearing. Use the Word Bank above, and the pictures below, to help you. The first one has been done for you.

**Ibu Maya dan Nina memakai kain kebaya, selendang dan sepatu selop.**
*Ibu Maya and Nina wear traditional costume, a sash and slip-on high heeled shoes.*

_____

_____ **dan** _____
**memakai ...**

_____ **memakai ...**

## ▌Cultural note: Indonesian weddings

Usually, people send out invitations for Indonesian weddings a week before the event. Weddings are an opportunity to recognize your family's ethnic background when a family is all from the same ethnic group, then obviously the traditions of that group will feature in the wedding costumes, decor and any traditional ceremonies (e.g. Sundanese people in Bandung, Balinese in Denpasar, etc.). However, many Indonesian families nowadays are ethnically mixed. Therefore, a bride might use a Sundanese costume at her religious ceremony to honor her mother, then a Javanese costume at the reception to honor her father.

# 4.5  Jam berapa sekarang? What time is it?

In Unit 3 we were introduced to the 24-hour clock when the boys travelled to Bali. Now we are going to use the 12-hour clock in combination with the time of day, as in English (e.g,. "8 o'clock in the evening").

Periods of time are expressed using the words **dari** ("from") and **sampai** ("to, until").  Generally, just **sampai** is used. So "8–9 o'clock" would be expressed as **(dari) jam delapan sampai sembilan**.

### Exercise 9

Look at the clocks below to see how one tells time in Indonesian, as well as how the day is divided up, and fill in the blanks to show the time.

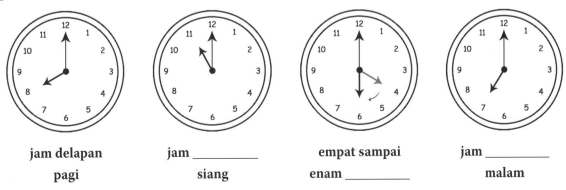

| jam delapan | jam _____ | empat sampai | jam _____ |
|:---:|:---:|:---:|:---:|
| pagi | siang | enam _____ | malam |

## Exercise 10

Now read the sentences below. Circle the correct time of day for each event.

| Event | Time of day (circle the correct answer) |
|---|---|
| 1. **Keluarga Adi tiba di Bandung jam 6.**<br>*Adi's family arrive in Bandung at 6 o'clock.* | (pagi) atau sore |
| 2. **Jam 8 akad nikah dilaksanakan di rumah Ranti.**<br>*At 8 o'clock the religious ceremony is held at Ranti's house.* | pagi atau sore |
| 3. **Semua berangkat ke gedung resepsi sekitar jam 9.**<br>*All depart for the reception venue around 9 o'clock.* | pagi atau malam |
| 4. **Resepsi diadakan jam 11 di gedung Bumi Sangkuriang.**<br>*The reception is held at 11 o'clock at the Bumi Sangkuriang building.* | siang atau malam |
| 5. **Jam 3 keluarga Adi kembali ke hotel.**<br>*At 3 o'clock Adi's family returns to the hotel.* | pagi atau sore |
| 6. **Dari jam 4 sampai jam 6 semuanya beristirahat.**<br>*From 4 to 6 o'clock all of them have a rest.* | pagi atau sore |
| 7. **Jam 7 mereka pergi makan malam.**<br>*At 7 o'clock they go out for dinner.* | sore atau malam |

## ▌Grammar note: *di-* / Passive *di-* verbs

So far we have learned active **meN-** verbs, such as the ones below. However, in Indonesian, the passive **di-** form of verbs is widely used. As in English, the word order changes when the passive voice is used:

ACTIVE FORM:   subject   **meN-** verb   object
PASSIVE FORM:   object   **di-** verb   subject

1. **melaksanakan** ("to hold, conduct")
**Jam 8 (keluarga Ranti) melaksanakan akad nikah di rumah Ranti.**
*At 8 o'clock (Ranti's family) held the reception at their home.*

   **dilaksanakan** ("to be held, conducted")
**Jam 8 akad nikah dilaksanakan di rumah Ranti.**
*At 8 o'clock the religious ceremony was conducted at Ranti's home.*

Here, the passive is used because there is an object focus on the religious ceremony. It is assumed we know who is holding the ceremony, so the focus shifts to the event itself.

2. **mengadakan** ("to hold, run")
**(Keluarga Ranti?) mengadakan resepsi jam 11 di Bumi Sangkuriang.**
*( ? ) held the reception at 11 o'clock at Bumi Sangkuriang.*

   **diadakan** ("to be held, run")
**Resepsi diadakan jam 11 di Bumi Sangkuriang.**
*The reception was held at 11 o'clock at Bumi Sangkuriang.*

Here, we are not really concerned with who is hosting or holding the reception (it would actually be the families of both the bride and groom). As this is either assumed, or unimportant, then the passive verb is used, to focus on the reception itself.

Why is the **di-** form common in Indonesian? There are a number of reasons.

- It focuses on the object, rather than the person doing the action. (You can even leave the person out completely.)
- It is considered more polite (as in English!, e.g. "Trespassers will be prosecuted.").
- It can be more formal. It is often used in public signs, as in the point above.

You will have noticed that the **meN-** form actually consists of **meng-**, **men-**, **me-** and **meny-**, among others. The letters after the **me-** may change, depending on the base or root word of the verb (as in the third example below). This is why it is called the **meN-** prefix.

| meN- prefix | base word | suffix/ending |
|---|---|---|
| meng- | ada | -kan |
| me- | laksana | -kan |
| men- | jemput | |

You can try to memorize which **meN-** prefix is used before which base words, or check the reference grammar or glossary in this book. It is often easier to just learn through practice. However, writing **di-** verbs is much easier, as the **di-** prefix never changes. It is always just added in front of the base word.

| di- prefix | base word | suffix/ending |
|---|---|---|
| di | ada | kan |
| di | laksana | kan |
| di | jemput | |

If you use a passive verb but still wish to mention who is doing the action, you can add **oléh** ("by") after the verb.

**Danny, Nyoman dan Adi dijemput oleh kakaknya Nyoman.**

*Danny, Nyoman and Adi were picked up by Nyoman's brother.*

## Exercise 11

These are all **meN-** verbs you have learned so far. Give their meanings and then rewrite them as passive **di-** forms. The first has been done for you.

| Active meN- form | Meaning | Passive di- form | Meaning |
|---|---|---|---|
| memutuskan | *to decide* | diputuskan | *to be decided* |
| membangun | | | |
| melakukan | | | |
| memakai (base word is **pakai**) | | | |
| memaafkan | | | |

## Exercise 12

Here are some new **di-** verbs from the wedding invitation, plus a few others. Rewrite them in the active **meN-** form. Check the glossary if you need to for the correct **meN-** form.

| Passive di- form | Meaning | Active meN- form | Meaning |
|---|---|---|---|
| dilakukan | | | |
| dilaksanakan | | | |
| dijemput | | | |
| dipesan | *to be ordered* | | |

# 4.6  Wanita di Indonesia  Indonesian women

Ibu Maya works in a bank. Indah is an engineer and Nina is a student.

Indonesian women work in many different professions, such as politician, journalist, teacher, homemaker, artist or civil servant, to name a few.

In a program from a Kartini Day concert, Danny is reading some mini biographies of three well-known Indonesian women who are patrons of the event.

After reading, decide whether the statements are true or false, and write down the phrase that justifies your answer.

## ▌ Basic Sentences: Mini Biographies

1. **Sri Mulyani adalah seorang ekonom. Sesudah menjadi menteri, pada tahun 2009 dia bekerja sebagai direktur Bank Dunia selama enam tahun. Pada tahun 2016 dia pulang untuk menjadi Menteri Keuangan di bawah Presiden Joko Widodo.**

   *Sri Mulyani is an economist. After becoming a minister, in 2009 she worked as director at the World Bank for six years. In 2016 she returned home to become Minister of Finance under President Joko Widodo.*

2. **Susi Pudjiastuti adalah seorang pengusaha. Dia mendapat ide untuk mengekspor ikan menggunakan pesawat terbang. Lalu dia mendirikan perusahaan Susi Air. Pada tahun 2014, dia diminta menjadi Menteri Perikanan dan Kelautan.**

   *Susi Pudjiastuti is a businessperson. She got the idea of exporting fish using aircraft. Then she founded the company Susi Air.  In 2014, she was asked to be Minister of Fisheries and Maritime Affairs.*

3. **Tri Rismaharini adalah orang perempuan pertama untuk dipilih langsung oleh rakyat sebagai walikota. Sejak tahun 2010 dia ikut mengubah Surabaya menjadi kota yang bersih, modern dan menarik. Surabaya lalu berkembang menjadi lebih baik.**

   *Tri Rismaharini was the first woman directly elected by the people as Mayor.  Since 2010 she has helped to change Surabaya into a clean, modern and attractive metropolis. The city has since developed for the better.*

## New Words and Phrases

**ékonom** *economist*

**menteri** *minister*

**sebagai** *as*

**diréktur** *director*

**Bank Dunia** *World Bank*

**keuangan** *finance*

**bawah** *below, beneath, under*

**Présidén** *President*

**pengusaha** *entrepreneur*

**mendapat** *to get, obtain*

**ide** *idea*

**mengékspor** *to export*

**ikan** *fish*

**menggunakan** *to use*

**terbang** *(to) fly*

**lalu** *then*

**mendirikan** *to establish, set up*

**perusahaan** *company*

**minta, meminta** *to ask, request*

**perikanan** *fisheries*

**kelautan** *maritime affairs*

**perempuan** *woman, female*

**pertama** *first*

**memilih** *to choose, elect*

**langsung** *direct, directly, straight*

**rakyat** *people, public*

**walikota** *mayor*

**ubah, mengubah** *to change*

**bersih** *clean*

**modérn** *modern*

**menarik** *attractive*

**berkembang** *develop, blossom*

**lebih** more

## Grammar note: Conjunctions

The mini-biographies contain some useful Indonesian conjunctions.

**Dia bekerja <u>sebagai</u> diréktur Bank Dunia.**
*She worked as a director at the World Bank.*

**<u>Lalu</u> dia mendirikan perusahaan Susi Air.**
*Then she founded the company Susi Air.*

**Dia wanita pertama untuk dipilih langsung oleh rakyat <u>sebagai</u> walikota.**
*She was the first woman to be directly elected by the people as Mayor.*

**<u>Sejak</u> tahun 2010 dia ikut mengubah Surabaya.**
*Since 2010, she has helped to change Surabaya.*

**Surabaya <u>lalu</u> berkembang menjadi lebih baik.**
*Surabaya then developed for the better.*

### Exercise 13

Answer the questions, based on the reading and the sentence structures above.

1. **Susi Pudjiastuti bekerja sebagai apa?**
   *What does Susi Pudjiastuti work as?*

2. **Sri Mulyani bekerja di Bank Dunia, lalu pulang menjadi apa?**
   *Sri Mulyani worked at the World Bank, then came home. What did she become?*

3. **Apakah Tri Rismaharini menjadi Walikota Surabaya sejak 2012?**
   *Has Tri Rismaharini been the Mayor of Surabaya since 2012?*

## Grammar note: Comparatives (*lebih*)

Making comparatives ("-er," "more") in Indonesian is very easy, by adding **lebih** before the adjective.

**Surabaya lalu berkembang menjadi lebih baik.**
*Surabaya has since developed for the better.*

If you want to make a negative comparison, simply use **kurang** ("less").  For a superlative ("most, -est"), use **paling** or the prefix **ter-**.

> **Pada tahun 2010, kota Surabaya kurang bersih.**
> *In 2010, the city of Surabaya was not so clean.*

> **Surabaya adalah kota paling bersih di Jawa Timur.**
> *Surabaya is the cleanest city in East Java.*

## Exercise 14

How would you say these words in Indonesian? All the adjectives are from this unit.

1. more modern _____

2. more interesting _____

3. straighter _____

4. shorter _____

5. not as long _____

6. largest _____

## | Unit review

Apart from Kartini, another famous early Indonesian feminist was Dewi Sartika. She was born in Bandung in 1884, and was able to attend a Dutch school. However, when her father was exiled to Ambon, she was forced to go and live with her uncle in the small town of Cicalengka. People there were amazed by the little Sundanese girl who could speak Dutch and liked teaching her friends to read and write. When her father died and Dewi Sartika finally returned to live in Bandung, she kept thinking of her friends in Cicalengka who had no school. This motivated her to open a school in Bandung, known as **Sakola Istri** in Sundanese (**Sekolah Perempuan** in Indonesian).

In 1906 Dewi Sartika married a fellow teacher. A few years later their school was renamed **Sakola Kautamaan Istri**. By 1912 there were nine of these schools around West Java.

Dewi Sartika's husband died in 1939, and a few years later Indonesia was invaded by Japan. This resulted in her schools closing. Dewi Sartika herself died in 1947, when she was evacuating from Bandung (then under siege from the Dutch), from a leg wound that, as a diabetic, she could not recover from. She is buried in Bandung.

Put the sentences in order, to create a mini-biography of Dewi Sartika in Indonesian.

A. **Dia besar di kampung, di Cicalengka.**

B. **Dewi Sartika lahir di kota Bandung pada tahun 1884.**

C. **Dia juga menikah dengan seorang guru.**

D. **Waktu kembali ke Bandung, dia menjadi guru, lalu mendirikan sekolah untuk anak-anak perempuan.**

E. **Waktu SD, dia belajar bahasa Belanda dan bahasa Sunda.**

## Unit 4 End-of-unit vocabulary list

**acara** *event, proceedings*
**adat** *tradition*
**akad nikah** *Islamic marriage ceremony*
**anak-anak** *children*
**apakah** *whether; forms a question*
**April** *April*
**badan** *body*
**balai** *hall*
**bangsa** *people, nation*
**batik** *traditional Indonesian wax-dyed cloth*
**bawah** *below, beneath, under*
**berambut** *to have hair*
**berangkat** *to depart, leave*
**berbadan** *-bodied*
**berkembang** *to develop, blossom*
**berkulit** *-skinned*
**bernyanyi** *to sing*
**berombak** *wavy*
**bersih** *clean*
**bertempat** *to take place*
**berwarna** *coloured*
**besar** *big, large*
**botak** *bald*
**Bu, Ibu** *you (to mother or older woman)*
**celana** *pants, trousers*
**cita-cita** *dreams, ambition*
**cokelat** *brown*
**dilaksanakan** *to be conducted (see melaksanakan)*
**diréktur** *director*
**dunia** *world*
**ékonom** *economist*
**foto** *photo*
**gelap** *dark*
**gemuk** *fat*
**guru** *teacher*
**hanya** *only, just*
**harum** *fragrant, smells good*
**Hindia Belanda** *Dutch East Indies*
**hitam** *black*
**HP ('handphone', hénpon)** *mobile (phone), cellphone*
**ide** *idea*
**ikal** *wavy*
**ikan** *fish*

**jalan** *street*
**jas** *suit jacket, blazer*
**Jawa** *Java*
**kain kebaya** *women's traditional dress, consisting of blouse and sarong*
**kamar** *room*
**kaum** *tribe, community*
**kecil** *small, little*
**kelautan** *maritime*
**kembar** *twin(s)*
**keméja** *shirt (with collar)*
**keriting** *curly, curled*
**keuangan** *finance, financial*
**kulit** *skin*
**kurus** *thin*
**lagi** *again, more*
**lalu** *then*
**langsung** *direct(ly), straight*
**lebih** *more*
**léwat** *past; via*
**lihat, melihat** *to see*
**lurus** *straight*
**matang** *cooked, ripe*
**méja** *table*
**melaksanakan** *to hold, conduct*
**memilih** *to choose, elect*
**meminta, minta** *to ask, request*
**menarik** *attractive*
**mendapat** *to get, obtain*
**mendirikan** *to establish, set up*
**mengekspor** *to export*
**menggunakan** *to use*
**mengubah** *to change something*
**menikah, nikah** *to marry*
**menteri** *minister*
**merdéka** *free, independent*
**minta, meminta** *to ask, request*
**mobil** *car*
**modérn** *modern*
**mulia** *lofty; pure*
**nasional** *national*
**oléh** *by*
**pahlawan** *hero, heroine*
**pakaian** *clothing*
**panjang** *long*
**para** *(more than one)*
**péci** *men's velvet cap*

**péndék** *short*
**pendékar** *fighter*
**pengusaha** *entrepreneur*
**pénsil** *pencil*
**perempuan** *woman, female*
**perikanan** *fisheries*
**pertama** *first*
**pertemuan** *meeting*
**perusahaan** *company, business*
**pirang** *blond(e)*
**potong, memotong** *to cut*
**Présidén** *President*
**pukul** *o'clock, :00*
**putra** *son; child*
**putri** *daughter*
**rakyat** *people, public*
**rambut** *hair*
**resépsi** *reception*
**Sabtu** *Saturday*
**sajikan, menyajikan** *to serve, present*
**sambil** *while, -ing*
**sayuran** *vegetables*
**sebagai** *as*
**sedang** *medium (of size, length)*
**sejak** *since, from*
**sejati** *real, true*
**sekarang** *now*
**seléndang** *shawl, sash*
**sepatu selop** *slip-on shoes*
**sungguh** *truly*
**tapi, tetapi** *but*
**télepon, menélepon** *to ring, telephone*
**tempat** *place*
**tempat pénsil** *pencil case*
**terang** *light; bright*
**terbang** *(to) fly*
**terpilih** *elected, chosen*
**tidak** *no, not (for adjectives)*
**tinggi** *tall; high*
**ubah, mengubah** *to change something*
**wahai** *O! Oh!*
**walikota** *mayor*
**ya** *yes; okay? (at the end of a sentence)*

**Belum masuk Jawa Tengah. Mungkin daerah Tasikmalaya?**
*We still haven't reached Central Java. Maybe the Tasikmalaya region?*

**Kita sudah sampai di mana, ya?**
*Where are we now?*

**Aku sudah tidak sabar tiba di Yogya. Menginap di hotel bagus, mengobrol dengan kawan-kawan, jalan-jalan ke Kaliurang... asyik!**
*I can't wait to reach Yogya. Stay in a nice hotel, chat with friends, visit Kaliurang... so much fun!*

**Sekarang aku ingin ke pantai Parangtritis. Paling terkenal di pantai selatan!**
*This time I'd like to go to the beach at Parangtritis. The most famous beach on the south coast!*

**Sebelum pulang, aku ingin mencari batik khas Yogya untuk ibuku.**
*While we're there, I want to find some special Yogya batik for my mum.*

**Kalau Danny, ingin mengunjungi daerah mana di Yogya?**
*What about you, Danny? Where do you want to visit in Yogya?*

**Saya hampir tidak sabar, mau melihat Candi Borobudur.**
*I can't wait to see the Borobudur temple.*

**Apalagi pada waktu matahari terbit!**
*Especially at sunrise!*

*This dialogue appears on pages 83 and 84.*

# 5

# Waisak di Yogya
## Waisak in Jogja

In this unit, we will:

- Discuss a visit to the cultural center of Yogyakarta,
- Learn how to express time and intention in Indonesian,
- Describe someone's personality,
- Learn how to state fractions (½ and ¼) and time to the quarter of the hour,
- Explore **pe-/peN-** words,
- Discuss professions, and interview someone about theirs,
- Use directions.

## 5.1 Jalan-jalan ke Yogyakarta  Trip to Jogjakarta

 **| Listening to a dialogue**

After their final exams in May, Adi and Danny are going on a school trip. They are going to the city of Jogjakarta in Central Java, by bus. Almost all their friends from their year group are coming. They will stay at a hotel in Jogja for four nights, before going back home to Jakarta.

Listen to them chatting on the bus going to Central Java.

DANNY: **Kita sudah sampai di mana, ya?**
*Where are we now?*

ADI: **Belum masuk Jawa Tengah. Mungkin daerah Tasikmalaya?**
*We still haven't reached Central Java. Maybe the Tasikmalaya region?*

RIRI: **Masih lama ya? Berapa jam lagi? Aku sudah tidak sabar tiba di Yogya. Menginap di hotel bagus, mengobrol dengan kawan-kawan, jalan-jalan ke Kaliurang ... asyik!**
*Is it still a long way to go? How many more hours? I can't wait to reach Yogya ... stay in a nice hotel, chat with friends, visit Kaliurang ... so much fun!*

ADI: **Kalau aku, sudah pernah ke Yogya. Sekarang aku ingin ke pantai Parangtritis. Paling terkenal di pantai selatan!**
*Well, I've been to Yogya before. This time I'd like to go to the beach at Parangtritis. The most famous beach on the south coast!*

NYOMAN:   **Kurasa pantainya kurang bagus, tidak seperti pantai di Bali. Sebelum pulang, aku ingin mencari batik khas Yogya untuk ibuku.**
*I don't think the beach is that good, not as good as the beaches in Bali. While we're there, I want to find some special Yogya batik for my mum.*

AYU:   **Kalau Danny, ingin mengunjungi daerah mana di Yogya?**
*What about you, Danny? Where do you want to visit in Yogya?*

DANNY:   **Saya hampir tidak sabar, mau melihat Candi Borobudur.**
*I can't wait to see the Borobudur temple.*

AYU:   **Apalagi pada waktu matahari terbit!**
*Especially at sunrise!*

## New Words and Phrases

**belum**  *not yet, no*
**daérah**  *area, region*
**tengah**  *central, middle*
**menginap**  *to stay overnight*
**masih**  *still*
**lama**  *long, far*
**bagus**  *good*
**mengobrol**  *to chat*

**jalan-jalan**  *go out (for a walk)*
**asyik**  *great, fun*
**kalau**  *as for; if*
**pernah**  *once, ever*
**ingin**  *would like, wish*
**terkenal**  *famous*
**mencari**  *to look for, find*

**khas**  *special, typical*
**kalau**  *if; when (in future)*
**hampir**  *almost*
**candi**  *(early Buddhist or Hindu) temple*
**apalagi**  *especially*
**terbit**  *rise; be published*

## Culture note: Yogyakarta

You may have noticed that Yogyakarta (Yogya for short) can also be spelt Jogjakarta. The reason for the two spellings lies in a historical error. After independence, Indonesia introduced spelling reform. Djakarta, as it was spelled under Dutch rule, became Jakarta, while names like Johan and Jasmin became Yohan and Yasmin. Djogdjakarta became Jogjakarta. However, some people over-corrected and started writing the name as Yogyakarta. Interestingly enough, the pronunciation has consistently remained Jogjakarta. Indonesians tend to write the city's name as Yogyakarta, but you may often see it spelt as Jogjakarta, especially in the tourist sector. In this book, we will spell it **Yogyakarta** in Indonesian, but "Jogjakarta" in English.

## Grammar note: Expressing tenses in Indonesian

In English, the tense is shown by a change in the verb form, e.g., *swim, swam, swum*, or by the addition of helping verbs. In Indonesian, tense is shown primarily by time markers such as **sudah** ("already"), **sesudah** ("after"), **sebelum** ("before"), and **waktu** ("when")—words you have already learned. The conversation above introduces the new time markers, **belum** ("not yet"), **pernah** ("ever" or "once"), and **masih** ("still").

### Time markers: *sudah, belum, tidak, pernah*

These words can be used to show whether or not something has happened.

   For example, Ibu Maya asks the boys, "**Sudah makan?**"

Danny replies, "**Sudah**" because he ate lunch at school. Adi replies, "**Belum**" because he had to see a teacher and hasn't had time to eat lunch.

**Belum** is a very useful word in Indonesian. It is quite common in Indonesia to ask someone you have just met, "**Sudah menikah belum?**" ("Are you married, or not yet?") If you are still single, the best answer is always "**Belum**," leaving open the possibility that it will happen. An answer of "**Tidak**" shows that you are not married and have no intention to marry, which suggests you think little of this important Indonesian social custom.

**Pernah** is a concept that Indonesians find tricky to translate. In questions, it means "ever," as in "**Sudah pernah ke Australia?**" ("Have you ever been to Australia?")

However, in statements, it either translates as "once" or puts the sentence into what can be translated as the present perfect tense:

**Saya pernah ke Sydney.**
*I've been to Sydney. / I once went to Sydney.*

You can leave out the **sudah** (although "**Saya sudah pernah ke Sydney**" is not wrong) as the **pernah** makes it clear that it happened in the past.

### Exercise 1

Answer the following questions.

1. **Sudah makan belum?**
2. **Sudah nikah belum?**
3. **Sudah pernah ke Indonesia?**
4. **Sudah bisa bahasa Inggris?**
5. **Sudah mandi belum?**

### Using *masih –, sudah tidak*

**Masih** means "still," while **sudah tidak** translates as "no longer." Both expressions were used in the conversation in the bus:

| Riri: | Masih | lama, | ya? | Berapa | jam | lagi? |
|-------|-------|-------|-----|--------|-----|-------|
|       | *Still* | *long* | *is it?* | *How many* | *hours* | *more?* |

They are still in West Java, so the answer is "**Masih lama**." If she asked the same question again near Wates, not far from Yogyakarta in Central Java, the answer would be:

| Sudah tidak | lama | lagi. | Hanya | satu jam | lagi. |
|-------------|------|-------|-------|----------|-------|
| *Already* | *long* | *more.* | *Only* | *one hour* | *more.* |

### Exercise 2

Answer the following questions about yourself.

1. **Sudah kuliah atau masih sekolah?**
2. **Sudah menikah atau masih sendiri?**
3. **Sudah bisa Bahasa Indonesia atau masih belajar?**
4. **Sudah pulang atau masih di sekolah?**

## ▍Grammar point: *ingin, mau, akan*

In Unit 3, Nyoman used the word **mau** when he wanted to order train tickets at the station. This was because he had already planned the trip and was definitely going to take the train.

In this unit, the friends in the bus use **ingin** ("wish," "would like") to talk about what they want to do in Yogya. They are on a school trip, but do not know the exact itinerary yet. Therefore, they use the word **ingin** to express their desire to visit somewhere, rather than the more definite **mau**:

> **Danny ingin mengunjungi Candi Borobudur.**
> *Danny would like to visit the Borobudur temple.*

> **Adi ingin ke pantai Parangtritis.**
> *Adi would like to go to Parangtritis Beach.*

> **Riri ingin mengunjungi daerah Kaliurang.**
> *Riri wishes to visit the Kaliurang area.*

> **Nyoman ingin mencari batik tulis.**
> *Nyoman wishes to find hand-made batik.*

**Mau** is also often used as a colloquial (spoken) form of the word **akan**, meaning "will":

> **Saya ingin ke sekolah.**
> *I want to go to school (but for some reason I can't, or I don't know if I can go).*

> **Saya mau ke sekolah.**
> *I want to go to school./ I will go to school./ I'm off to school now.*

> **Saya akan ke sekolah.**
> *I will go to school (although I may not want to).*

### Exercise 3

Which word would you use in the following situations: **ingin**, **mau**, or **akan**?

1. **Saya** _____ **pulang ke rumah.** (and you are offering a lift to someone else)

2. **Saya** _____ **pulang ke rumah.** (but you have to sit an exam at school)

3. **Saya** _____ **pulang ke rumah.** (although someone has asked you to go out clubbing)

4. **Saya** _____ **pulang ke rumah.** (you have just heard that your mum is not well)

5. **Saya** _____ **pulang ke rumah.** (but you are in Jakarta)

## 5.2 **Teman di bis** Friends on the bus

Let's learn a little about Adi and Danny's school friends, while reviewing descriptions from Unit 4.

## Basic Sentences

1. **Danny yang orang Australia itu berbadan kurus. Rambut dan matanya hitam. Dia sensitif dan keras kepala, tapi selalu ramah. Danny tiga bersaudara.**
   *Danny, the Australian, is thin. His hair and eyes are black. He is sensitive and stubborn, but always friendly. Danny is one of three children.*

2. **Adi yang kawan baiknya Danny itu juga kurus, tapi tinggi dan berkulit gelap. Rambut dan matanya juga berwarna hitam.**
   *Adi, who is Danny's good friend, is also thin, but tall and dark-skinned. His hair and eyes are also black.*

3. **Riri, yang Danny sangat suka itu, lucu dan pandai. Rambutnya yang hitam itu lurus dan panjang. Riri berbadan kecil dan berkulit gelap.**
   *Riri, whom Danny really likes, is cute and clever. Her black hair is straight and long. Riri is small and dark-skinned.*

4. **Salah seorang dari tiga berkawan yang ikut ke Bali adalah Nyoman. Dia menyenangkan tapi sedikit pemarah. Nyoman yang beragama Hindu itu bermata hitam dan berambut cokelat.**
   *One of Danny's three friends who went to Bali is Nyoman. He is pleasant but a bit bad-tempered. Nyoman, who is Hindu, has black eyes and brown hair.*

5. **Ayu yang ibunya orang Yogyakarta itu sabar, rajin dan jujur. Rambutnya yang cokelat pendek dan ikal. Ayu berbadan sedikit gemuk.**
   *Ayu, whose mother is from Yogya, is patient, diligent and honest. Her brown hair is short and wavy. Ayu is a little plump.*

## New Words and Phrases

**selalu** *always*
**sangat** *very*

**sedikit** *a little*
**beragama** *to have a religion*

## Grammar note: Detailed descriptions using *yang*

We have already learned how to describe someone's personality in Unit 1, and how to describe their physical appearance in Unit 4. We can give more detailed, lengthy descriptions of both people, places and events if we use the word **yang** ("which" or "that").

We read this in the description of Adi's twin brothers in Unit 4: **Sena, kakaknya Adi yang satu lagi, juga tinggi tapi kurus dan berkulit terang. Hari dan Sena itu kembar. Sena yang lahir pertama itu rajin dan baik hati. Hari yang adiknya lucu dan sabar.**

Instead of just using adjectives to describe the nouns (**keluarga**, Danny, and **cerita**), we use **yang** to make a highlighted noun phrase, which is longer and more detailed, as you can see in the examples below:

**Keluarga Adi baik, ramah dan sabar. Keluarga Adi tinggal di Bintaro, Jakarta Selatan.**
*Adi's family is kind, friendly and patient. Adi's family lives in Bintaro, South Jakarta.*

→ **Keluarga Adi <u>yang</u> baik, ramah dan sabar itu tinggal di Bintaro, Jakarta Selatan.**
  *Adi's family, who is kind, friendly and patient, lives in Bintaro, South Jakarta.*

**Danny di kelas III B 2. Dia belajar IPS, Ekonomi, dan Bahasa Indonesia.**
*Danny is in the III B 2 class. He studies Social Studies, Economics and Indonesian.*

→ **Danny <u>yang</u> duduk di kelas III B 2 belajar IPS, Ekonomi, dan Bahasa Indonesia.**
  *Danny, who is in the III B 2 class, studies Social Studies, Economics and Indonesian.*

**Cerita ini lucu. Ceritanya tentang Bali.**    →    **Cerita <u>yang</u> lucu ini tentang Bali.**
*This story is funny. The story is about Bali.*       *This funny story is about Bali.*

You will sometimes see the word **itu** (or **ini**) at the end of a noun phrase. While it literally means "that" (or "this"), it will not be translated into English. It simply marks the end of the noun phrase, so that the reader can then expect that a verb (or another noun phrase) will follow.

**Exercise 4**

Join the sentences below using **yang**, using a similar structure to the sentences above.

1. **Danny berasal dari Australia. Danny kurus badannya.**
2. **Adi juga kurus. Adi kawan baiknya Danny.**
3. **Riri lucu dan pandai. Riri berambut panjang.**
4. **Nyoman orang Hindu. Dia berasal dari Bali.**
5 **Ayu sabar dan jujur. Ayu juga rajin.**

## 5.3 Karyawisata School trips

As in any country, school trips are a highlight of every Indonesian student's year. From kindergarten to senior high schools, there is a thriving industry around **karyawisata** ("school trips"). Relatively inexpensive transport, accommodation, and entrance costs means that nearly all levels of society can have the chance to go somewhere with their school friends. For some Indonesians, these will be one of the few holidays away from home that they will experience, apart from possibly returning to their ancestral village on religious holidays.

On school trips, young children in lower socioeconomic areas might have the chance to visit a town square or place of worship in a town nearby. Those in wealthier areas may get to go on a package tour out of town to hot springs or the nearest big city, staying a few nights and travelling by bus. High-end schools catering to a more international market offer trips either locally or abroad, in Southeast Asia or beyond.

As with many group activities in Indonesia, building and maintaining a sense of community is one of the most important goals. Participants may wear uniform caps or T-shirts, frequently pose for photos against a school banner, be grouped into smaller teams and enjoy competitive activities accompanied by team war-cries (**yél**). It is important to be part of a group.

## Listening: *Jam berapa?*

The tour bus has arrived in Yogya. Danny has taken the itinerary out, so Ayu is asking him what time the different activities will be on Tuesday. Listen to their conversation.

AYU: **Besok, jam berapa kita sarapan?** *Tomorrow, what time do we have breakfast?*

DANNY: **Jam enam lewat seperempat.** *A quarter past six.*

AYU: **Jam berapa kita ke Candi Borobudur?** *What time are we going to Borobudur?*

DANNY: **Jam delapan.** *Eight o'clock.*

AYU: **Jam berapa kita makan siang?** *What time are we eating lunch?*

DANNY: **Jam setengah dua belas.** *Half past eleven.*

AYU: **Jam berapa kita ke Candi Prambanan?** *What time are we going to Prambanan?*

DANNY: **Jam satu lewat empat puluh menit.** *One forty.*

AYU: **Jam berapa kita jalan ke Kotagede?** *What time will we go to Kotagede?*

DANNY: **Jam lima kurang seperempat.** *A quarter to five.*

AYU: **Jam berapa kita makan malam?** *What time are we eating dinner?*

DANNY: **Jam setengah delapan.** *Half past seven.*

Here is the travel itinerary for the school trip to Yogya that Danny was looking at.

| | *Pagi/siang* | *Sore/malam* |
|---|---|---|
| **Senin tgl 21 Mei** | 06.00  Berangkat dari sekolah<br>12.00  makan siang di Purwokerto | 18.00  tiba di Hotel<br>20.00  makan malam di Jalan Malioboro |
| **Selasa tgl 22 Mei** | 06.15  sarapan di hotel<br>08.00  tur kota lalu berangkat ke Candi Borobudur<br>12.30  makan siang di Magelang | 14.00  mengunjungi Candi Prambanan<br>17.00  jalan-jalan di Kotagede<br>19.30  makan malam di warung gudeg |
| **Rabu tgl 23 Mei** | 06.15  sarapan di hotel<br>08.00  berangkat ke pantai Parangtritis 12.00  makan siang di Kasongan | 14.00  tiba di makam kerajaan Imogiri<br>19.00  makan malam di angkringan |
| **Kamis tgl 24 Mei** | 06.15  sarapan di hotel<br>08.00  mengunjungi kraton dan Taman Sari<br>12.00  makan siang di Wijilan | 14.00  tiba di Kaliurang<br>18.00  makan malam di Kaliurang |
| **Jumat tgl 25 Mei** | 06.15  sarapan di hotel<br>08.00  berangkat ke Jakarta<br>13.00  makan siang di Purwokerto | 18.00  makan malam di Cikampek<br>20.00  tiba di sekolah |

## New Words and Phrases

**bésok** *tomorrow*
**sarapan** *breakfast*
**seperempat** *a quarter*
**makan** *eat*
**setengah** *half*
**menit** *minute*
**(hari) Senin** *Monday*

**(hari) Selasa** *Tuesday*
**tur** *tour*
**warung** *roadside stall*
**gudeg** *cooked jackfruit (a Jogja specialty)*
**(hari) Rabu** *Wednesday*
**makam** *grave*

**angkringan** *traditional Jogja roadside eatery*
**(hari) Kamis** *Thursday*
**keraton, kraton** *(Javanese) palace*
**Taman Sari** *water gardens*
**(hari) Jumat** *Friday*

## Language note: Telling time using fractions

In Indonesian, as in English, there are two ways of telling the time, both using the word **jam** ("o'clock"). Digital (or 24-hour) time, which is perhaps easier, simply uses **jam** followed by the relevant numbers, so 13:00 is read as **jam tiga belas**, or **jam satu** (**siang**, to distinguish it from **jam satu pagi** or "1:00 a.m.").

If you want to tell the minutes past an hour, you use the word **léwat** ("past"). So, to say 2:10:

| Jam | dua | lewat | sepuluh | (menit) |
|-----|-----|-------|---------|---------|
| *hour* | *two* | *past* | *ten* | *(minutes)* |

The word **menit** is optional. **Léwat** is used only for times that are until thirty minutes past the hour. After that, we use **kurang**, meaning "less than." In English, we would say "It's ten (minutes) to two." In Indonesian, this would be "**jam dua kurang sepuluh (menit)**."

Another way of telling time is by using expressions such as "half past," "a quarter past," or "a quarter to."

### *Setengah*

**Setengah** literally means "half." In Indonesian, the number used with **setengah** is the next hour, so **jam setengah tiga** means "2:30," and not "3:30." (This is the same in Dutch, the colonial language, from where it probably originated.)

**Jam setengah tiga (2.30)**
*half past two*

**Jam setengah empat (3.30)**
*half past three*

### *Seperempat*

**Seperempat** means "a quarter." "A quarter past two" is therefore **jam dua léwat seperempat**. Sometimes **léwat** is omitted, and just **jam dua seperempat** is used.

**Léwat** means "past." (It can also mean "via," in directions.)

**Lewat** can be used for any time that passed, by adding the word **menit** ("minutes") at the end.

**Jam dua lewat seperempat**
*a quarter past two*

**Jam dua lewat sepuluh (menit)**
*ten (minutes) past two*

The opposite of **léwat** is **kurang**, meaning "less than." In English, we would say, "It's ten (minutes) to two." In Indonesian, this would be **jam dua kurang sepuluh (menit)**.

The phrase "a quarter to two" would use **kurang**:

| | |
|---|---|
| **jam dua kurang seperempat** | **jam dua kurang sepuluh (menit)** |
| *a quarter to two* | *ten (minutes) to two* |

### *Pagi, siang, sore, malam* / times of the day

You will see that different periods of a day can have one of these words ("morning," "middle of the day," "afternoon," "night") after them, to differentiate between two possible times. In English we sometimes do the same, such as "1 a.m.," "1 o'clock in the morning," and so on. **Pagi, siang, sore** and **malam** do not have to be used, but they can be useful for clarifying time when the 24-hour clock is not used.

### Exercise 5

Write down these times in Indonesian. The first has been done for you.

1. 2:03 **jam dua lewat tiga menit**

2. 2:05 _____

3. 2:15 _____

4. 2:20 _____

5. 2:30 _____

6. 2:45 _____

### Exercise 6

Look at the itinerary and answer the following questions. Try to use **pagi** / **siang** / **sore** / **malam** in your answers.

1. **Jam berapa berangkat dari sekolah?**
2. **Jam berapa makan malam di Jalan Malioboro?**
3. **Jam berapa ke Kotagede?**
4. **Jam berapa ke Taman Sari?**
5. **Jam berapa tiba di Kaliurang?**
6. **Jam berapa makan malam di Cikampek?**

### Exercise 7

Answer the following questions.

1. **Jam berapa sarapan?**
2. **Jam berapa berangkat ke sekolah?**
3. **Jam berapa makan siang?**
4. **Jam berapa pulang sekolah?**
5. **Jam berapa makan malam?**

Next, ask a friend the same questions.

## 5.4  Mengobrol dengan pemandu wisata
Chatting with a tour guide

In Yogyakarta, the students will be accompanied by a travel guide, Dea. While the students are at Borobudur, she starts chatting with Riri.

> **Mbak Dea, sudah berapa lama menjadi pemandu wisata?**
> *Dea, how long have you been a tour guide?*

> **Saya sudah tiga tahun bekerja sebagai pemandu wisata.**
> *I've worked for three years now as a tour guide.*

### Listening to a dialogue

RIRI: **Mbak Dea, sudah berapa lama menjadi pemandu wisata?**
*Dea, how long have you been a tour guide?*

DEA: **Saya sudah tiga tahun bekerja sebagai pemandu wisata.**
*I've worked for three years now as a tour guide.*

RIRI: **Dulu sekolah di mana?**
*Where did you study? (lit., "go to school")*

DEA: **Saya kuliah di Akademi Pariwisata di Yogya .**
*I was a student at the Tourism Academy in Jogja.*

RIRI: **Apakah itu enak, menjadi pemandu wisata?**
*Is it enjoyable, being a tour guide?*

DEA: **Enak, hanya kadang-kadang capek.**
*It's good, only sometimes tiring.*

RIRI: **Waktu Mbak kecil, cita-citanya nanti menjadi apa?**
*When you were little, what did you dream of becoming?*

DEA: **Dulu saya ingin menjadi guru. Tetapi sejak SMA, saya sudah mau bekerja di bidang pariwisata.**
*I used to want to become a teacher. But since senior high school, I wanted to work in the tourism field.*

RIRI: **Apa pengalaman yang paling enak selama ini?**
*What has been your most enjoyable experience up until now?*

DEA: **Waktu saya memandu rombongan dari Jepang, mengunjungi Gunung Merapi. Mereka suka mendaki gunung dan berkemah!**
*When I guided a group from Japan who were visiting Mount Merapi. They liked mountain climbing and camping!*

RIRI:  **Apa ada keluarga lain yang juga pemandu wisata?**
*Is anyone else in your family also a tour guide?*

DEA:  **Kedua orang tua saya petani. Kakak saya pegawai negeri dan adik saya pelukis!**
*Both my parents are farmers. My older sibling is a civil servant and my younger sibling is an artist!*

## New Words and Phrases

**Mbak** *term of address, lit., "big sister"*
**pemandu** *guide*
**wisata** *tourism; tourist* (adj)
**pariwisata** *tourism*
**énak** *nice, pleasant*
**hanya** *only*
**kadang-kadang** *sometimes*
**tetapi, tapi** *but*
**bidang** *area, field*
**pengalaman** *experience*

**selama ini, sampai sekarang** *until now*
**memandu** **to** *guide*
**rombongan** *group*
**mendaki** *to climb (mountains, trees)*
**berkémah** *to camp, go camping*
**kedua** *both*
**petani** *farmer*
**pegawai negeri** *civil servant*
**pelukis** *artist*

## Occupations: new words and phrases

**pengacara** *lawyer*
**ibu rumah tangga** *housewife*
**penerjemah** *translator*
**karyawan/karyawati** *employee (m/f)*

**perawat** *nurse*
**supir** *driver, chauffeur*
**perancang** *designer*
**juru masak** *chef, cook*

**arsiték** *architect*
**dokter** *doctor*
**insinyur** *engineer*

## Language note

**Wisata** is generally used as an adjective for "tourism/tourist," so a tour guide is **pemandu wisata**, and a "tour agency" is **biro wisata**. **Pariwisata** is a noun, meaning "tourism" (literally, "tourist matters"). Tour buses will have signs on them saying **pariwisata**, meaning they are not public buses.

## ▌Grammar note: *Apa / Apakah*

**Apa** means "what," but it can also be short for **apakah**. Put **apakah** or **apa** at the beginning of any sentence, and it will become a question. It works like a question mark, but goes first.

**Apa pengalaman yang paling enak selama ini?**
*What is your most enjoyable experience up to now?*

**Apakah itu enak, menjadi pemandu wisata?**
*Is it enjoyable, being a tour guide?*

**Apakah** is more formal than **apa**.  It is also used to make any statement into a question.

| | |
|---|---|
| **Danny belajar Bahasa Indonesia.** | **Apakah Danny belajar Bahasa Indonesia?** |
| *Danny studies Indonesian.* | *Does Danny study Indonesian?* |

## ▌Grammar note: *Pe-/peN-* words

You may have noticed that several occupations, such as **pemandu wisata**, **petani**, **pengusaha**, and **pelajar**, begin with the prefix **pe-** or **peN-**. We have also encountered the following words that start with **pe-** or **peN-**:

| | | | |
|---|---|---|---|
| **pemarah** | *angry person* | **penduduk** | *inhabitant, resident* |
| **pendekar** | *fighter* | **penggemar** | *fan, supporter* |

The **pe-/peN-** prefix indicates someone or something that is an actor or doer of an action. In many ways, it works like the **meN-** prefix already studied, in that the first letter of a base word may change when the **peN-** prefix is added. Many occupations start with this prefix. If you look at the rest of the word (almost always a noun) following this prefix, you can often get the meaning immediately.

### Exercise 8

Complete the sentence using the words in the box below. An English translation has been provided to help you.

| | | | |
|---|---|---|---|
| pegawai negeri | pelajar | pelukis | pemandu wisata |
| pembantu | pengajar | pengusaha | petani |

1. Seorang _____ memandu wisatawan. *(A tour guide guides tourists.)*

2. Seorang _____ bertani. *(A farmer farms.)*

3. Seorang _____ mempunyai perusahaan. *(An entrepreneur owns a business.)*

4. Seorang _____ membantu di rumah. *(A maid (helper) helps at home.)*

5. Seorang _____ mengajar di sekolah. *(A teacher teaches at school.)*

6. Seorang _____ belajar di sekolah. *(A student studies at school.)*

7. Seorang _____ bekerja untuk negara. *(A civil servant works for the nation.)*

8. Seorang _____ melukis lukisan. *(A painter (artist) paints paintings.)*

You can see the relationship between the **peN-** nouns and their corresponding **meN-** verbs.

## ▌Indonesian and me

**Exercise 9**

Fill in the blanks below using information about yourself and your family, using words for the professions. You may need to consult the glossary or an English-Indonesian dictionary.

1. **Sekarang, saya seorang** _____ .

2. **Ayah saya seorang** _____ .

3. **Ibu saya seorang** _____ .

4. **Kakak saya seorang** _____ .

5. **Adik saya seorang** _____ .

6. **Cita-cita saya waktu kecil adalah menjadi seorang** _____ .

7. **Sekarang saya ingin menjadi seorang** _____ .

8. **Saya tidak ingin menjadi seorang** _____ .


# 5.5 Melamar pekerjaan Applying for a job

This is the advertisement Dea saw when she applied for a job as a tour guide.

---

MENCARI: **PEMANDU WISATA**
- **Tamat SMA, DIII, S1**
- **Pria/Wanita**
- **Umur 20 – 30 tahun**
- **Jujur dan rajin**
- **Sudah bekerja selama 1 tahun**
- **Tinggal di Yogyakarta atau Jawa Tengah**
- **Berbahasa Inggris DAN bahasa Mandarin/Jepang/Korea**

---

This was Dea's application letter for the job:

---

**Yogyakarta, 20 September 2012**

**Bapak/Ibu yang terhormat,**

**Saya ingin melamar sebagai pemandu wisata. Saya dari keluarga petani, tapi sejak SMA saya ingin bekerja di pariwisata. Saya lulusan Akademi Pariwisata Yogyakarta pada tahun 2007. Sejak itu, saya bekerja sebagai pemandu wisata di Yogyakarta, Solo dan Jawa Tengah. Saya berbahasa Indonesia, Jawa, Inggris dan Jepang dengan baik.**

**Hormat saya,**
**Dea Handayani**

---

*Jogjakarta, 20 September 2012*

*Dear Sir/Madam,*

*I would like to apply to be a tour guide. I am from a <u>farming</u> family, but since senior high school I have wanted to work in tourism. I graduated from the <u>Jogjakarta Tourist Academy</u> in <u>2007</u>. Since <u>then</u>, I have worked as a tour guide in <u>Jogjakarta, Solo and Central Java</u>. I speak <u>Indonesian, Javanese, English and Japanese</u> well.*

*Regards,*
*Dea Handayani*

## ▌New Words and Phrases

**mencari** *to look for, seek; find*
**tamat** *finish, graduate*
**pria** *male*
**wanita** *female*
**berbahasa** *to speak (a language)*

**bahasa Mandarin** *Mandarin, Chinese*
**Koréa** *Korea, Korean*
**melamar** *apply; propose*

**yang terhormat** *Dear (for formal letters)*
**hormat saya** *yours sincerely (my respects)*

### Exercise 10

Imagine that you are applying for the same position of tour guide. Practice using the letter format by writing your own application letter, changing the underlined words to fit your own personal situation as below:

- you are writing from Bandung on 13 June 2017
- you are from a family of teachers
- you have wanted to work in tourism since junior high school
- you graduated from the University of Indonesia in 2008
- since then, you have worked as a tourist guide in Bandung and West Java
- you speak Indonesian, Sundanese and English

## ▌Cultural note

Tourism is a growing industry in Indonesia. While Bali remains Indonesia's premier destination for both foreign tourists (officially known as **wisatawan mancanegara** or **wisman**) and locals (**wisatawan Nusantara** or **wisnu**), other parts of the nation now want a slice of the tourism market. Regions such as Danau Toba (Lake Toba, right), Gunung Bromo, Lombok, and Toraja all promote their local sights and activities, while hotels and other supporting infrastructure have sprung up along the way. You will not hear the words **wisman** or **wisnu** used often on the street. In bigger cities, where the outside influence is stronger, tourists may be simply referred to as **turis**, although **wisatawan**

is the more proper Indonesian term. Hotel staff, people in the hospitality industry, and taxi drivers refer to tourists as **tamu** (guests), while in Malay areas, visitors may be known as **pelancong** (especially if they come from Malaysia).

## 5.6 Tur keliling kota Yogya Tour around Jogja

The students are on the bus taking a quick city tour of Jogja before they leave for Borobudur.

### Exercise 11

Listen to the audio for the commentary, and try to mark the route the students took, on the map. (Refer to the transcript on the next page if you have difficulties in following the audio instructions.)

1. **Kita mau keliling kota Yogyakarta. Kita keluar dari hotel, lewat setasiun Tugu, lalu belok kanan masuk Jalan Malioboro. Di sini bisa belanja banyak oleh-oleh di pinggir jalan atau Pasar Beringharjo. Di ujung Jalan Malioboro ada kantor pos.**

   *We are going around the city of Jogjakarta. We go out of the hotel, past Tugu railway station, then turn right into Malioboro Street. Here you can shop for lots of souvenirs by the side of the road or at Beringharjo Market. At the end of Malioboro Street is the post office.*

2. **Sekarang kita menuju kraton. Di depannya ada alun-alun utara. Dari sini, kita ke kanan lewat Mesjid Kauman dan Pasar Burung.**

   *Now we are heading for the palace. In front of it is the northern town square. From here, we go right past the Kauman Mosque and Bird Market.*

3. **Sekarang kita masuk jalan raya yang menuju Bantul. Kalau terus, sampai di pantai selatan.**

   *Now we enter the main road towards Bantul. If you keep going, you reach the south coast.*

4. **Tapi kita mau belok kiri ke timur. Di sebelah kiri masih daerah kraton, dan alun-alun selatan. Sekarang kita mau belok kiri lagi, masuk Jalan Taman Siswa. Di sebelah kiri ada gereja Jawa. Di ujung jalan ada sekolah Taman Siswa yang terkenal itu.**

   *But we want to turn left, to the east. On the left side is still the palace district, and the southern town square. Now we will turn left again, into Taman Siswa Street. On the left hand side is a Javanese church. At the end of the street is the famous Taman Siswa school.*

5. **Sekarang kita sampai di Jalan Kusumanegara. Kalau ke kanan, ke kebun binatang Gembira Loka. Tapi kita akan jalan terus ke utara, lewat Universitas Gajah Mada atau UGM. Siapa yang ingin kuliah di UGM?**

   *Now we have reached Kusumanegara Street. If you turn right, you go to the Gembira Loka zoo. But we will keep travelling north, past Gajah Mada University or UGM. Who wants to study at UGM?*

6. **Sekarang kita belok kiri, menuju Jalan Magelang. Tujuan kita hari ini adalah Candi Borobudur.**

   *Now we turn left, towards Magelang Road. Our destination today is the Borobudur temple.*

## ▌ New Words and Phrases

| | | |
|---|---|---|
| **keliling** *around* | **belanja** *shop, shopping* | **mesjid** *mosque* |
| **keluar** *go out, exit* | **oléh-oléh** *souvenirs* | **burung** *bird* |
| **hotél** *hotel* | **pinggir** *edge, side* | **jalan raya** *main road, highway* |
| **tugu** *monument* | **pasar** *market* | **pantai** *beach* |
| **bélok** *turn* | **ujung** *end, point* | **sebelah** *beside; next to* |
| **masuk** *go in, enter* | **kantor pos** *post office* | **geréja** *church* |
| **depan** *front* | **alun-alun** *town square* | **kebun binatang** *zoo* |

## ▎Cultural note: *Hari Raya Waisak* / the Waisak holiday

The Buddhist holiday of Waisak is a public holiday. Buddhism is one of the six religions recognized in Indonesia (Islam, Christianity, Catholicism, Hinduism, and Confucianism are the others). Waisak usually falls in May or early June.  While there are only around one million Buddhists in Indonesia, temples are busier during Waisak. Many Buddhists from around the country go to Borobudur Temple in Central Java, and parade from Candi Mendut and Candi Pawon to celebrate the life of Gautama Siddharta, Buddhism's founder. In recent years, the celebration has ended with thousands of paper lanterns (**lampion**) being lit then released into the sky over Borobudur.

Borobudur is the world's largest Buddhist place of worship, built by the Syailendra dynasty in the 8th or 9th century AD. At that time Buddhism was a major religion in the Indonesian archipelago, as shown by the number of temples still remaining in Java. Centuries later, Borobudur fell into disrepair until it was uncovered in colonial times and restored to its former grandeur in the 1970s.

## ▎Language notes

The word **candi** refers to a historic Buddhist building, and should not be confused with other words for such as **klénténg** (a Confucian temple of Chinese-style architecture which also serves as a community meeting place), or **wihara** or **kuil** (Buddhist temples of local design).

Similarly, the word **kraton** or **keraton** is a Javanese word referring to a palace. The most famous is the Ngayogyakarta **kraton** where Sri Sultan Hamengkubowono X resides, but there are others in Yogya, Solo and around Java. The word **istana** is a Malay word meaning "palace," and is found across Sumatra, Singapore, and the Malay Peninsula.

## Unit Review

1. How would you say the following in Indonesian?

    a. 3.15 am

    _____

    b. 8.30 pm

    _____

    c. a quarter to twelve

    _____

    d. fifteen minutes past midnight

    _____

2. What is the Indonesian word for the following?

    a. an angry person

    _____

    b. a student

    _____

    c. a worker

    _____

    d. maid or household helper

    _____

3. Follow these instructions on the map of Jogja city. Where would you end up?

**Dari setasiun kereta api, jalan ke utara lewat Jalan Malioboro. Di tugu belok kanan. Jalan terus sampai Jalan Cik di Tiro, lalu belok kiri. Apa yang ada di ujung jalan itu?**

## Unit 5 End-of-unit vocabulary list

**alun-alun** _town square_
**angkringan** _traditional Jogja roadside eatery_
**apa** _what_
**apakah, apa** _whether, if; makes a question_
**apalagi** _especially_
**arsiték** _architect_
**asyik** _great, fun_
**bagus** _good_
**belanja** _to shop, go shopping_
**bélok** _to turn_
**belum** _not yet_
**beragama** _religious, to have a religion_
**berbahasa** _to speak a language_
**berkémah** _to camp, go camping_
**bésok** _tomorrow, the next day_
**bidang** _field, area_
**bis** _bus_
**burung** _bird_
**candi** _(Hindu) temple_
**daérah** _region, area_
**depan** _front_
**dokter** _doctor_

**énak** _nice, pleasant_
**geréja** _church_
**gudeg** _cooked jackfruit_
**hampir** _almost, nearly_
**hanya** _only_
**hormat** _respect_
**hotél** _hotel_
**ibu rumah tangga** _housewife_
**ingin** _to wish_
**insinyur** _engineer_
**jalan raya** _main road, highway_
**jalan-jalan** _to go out_
**Jepang** _Japan, Japanese_
**Jumat** _Friday_
**juru masak** _chef, cook_
**kadang-kadang** _sometimes_
**kalau** _if; when (in future)_
**Kamis** _Thursday_
**kantor** _office_
**karyawan, karyawati** _employee (m/f)_
**kebun binatang** _zoo_
**kedua** _both; second_
**keliling** _around_
**keluar** _to go out, exit_

**kemarin** _yesterday_
**keraton** _Javanese palace_
**khas** _special, typical_
**Koréa** _Korea_
**kraton** _Javanese palace_
**kurang** _less, fewer; to (the hour)_
**lama** _long, far_
**makam** _grave_
**makan** _eat_
**mancanegara** _international_
**masih** _still_
**masuk** _go in, enter_
**matahari** _sun_
**mbak** _term of address, lit., older sister_
**Mei** _May_
**melamar** _to apply, propose_
**memandu** _to guide_
**mencari** _to look for, find_
**mendaki** _to climb (a mountain, tree)_
**menginap** _to stay overnight_
**mengobrol** _to chat_
**menit** _minute_
**menuju** _to head for, approach_

**mesjid** *mosque*
**mungkin** *maybe, perhaps*
**Nusantara** *another name for Indonesia ("the islands between")*
**oléh-oléh** *souvenirs*
**paling** *most, -est*
**pantai** *beach*
**pariwisata** *tourism*
**pasar** *market*
**pegawai negeri** *civil servant*
**pelukis** *painter, artist*
**pemain** *player*
**pemandu** *guide*
**pembantu** *maid, helper*
**penerjemah** *translator, interpreter*
**pengacara** *lawyer*
**pengajar** *teacher*
**pengalaman** *experience*
**perancang** *designer*
**perawat** *nurse*

**pernah** *once, ever*
**petani** *farmer*
**pinggir** *side, edge*
**pos** *post*
**pria** *male*
**Rabu** *Wednesday*
**rasa** *think, feel, taste*
**rombongan** *group*
**salah seorang** *one of (person)*
**sangat** *very*
**sarapan** *breakfast*
**sebelah** *beside, next to*
**sedikit** *a little*
**selalu** *always*
**selama ini** *until now*
**Selasa** *Tuesday*
**Senin** *Monday*
**seperempat** *quarter*
**setengah** *half*
**siswa** *(school) student, pupil*

**sudah** *already*
**supir** *driver, chauffeur*
**taman** *garden, park*
**tamansari** *water gardens*
**tamat** *graduate*
**tamu** *guest*
**tengah** *central, middle*
**terbit** *rise; be published*
**terhormat** *respected*
**terkenal** *famous*
**terus** *straight; then, so*
**tetapi, tapi** *but*
**tidur** *sleep*
**tugu** *monument*
**ujung** *end, point*
**wanita** *woman, female*
**warung** *roadside stall*
**wisata** *tourist, tourism*
**wisatawan** *tourist*

**How to Download the Audio Recordings and Answer Key for this Book.**

1. Check your Internet connection.
2. Type the URL below into your web browser.

https://www.tuttlepublishing.com/Indonesian-for-Beginners

For support email us at info@tuttlepublishing.com

*This dialogue appears on page 110.*

# UNIT

# 6

# Hore, Liburan Sekolah!
Hooray! It's School Holidays!

In this unit, we will:

- Learn the names of popular sports and hobbies in Indonesia,
- Understand how school reports work,
- Evaluate and rank performances using simple maths,
- Learn how to say something is a favorite (**paling**),
- Build on our vocabulary of clothing items,
- Understand the seasons in Indonesia,
- Build on our vocabulary of colors,
- Understand Indonesian geography through soccer teams.

## 6.1 Porseni  Sports and Arts Week

At the end of the school year, there is usually a fun week where students focus on sporting and cultural activities. These events are known as Sports and Art Week, which can be translated as **Porseni (Pekan Olahraga dan Seni)** or **PORSA (Pekan Olahraga, Seni dan Agama**; i.e., sports, arts, and religion).

Afterwards, there may be ceremonies with awards for various student achievements. Danny and Adi are now at the awards ceremony, listening to the principal announce the awards.

1. **Para siswa SMA3 yang kita sayangi,**

   *Dear SMA3 students,*

2. **Selamat datang di upacara penutupan Porseni tahun ini.**

   *Welcome to this year's Sports and Culture Week's closing ceremony.*

3. **Kami senang bahwa hampir semua murid dari kelas II SMA berhasil naik kelas, sesudah masa ujian selesai.**

   *We are glad that nearly all students from second grade were promoted after finishing their exams.*

4. **Sekarang saatnya mengumumkan juara dari perlombaan Porseni tahun ini.**

*Now it's time to announce the winners of this year's Sports and Culture Week competitions.*

5. **Juara Lomba Sepak Bola adalah … tim dari kelas II B 1!**

*The winner of the soccer competition is … the team from class II B 1!*

6. **Juara Lomba Menyanyi adalah Lina Sitorus!**

*The winner of the singing contest is Lina Sitorus!*

7. **Juara umum Porseni adalah kelas III A 2!**

*The overall winner of Sports and Culture Week is class III A 2!*

8. **Sekarang kita mengucapkan selamat kepada semua!**

*Now let's congratulate everyone!*

## New Words and Phrases

**menyayangi** *to love (a person)*
**penutupan** *closing*
**Porseni** *Sports and Art Week*
**olahraga** *sport(s)*
**seni** *art(s)*
**bahwa** *that*
**murid** *student*
**berhasil** *to succeed*

**lomba** *race, contest*
**naik kelas** *graduate or be promoted to the next grade*
**masa** *time, period*
**ujian** *examination*
**saat** *moment*
**mengumumkan** *to announce, make public*

**juara** *champion, winner*
**perlombaan** *competition*
**sépak bola** *soccer, football*
**tim** *team*
**menyanyi** *to sing*
**umum** *general*
**kepada** *to, for (a person)*

## Cultural note: School terms

The end of the Indonesian school year is in June, when school takes a holiday for several weeks. The school year runs from July to June, roughly following the European schedule inherited from the Dutch colonizers, who set up the first schools and inspired local schools such as **Taman Siswa**. There are usually two terms: **semester ganjil** (literally, "odd semester") from July until December, then **semester genap** ("even semester") from January to June. There may be a mid-semester break, which is usually a one- or two-week holiday at Christmas.

## Cultural note: Graduating to the next grade

Students in Indonesia do not automatically graduate (**naik kelas**) to the next grade. They must pass their exams and, traditionally, receive no less than an average of 6 (out of a maximum 10) on their school report (**rapot**). Those who do not may have to resit exams or repeat that school year. Nowadays, grades are increasingly given in percentages. This means that a grade of 50% or less could result in a fail.

## Grammar note: Cardinal numbers

It is very easy to make cardinal numbers ("first, second, third," etc.) in Indonesian. All you have to do is add **ke-** to the number. One exception is the word for "first," which is almost always **pertama**, although occasionally you may hear **kesatu**.

This is useful for class rankings. Traditionally students are ranked based on their report grades into the top ten in each class. It is a matter of pride to be ranked **satu** or to be among the **masuk ranking** (i.e., be one of the top ten).

## Language note: Winners and rankings

In Indonesian, **juara** is the word for "winner," while the word for the person in second place is **juara kedua** ("second winner"). "Third place" is **juara ketiga**, while **juara harapan** means "special mention."

### Exercise 1

Look at the overall grades for Adi and Danny's class, and answer the questions below.

| Peringkat Ranking | Nama Name | Nilai Rata-Rata Average Score |
|---|---|---|
| 1 | Isfandari | 88.74 |
| 2 | Suriadi Wulandaru | 84.80 |
| 3 | M. Akbar | 84.52 |
| 4 | Riri Rahmawati | 82.45 |
| 5 | Sri Ayu Lestari | 81.98 |

1. **Siapa yang juara kelas?**

2. **Siapa yang juara kedua?**

3. **Siapa yang ranking tiga?**

4. **Apakah Danny masuk ranking?**

## 6.2  Bagi rapot  Handing out report cards

### Listening to a dialogue

Look at the student reports in more detail. Listen to the class comparing their results.

ADI: **Nilai Matematikamu berapa ya?** *What was your Math grade?*

RIRI: **Aku hanya 74. Matematika itu susah.** *I only got 74. Math is difficult.*

DANNY: **Nilaiku lebih baik, 87.** *My grade is higher, 87.*

AYU: **Wah, kamu hebat, Dan! Kalau IPA, siapa yang dapat nilai paling tinggi?**
*Wow, you're wonderful, Dan! What about Science, who got the highest grade?*

ADI: **Mungkin Rini, ya? Nilai dia selalu tinggi.** *Maybe it's Rini? Her grades are always high.*

RIRI: **Aku senang dengan Bahasa Indonesia. 91!** *I'm happy with my Indonesian mark. 91!*

DANNY: **Kalau aku, Bahasa Indonesia kurang baik. Nilaiku yang paling tinggi itu Bahasa Inggris.**
*As for me, my Indonesian grade isn't so good. My highest grade is English.*

| Nama | Suriadi Wulandaru |
|---|---|
| IPA | 86 |
| Bahasa Indonesia | 89 |
| Bahasa Inggris | 87 |
| Matematika | 81 |
| Agama | 88 |
| Pendidikan Pancasila & Kewarganegaraan | 78 |
| Nilai rata-rata | 84.80 |

| Nama | Sri Ayu Lestari |
|---|---|
| IPA | 80 |
| Bahasa Indonesia | 92 |
| Bahasa Inggris | 88 |
| Matematika | 74 |
| Agama | 73 |
| Pendidikan Pancasila & Kewarganegaraan | 85 |
| Nilai rata-rata | 81.98 |

| Nama | Riri Rahmawati |
|---|---|
| IPA | 74 |
| Bahasa Indonesia | 91 |
| Bahasa Inggris | 89 |
| Matematika | 74 |
| Agama | 85 |
| Pendidikan Pancasila & Kewarganegaraan | 80 |
| Nilai rata-rata | 82.45 |

| Nama | Danny Lee |
|---|---|
| IPA | 60 |
| Bahasa Indonesia | 65 |
| Bahasa Inggris | 99 |
| Matematika | 87 |
| Agama | 62 |
| Pendidikan Pancasila & Kewarganegaraan | 58 |
| Nilai rata-rata | 71.9 |

## New Words and Phrases

**sulit, susah** *difficult, hard*
**wah!** *wow! (exclamation)*
**hébat** *great, wonderful*
**dapat** *can; to get*

**Pendidikan Pancasila dan Kewarganegaraan**
*Pancasila (PPKn, state philosophy) and Civics*

**bagi, membagi** *to hand out*
**dibandingkan** *compared with*
**daripada** *than*

## Grammar: Comparatives and Superlatives / *Lebih/kurang/paling*

When making comparatives and superlatives in Indonesian, we simply use the words **lebih** ("more"), **kurang** ("less"), and **paling** ("most") before the adjectives they modify. For example:

| | |
|---|---|
| **lebih baik** | *better* |
| **Nilaiku lebih baik, 87.** | *My grade was better, 87.* |
| **kurang baik** | *not so good, worse* |
| **Kalau aku, Bahasa Indonesia kurang baik.** | *My Indonesian wasn't so good.* |
| **paling tinggi** | *highest* |
| **Siapa dapat nilai paling tinggi?** | *Who got the highest grade?* |
| **Nilaiku yang paling tinggi itu Bahasa Inggris.** | *My highest grade was English.* |

## Exercise 2

Answer the following questions using information in the student reports above.

1. **Siapa yang paling pandai di kelas Matematika?**

2. **Siapa yang lebih pandai di kelas IPA, Adi atau Riri?**

3. **Apakah nilai Ayu di kelas Agama kurang dari nilai Danny?**

4. **Nilai Riri yang paling baik adalah _____.**

5. **Nilai Danny yang paling tinggi adalah untuk _____.**

## Exercise 3

Complete the following comparisons using **lebih**, **kurang**, or **paling**.

1. **Di kelas Agama, nilai Adi _____ tinggi dari nilai Riri.**

2. **Di kelas Agama, nilai Riri _____ tinggi daripada nilai Adi.**

3. **Bagi Ayu, Bahasa Indonesia _____ sulit dibandingkan Bahasa Inggris.**

4. **Danny _____ pandai di kelas Bahasa Inggris.**

## ▌Cultural note: Teacher's comments

Indonesian school reports are usually short and to the point. Teachers may also write brief comments in the student reports. Look at the comments for Riri and Danny.

| Nama | | Riri Rahmawati |
|---|---|---|
| IPA | 74 | cukup baik |
| Bahasa Indonesia | 91 | sangat baik |
| Bahasa Inggris | 89 | baik |
| Matematika | 74 | cukup baik |
| Agama | 85 | baik |
| Pendidikan Pancasila & Kewarganegaraan | 80 | baik |
| Nilai rata-rata | | 82.45 |

| Nama | | Danny Lee |
|---|---|---|
| IPA | 60 | kurang |
| Bahasa Indonesia | 65 | kurang |
| Bahasa Inggris | 99 | sangat baik |
| Matematika | 87 | baik |
| Agama | 62 | kurang |
| Pendidikan Pancasila & Kewarganegaraan | 58 | kurang |
| Nilai rata-rata | | 71.9 |

## ▌New Words and Phrases

**kurang** *lacking, unsatisfactory*
**cukup baik** *quite good*

**baik** *good*
**sangat baik** *very good*

**Exercise 4**

Write in the correct comments for Ayu, following the example above.

| Nama | | Sri Ayu Lestari |
|---|---|---|
| IPA | 80 | |
| Bahasa Indonesia | 92 | |
| Bahasa Inggris | 88 | |
| Matematika | 74 | |
| Agama | 73 | |
| Pendidikan Pancasila & Kewarganegaraan | 85 | |

## Indonesian and Me

**Exercise 5**

Describe your performance in the following school subjects:

Matematika    _____        Bahasa Indonesia _____

Bahasa Inggris _____        IPS               _____

IPA            _____

## 6.3 Hobi  Hobbies

## Dialogue

Danny and Ayu are discussing their hobbies. Listen to their conversation.

DANNY:  **Ayu suka hobi apa, ya?**  *What hobbies do you have?*

AYU:    **Aku paling suka bulu tangkis dan menyanyi.  Kalau Danny?**
       *I like badminton and singing most. What about you?*

DANNY:  **Saya suka memasak, sepak bola dan futsal.**
       *I like cooking, soccer and indoor soccer.*

AYU:    **Aku juga suka memasak! Tapi aku tidak suka futsal.**
       *I like cooking too! But I don't like indoor soccer.*

DANNY:  **Kalau menonton, suka?**
       *What about watching films? Do you like doing that?*

AYU:    **Aku kurang suka menonton. Tapi bersama Danny, aku mau!**
       *Not really. But with you, I would!*

## Language note: *Suka*

To express likes, you simply use the base verb **suka**.

**Saya suka memasak.**        *I like cooking.*

To express what you like most of all, using **paling** before **suka**.

**Saya paling suka memasak.**        *I like cooking most of all.*

To express that you don't really like something, use **kurang** before **suka**.

**Saya kurang suka memasak.**     *I don't really like cooking.*

To express that you don't like something, use **tidak** before **suka**.

**Saya tidak suka masak.**     *I don't like cooking.*

## Language note: *Kalau*

We have learned that **kalau** means "if" or "when." However, as you can see in the conversation above, it can also be used at the start of a sentence in a construction which roughly translates to "as for," "how about" or "what about." It is hard to find an English equivalent: **kalau** marks the rest of the sentence as an idea or possibility to consider.

   Look back at the activities from PORSENI. Lots of these are actually hobbies that young people do either as an after-school activity, or outside school. Here are some hobbies that are enjoyed by students in Indonesia, as well as around the world.

futsal     bola voli     bulu tangkis     bola basket

fotografi     lukis     menyanyi     tari tradisional

memancing     menonton     memasak     sepak bola

## New Words and Phrases

**futsal** *indoor soccer*
**bola voli** *volleyball*
**bulu tangkis** *badminton*
**bola baskét** *basketball*
**fotografi** *photography*

**lukis** *painting*
**menyanyi** *singing*
**tari tradisional** *traditional dance*
**memancing** *fishing*

**menonton** *watching films*
**memasak** *cooking*
**sépak bola** *soccer, football*

## Exercise 6

Arrange all the hobbies listed on page 109 into those that you like best (**paling suka**), those you like (**suka**) and those you don't really like (**kurang suka**).

| paling suka | suka | kurang suka |
|---|---|---|
|  |  |  |

## Exercise 7

Write sentences about how you feel about certain hobbies.

**Saya suka** _____

**Saya kurang suka** _____

**dan tidak suka** _____

## Exercise 8

Ask a friend what hobbies they like and those they dislike, and write down the answers.

**Kawan saya suka** _____

**Dia kurang suka** _____

**dan tidak suka** _____

# 6.4 Menonton sepak bola di Makasar
## Going to the soccer game in Makassar

As mentioned in the dialogue, one of Danny and Adi's hobbies is soccer. They love any form of the game. After school is over for the year, they are going to fly to Makassar in Sulawesi to see a match. Listen to their conversation as they are packing.

### Listening to a dialogue

ADI:    **Tas kamu sudah siap belum?** *Is your bag ready yet?*

DANNY:    **Sudah. Saya bawa celana pendek, kaus, topi dan sendal jepit.**
*Yes. I'm bringing shorts, shirts, a hat and plastic sandals.*

ADI:    **Lebih baik bawa sepatu sendal saja, kalau kita mau nonton di stadion.**
*Better to just bring ordinary sandals, if we're going to the stadium to watch.*

DANNY:    **Terus, apa lagi yang harus kubawa? Piyama?** *So, what else should I bring? Pajamas?*

ADI:    **Saya bawa sarung, bukan piyama. Saya juga bawa jaket buat di pesawat.**
*I'm bringing a sarong, not pajamas. I'm also bringing a jacket for the plane.*

DANNY:    **O ya, kaus kaki buat di pesawat. Kaki saya suka kedinginan.**
*Oh yes, socks for the plane. My feet often get cold.*

## New Words and Phrases

| | | |
|---|---|---|
| **celana péndék** *shorts* | **sepatu sendal** *sandals* | **jakét** *jacket* |
| **kaus** *(collarless) shirt, T-shirt* | **stadion** *stadium* | **kaus kaki** *sock(s)* |
| **topi** *hat, cap* | **harus** *must, have to* | **suka** *often, tends to [colloquial]* |
| **sendal jepit** *plastic sandals, thongs, flip flops* | **piyama** *pajamas* | **kedinginan** *to feel cold* |

## Language note: *Suka*

We have learned that **suka** means "to like." However, an extended, colloquial meaning of **suka** is also "tend to" or "often." In the dialogue, Danny talks about his feet getting cold in planes.

**Kaki saya suka kedinginan.**      *My feet often get cold.*

This use of **suka** is in contrast to the previous dialogue talking about hobbies.

**Saya kurang suka menonton.**      *I don't really like watching films.*

In most situations, **suka** will mean "like," but be aware of the other meaning. It is usually obvious from the context.

## Language note: *Harus*

**Harus** means "must" or "have to." In English, these are modal verbs that require another verb to follow. Modal verbs are mostly used the same way in Indonesian, but can exist alone, especially in informal speech.

**Apa lagi yang harus kubawa?**      *What else do I need to bring?*

Here, **bawa** (from **membawa**) is the verb that follows. In the example below, it is **pergi**.

**Saya harus pergi ke Jakarta.**      *I need to go to Jakarta.*

However, it is also perfectly acceptable to say, **Saya harus ke Jakarta**.

Other verbs previously learned that work like **harus** are **bisa** ("can"), **mau** ("want to, will") and **boleh** ("may, allowed"). However, **akan** can only be used with a verb following it.

## Cultural note: Unofficial dress code

Many overseas visitors are not aware of the unofficial dress codes that exist in Indonesia. Tourists on holiday in Bali, who find the climate very hot, often wear singlets or tank tops, shorts, and plastic sandals as a means of coping with the heat. While in tourist areas (such as Kuta in Bali) this may be acceptable, ordinary Indonesians would only dress like this at home, and would never wear a singlet (i.e. item of underclothing) out in public. To go out, they put on sandals with straps (**sepatu sendal**), or more formal-looking shoes, and men generally wear long trousers. To go into a government office, shoes with closed toes (**sepatu**) are required, and women should make sure their tops have sleeves. Very short shorts and bare midriffs are frowned upon, especially over the last few years as the popularity of the hijab has increased among Muslim women, many of whom are now wearing clothing that reveals less of the body. You will find that you blend in better if you follow what the locals are doing.

## Exercise 9

Read again Adi and Danny's conversation about what clothes they are taking to Makassar. Fill in the blanks below, following the sentence structure given, suggesting the appropriate clothing for each situation.

**Di pantai, lebih baik Danny memakai kaus dan celana pendek.**

*At the beach, it's better that Danny wears a shirt and shorts.*

1. **Di pesawat, lebih baik Danny memakai** _____

2. **Di hotel, lebih baik** _____

3. **Di stadion,** _____

4. **Di kantor** _____

## Language note: *Musim apa?* / What season is it?

There are two main seasons: **musim hujan** ("rainy" or "wet season") and **musim kemarau** ("dry season"). In the past, the wet season, or monsoon season, lasted from October to March, while the dry season ran from April to September. **Perubahan iklim** (climate change) has to some degree affected the seasons in Indonesia, so that the timing of the seasons is less predictable than in the past. Colloquially, Indonesians also talk about **musim pancaroba**, or a time of change between seasons, when it is believe people are more likely to catch colds or become unwell.

Here are the names in Indonesian for the seasons in temperate countries:

| | | | |
|---|---|---|---|
| *summer* | **musim panas** | *spring* | **musim semi** |
| *winter* | **musim dingin** | *snow season* | **musim salju** |
| *autumn, fall* | **musim gugur** | *holiday season* | **musim liburan** |

## New Words and Phrases

| | | |
|---|---|---|
| **Mei** *May* | **Agustus** *August* | **Novémber** *November* |
| **Juni** *June* | **Séptémber** *September* | **Désémber** *December* |
| **Juli** *July* | **Oktober** *October* | |

The names of months of the year were originally taken from Dutch, so these resemble their English equivalents.

**Exercise 10**

Write down the seasons in your country, and the months they occur.

| Season | Months |
|--------|--------|
| e.g. summer (**musim panas**) | **Desember, Januari, Februari** |
| | |
| | |
| | |

The Western calendar is not the only one in operation in Indonesia. Calendars showing Islamic dates are also common, as this determines when the fasting month and other Muslim holidays fall. **Bulan puasa** ("fasting month") is the most common way to refer to Ramadan (Unit 7). The Chinese calendar also dictates when **Imlék** (Unit 1) falls.

## 6.5 Tim-tim sepak bola di Indonesia   Indonesian soccer teams

The word **musim** can also be used to talk about sporting seasons, such as football. Below you can see a list of the top nine teams from **PSSI (Persatuan Sepak Bola Seluruh Indonesia)**, the Football Association of Indonesia.

| Kesebelasan / Tim<br>Team | Asal<br>Origin | Provinsi<br>Province | Warna<br>Colors |
|---------------------------|----------------|----------------------|-----------------|
| **Aréma** | **Malang** | | biru, kuning |
| **Semen Padang** | **Padang** | | merah, hitam |
| **Persebaya** | **Surabaya** | | hijau |
| **Persib** | **Bandung** | | biru, putih |
| **Persiba** | **Balikpapan** | | biru, putih |
| **Persija** | **Jakarta** | | jingga, putih |
| **Persipura** | **Papua** | | merah, hitam |
| **PSM** | **Makassar** | | merah, putih |
| **PSMS** | **Medan** | | hijau, putih |

## New Words and Phrases

**kesebelasan** *team (literally, "eleven")*
**provinsi** *province*
**warna** *color*
**biru** *blue*
**kuning** *yellow*

**hijau** *green*
**putih** *white*
**jingga** *orange*
**Sumatera** *Sumatra*
**Kalimantan** *Kalimantan, Indonesian Borneo*

**khusus** *special*
**ibukota** *capital city*
**Sulawési, Sulawesi** *Sulawesi (formerly Celebes)*

## Exercise 11

1. Use the map of Indonesia below to help you complete the above table (on page 113) showing the nine home provinces of these teams.

2. Then color the area around each team's hometown (or home province) in the correct team colors.

## Exercise 12

Reading comprehension: True or false?

| | T (✓) | F (✗) |
|---|---|---|
| 1. **Ada lima tim dari pulau Jawa.** | ___ | ___ |
| 2. **PSMS berasal dari Sumatera Utara.** | ___ | ___ |
| 3. **Hanya satu tim yang seragamnya warna hijau.** | ___ | ___ |

4. Here is the league ladder. At the end of Round 10, all teams have played 10 times, except for Persija and PSM. Teams score three points for a win, two points for a draw and none for a loss. Can you calculate the final team points from their win-loss record, and work out their ranking?

| Kesebelasan / Tim Team | Menang (3) Wins | Seri (2) Draws | Kalah Losses | Nilai Points | Peringkat Ranking |
|---|---|---|---|---|---|
| Arema | 2 | 3 | 5 | | |
| Semen Padang | 4 | 1 | 5 | | |
| Persebaya | 2 | 6 | 2 | | |
| Persib | 6 | 3 | 1 | | |
| Persiba | 2 | 5 | 3 | | |
| Persija | 3 | 4 | 3 | | |
| Persipura | 1 | 5 | 4 | | |
| PSM | 5 | 4 | 1 | | |
| PSMS | 0 | 3 | 7 | | |

## 6.6 PSM melawan Persija PSM versus Persija

Here is a short news report about the match that Adi and Danny went to see.

(Makassar, Minggu 30 Mei) Kesebelasan PSM bermain baik kemarin (Sabtu 29 Mei) dengan nilai 2-2 melawan Persija. Pada menit ke20, pemain belakang PSM mendapat gol. Tapi sebelum istirahat, Persija juga mendapat gol.

*(Makassar, Sunday 30 May) PSM played well yesterday (Saturday 29 May) with a score of 2-2 against Persija. In the 20th minute, a PSM defender scored a goal. But before the break, Persija also scored a goal.*

Golnya Riki Rifai di menit ke76 membuat para penonton PSM sangat gembira. Tetapi akhirnya PSM tidak jadi menang karena Persija mendapat gol lagi hanya beberapa menit sebelum akhir pertandingan.

*Riki Rifai's goal in the 76th minute made the PSM spectators very excited. But finally PSM did not end up winning as Persija got another goal only several minutes before the end of the match.*

Minggu depan Persija akan melawan Persib Bandung.

*Next week Persija will face Persib Bandung.*

## New Words and Phrases

seri *draw*

kalah *lose*

(hari) Minggu *Sunday*

melawan *to oppose, fight back*

belakang *back, behind*

gol *goal (score)*

istirahat *rest, break*

membuat *to make*

penonton *viewer, audience, crowd*

gembira *happy, joyous*

beberapa *several*

atas *above, over*

menang *win*

karena *because*

akhir *end*

pertandingan *match, competition*

minggu *week*

## Exercise 13

Answer the following questions.

1. Which team won?

   a) PSM        b) Persib        c) it was a draw (neither team won)

2. How many goals were scored before the half-time break?

   a) 0          b) 1          c) 2

3. How many goals were scored after the break?

   a) 0          b) 1          c) 2

## Language note: *Warna tua dan muda* / Light and dark colors

After learning the words for red and white in previous units, we looked at colors in this unit when describing team uniforms. Here is a recap of the basic colors in Indonesian:

| | | | | |
|---|---|---|---|---|
| putih | *white* | | kuning | *yellow* |
| jingga, oranye | *orange* | | mérah | *red* |
| ungu | *purple* | | biru | *blue* |
| hijau | *green* | | cokelat | *brown* |
| abu-abu | *grey* | | hitam | *black* |

For different shades of colors, we simply add **tua** (literally "old," but meaning "dark") or **muda** (literally, "young," but meaning "light") after the color. Therefore:

| | | | |
|---|---|---|---|
| ungu muda | *light purple, violet* | ungu tua | *dark purple* |
| biru muda | *light blue, sky blue* | biru tua | *dark blue, navy blue, indigo* |
| mérah muda | *pink* | | |

As in any language, colors are very subjective. Some Indonesians would describe any shade of orange, pink, red, and purple as **mérah**. Others would debate whether aqua was **biru** or **hijau**. Some regional languages did not even have a word for green until Europeans came to Indonesia.

# 6.7 Menonton di bioskop  Going to the cinema

Adi and Danny decide to go to the cinema. They are queue-
ing to buy tickets. Nine people are standing in front of them.

## | Cultural note

Going to the cinema is very popular in Indonesia, partly
because people love watching movies, both local and import-
ed, and partly because cinemas are an air-conditioned escape
from the tropical heat outside. The cinema is particularly
popular with students, couples, and of course families.

In recent years, the Indonesian film industry has enjoyed
great growth, with a variety of historical-themed movies,
comedies, films for children, and, interestingly, horror films.
While most foreign films are either mainstream American features or from Bollywood, some more
independent films do make it to Indonesia, often in smaller cinemas or cultural centers such as the
Alliance Francaise, Goethe-Institut or Erasmus Huis.

School holidays are peak times for visits to the cinema. Many films are released to coincide with
school holidays, as well as with the Idul Fitri break and (to a lesser extent) Christmas and New Year.

| Title of the show | Timing |
|---|---|
| Jokowi Adalah Kita | jam 14.00, jam 17.00 |
| Cinta 2 | jam 10.00 |
| Garuda 19 | jam 11.00, jam 14.30, jam 17.00 |

## | Unit review

Use your knowledge of Indonesian to complete Adi and Danny's conversation at the cinema below.

ADI:       **Pagi. Dua orang untuk "Garuda 19."** *Morning. Two tickets to "Garuda 19."*

PETUGAS:   **Baik. Kalau jam 11, sudah tidak ada tiket lagi. Kalau jam 14.30?**
           *Right. For 11.00, there are no tickets left. What about 2.30?*

ADI:       **Masih lama ya, Danny?** *That's still a while, isn't it, Danny?*

DANNY:     **Saya tidak apa-apa.** *I don't mind.*

PETUGAS:   **Kalau film lain, ada "Ada apa dengan Cinta 2" sebentar lagi jam 10. Atau "Jokowi ada-
           lah Kita" nanti jam 2 siang.**
           *Among the other films, there's "Ada apa dengan Cinta 2" soon at 10.00. Or "Jokowi is
           Us" later at 2 in the afternoon.*

ADI:       **Mau nonton "Jokowi"? Atau kita makan dulu, baru nonton "Garuda 19"?**
           *Do you want to watch "Jokowi"?  Or shall we eat first, then watch "Garuda 19"?*

DANNY:     _____

PETUGAS:   **Mau duduk di depan, di kelas biru, atau belakang, di kelas merah?**
           *Do you want to sit at the front, in blue class, or the back, in red class?*

DANNY: _____

PETUGAS: **Mau di kiri atau kanan?** _Do you want the left or right side?_

ADI: _____

PETUGAS: **Seratus ribu rupiah. Ini, dua orang untuk** _____, **jam** _____, **bioskop 3. Terima kasih.**
_One hundred thousand rupiah. Here, two tickets for_ _____ _at_ _____, _cinema 3. Thank you._

DANNY, ADI: _____.

## ▌Unit 6 End-of-unit vocabulary list

**agama** _religion_
**Agustus** _August_
**akhir** _end_
**atas** _above, over_
**bagi** _for, to (usually a person)_
**bahwa** _that_
**beberapa** _several_
**belakang** _back, behind_
**berhasil** _to succeed_
**bioskop** _cinema_
**biru** _blue_
**bola baskét** _basketball_
**bola voli** _volleyball_
**bulan** _month_
**bulu tangkis** _badminton_
**cukup** _quite, enough; satisfactory_
**dapat, bisa** _can, be able_
**dari, daripada** _than_
**Désémber** _December_
**dibandingkan** _compared with_
**fotografi** _photography_
**futsal** _indoor soccer_
**ganjil** _odd_
**gembira** _happy, excited_
**genap** _even_
**gol** _goal (score)_
**harapan** _hope_
**harus** _must_
**hébat** _great, wonderful_
**hijau** _green_
**horé** _hooray, hurrah_
**hujan** _rain_
**ibukota** _capital city_
**istirahat** _rest_
**jakét** _jacket_

**jingga** _orange_
**juara** _winner, champion_
**Juli** _July_
**Juni** _June_
**kalah** _lose_
**karena** _because_
**kaus** _(collarless) shirt, T-shirt_
**kaus kaki** _sock, socks_
**kedinginan** _to feel cold_
**kemarau** _dry (season)_
**kepada** _to, for (a person)_
**kesebelasan** _team_
**khusus** _special_
**kuning** _yellow_
**kurang** _less, -er; unsatisfactory_
**liburan** _holiday_
**lomba** _race, contest_
**lukis** _painting, drawing_
**main** _play_
**masa** _time, period_
**Mei** _May_
**melawan** _to oppose, fight back_
**memancing** _to fish, go fishing_
**memasak** _to cook_
**membagi** _to hand out, share, divide up_
**membandingkan** _to compare_
**membuat** _to make_
**menang** _win_
**mengumumkan** _to announce, make public_
**menit** _saat, minute_
**menonton** _to watch (a film, TV)_
**menyanyi** _to sing_
**menyayangi** _to love (someone)_

**Minggu** _Sunday_
**minggu** _week_
**muda** _light (of color); young_
**murid** _pupil, student_
**musim** _season_
**musim gugur** _fall, autumn_
**musim semi** _spring (season)_
**naik kelas** _graduate or be promoted to the next grade_
**nilai** _score, points_
**nonton, menonton** _to watch (a film, TV)_
**Novémber** _November_
**nyanyi** _sing_
**Oktober** _October_
**olahraga** _sport_
**pakai, memakai** _use; wear; with_
**panas** _hot_
**pancaroba** _changeover (season)_
**penonton** _viewer, audience, crowd_
**penutupan** _closing_
**peringkat** _rank_
**perlombaan** _competition_
**pertandingan** _match, competition_
**piyama** _pajamas_
**Porseni** _Sports and Art Week_
**PPKn** _Civics & Pancasila_
**provinsi** _province_
**puasa** _to fast_
**putih** _white_
**ranking** _rank_
**rapot** _(school) report_
**rata-rata** _average_
**saat** _moment_
**salju** _snow_

**seméster** *term, semester*
**sendal** *sandal*
**sendal jepit** *plastic sandals, thongs, flipflops*
**seni** *art*
**sépak bola** *soccer, football*
**Séptémber** *September*
**seragam** *uniform*
**seri** *draw*

**siap** *ready*
**stadion** *stadium*
**suka** *often, tend to (colloquial)*
**sulit** *difficult, hard*
**susah** *difficult, hard*
**Sumatera** *Sumatra*
**tari** *(traditional) dance*
**tas** *bag*
**tim** *team*

**topi** *hat, cap*
**tradisional** *traditional*
**tua** *dark (of color); old*
**umum** *general, public*
**ujian** *exam, test*
**wah** *wow! (exclamation)*
**warna** *color*

**How to Download the Audio Recordings and Answer Key for this Book.**

1. Check your Internet connection.
2. Type the URL below into your web browser.

https://www.tuttlepublishing.com/Indonesian-for-Beginners

For support email us at info@tuttlepublishing.com

**Apa itu Ramadan, Pak?**
*What is Ramadan?*

**Ramadan atau bulan puasa di sini berbeda dengan bulan biasa.**
*Ramadan or fasting month here is different from an ordinary month.*

**Saya lihat banyak warung yang menjual makanan. Apa itu, Pak Johan?**
*I see a lot of roadside stalls selling food. What's all that about?*

**Biasanya setiap kota mempunyai pasar murah yang menjual sembako.**
*Usually every town has a bazaar selling staple food items.*

**Mengapa banyak orang keluar sore hari?**
*Why do lots of people go out in the afternoon?*

**Itu karena orang mau ngabuburit, atau menghabiskan waktu sambil menunggu buka puasa.**
*That's because people want to 'ngabuburit' or fill in time as they wait to break the fast.*

**Kalau makanan ini apa ya?**
*What's this food, then?*

**Itu kolak pisang. Kalau ini, bubur.**
*That's a kind of banana pudding. This one is porridge.*

This dialogue appears on page 124.

# 7

# Ramadhan dan Idul Fitri
## Fasting Month and Eid-Ul-Fitr

In this unit, we will:
- Learn about customs during the Islamic holy month,
- Ask and answer questions in a survey,
- Read and write comments,
- Learn about a special tradition in Aceh,
- Practice the language of shopping for food,
- Recognize the different ways **ter-** is used.

## 7.1 Menyambut Ramadhan  Welcoming Ramadan

Ramadan is a very special month for Muslims. This is the time when Muslim people do not eat and drink in the day, the time between sunrise and sunset. As Muslims, Adi and his family happily welcome this special month with various activities.

### ▌Basic Sentences

1.  **Ibu pergi ke pasar untuk membeli makanan, terutama untuk sahur pertama.**
*Mother goes to the market to buy food, especially for the first pre-dawn meal.*

2.  **Adi ikut kuliah subuh di mesjid terdekat.**
*Adi goes to the dawn sermon at the nearest mosque.*

3.  **Ayah membersihkan mushola keluarga untuk sholat taraweh.**
*Father cleans the family prayer room for Ramadan prayers.*

4. **Banyak sekolah (termasuk sekolah Adi) meliburkan murid-muridnya selama Ramadhan, supaya mereka bisa beristirahat.**
*Lots of schools (including Adi's school) give their students a holiday during Ramadan, so they can rest.*

5. **Pak RW membuat spanduk yang tertulis, "Selamat Berpuasa" di depan mesjid.**
*The neighborhood head makes a banner saying "Happy Fasting" in front of the mosque.*

6. **Terbentuk panitia zakat di mesjid, terdiri dari warga.**
*An alms committee, consisting of local residents, is formed at the mosque.*

## New Words and Phrases

**sahur** *pre-dawn meal*
**membeli** *to buy*
**makanan** *food*
**terutama** *especially, particularly*
**subuh** *pre-dawn prayer*
**terdekat** *nearest, closest*
**membersihkan** *to clean*
**mushola** *small prayer room*

**sholat taraweh** *voluntary evening prayers during Ramadan*
**termasuk** *including*
**meliburkan** *to give a holiday to someone*
**supaya** *in order to*
**beristirahat** *to rest, take a break*

**Pak RW (Rukun Warga)** *local neighborhood head*
**spanduk** *poster*
**tertulis** *written, inscribed*
**berpuasa, puasa** *to fast*
**terbentuk** *formed, created, shaped*
**panitia** *committee*
**zakat** *(Islamic) alms*

## Cultural note: Ramadan

Indonesia is the world's largest Muslim nation, with over 85% of its 260 million population Muslim. The holy month of Ramadan, followed by **Idul Fitri** (Eid-ul-Fitr), is therefore a huge annual event which impacts on the whole country, including those who are not very religiously observant and non-Muslims. Many restaurants close during the day, only to open later in the evenings. Often, offices will let their employees leave work an hour earlier, in order that they reach home to break the fast. Gatherings to break the fast together (**buka puasa bersama**) are also important, and include friends, family, colleagues or neighbors.

## Grammar note: *Ter-* for passive sentences

**Ter-**, a very useful prefix in Indonesian, is used in a number of ways. Generally speaking, **ter-** reflects an action which is passive, has already occurred, and in which the actor or doer is less important than the effect. Let's look at some **ter-** words in the reading above:

| | | | | |
|---|---|---|---|---|
| ter + | **tulis** *(write)* | = | **tertulis** | *written* |
| ter + | **kenal** *(know)* | = | **terkenal** | *well-known, famous* |
| ter + | **diri** *(self, stand)* | = | **terdiri** | *consisting* |
| ter + | **pilih** *(choose)* | = | **terpilih** | *chosen, elected* |
| ter + | **masuk** *(enter)* | = | **termasuk** | *including* |

**Ter-** differs from **di-** in that there is very little, if any, emphasis on the actor or doer of the action. Compare the following sentences:

**Pak RT membuat spanduk yang tertulis, "Selamat berpuasa."**
*The neighborhood head made a banner on which was written, "Happy fasting."*

**"Selamat berpuasa" ditulis di spanduk (oleh Pak RT?)**
*"Happy fasting" was written on the banner (by the neighborhood head?)*

**Pak RT menulis "Selamat berpuasa" di spanduk.**

*The neighborhood head wrote "Happy fasting" on the banner.*

### Exercise 1

Match the meanings to the following **ter-** words. (Hint: you have previously learned all the base words.)

| | |
|---|---|
| 1. **terpakai** | *obtained, available* |
| 2. **terlukis** | *fallen* |
| 3. **terdapat** | *painted, illustrated* |
| 4. **terpelajar** | *used* |
| 5. **terjatuh** | *educated* |

### ▌Grammar note: *Ter-* for superlatives vs *paling*

The other use of **ter-** is also as a superlative ("most," "-est"), in effect an alternative way of using **paling** as studied in Unit 5. **Terdekat** is therefore another way of saying **paling dekat** (closest), and **tertua** would be an alternative way to say **paling tua** (oldest). However, there are some words which form the superlative only with **paling** (eg. **paling gemuk** means "fattest"). The main point is to be aware that **ter-** either indicates a superlative or a passive meaning. The individual meaning should be clear from the context.

| | | | | |
|---|---|---|---|---|
| **ter** + **utama** *(main)* | = | **terutama** | *especially, particularly* |
| **ter** + **dekat** *(near, close)* | = | **terdekat** | *nearest, closest* |
| **ter** + **atas** *(over, above)* | = | **teratas** | *highest* |

### Exercise 2

How would you say the following superlatives in Indonesian, using **ter-**?

| | ADJECTIVE | SUPERLATIVE | |
|---|---|---|---|
| 1. **lama** | *long* | _____ | *longest* |
| 2. **besar** | *big, large* | _____ | *biggest, largest* |
| 3. **muda** | *young* | _____ | *youngest* |
| 4. **baik** | *good* | _____ | *best* |
| 5. **baru** | *new* | _____ | *newest* |

## 7.2  Kegiatan selama Ramadhan  Activities during Ramadan

It is the first time Danny has experienced the Islamic fasting month. He is asking Pak Johan, Adi's father, about what happens during Ramadan, while Adi's family is waiting to break the fast. Listen to their conversation.

## Listening to a dialogue

DANNY:       **Apa itu Ramadan, Pak?** *What is Ramadan?*

PAK JOHAN:   **Ramadan sangat ditunggu oleh setiap orang Islam di dunia, termasuk di Indonesia. Bulan puasa di sini berbeda dengan bulan biasa.**
*Ramadan is always a much-anticipated time for every Muslim in the world, including in Indonesia. Fasting month here is different from an ordinary month.*

DANNY:       **Saya lihat banyak warung yang menjual makanan. Apa itu, Pak Johan?**
*I see a lot of roadside stalls selling food. What's all that about?*

PAK JOHAN:   **Biasanya setiap kota mempunyai pasar murah yang menjual sembako. Pasar Murah biasanya diadakan di alun-alun kota supaya warga bisa dengan mudah datang membeli.**
*Usually every town has a bazaar selling staple food items. Bazaars are usually held in the town square so that locals can come easily to shop.*

DANNY:       **Mengapa banyak orang keluar sore hari?**
*Why do lots of people go out in the afternoon?*

PAK JOHAN:   **Itu karena adanya ngabuburit, Danny. Menjelang sore, orang tertarik untuk menghabiskan waktu sambil menunggu saatnya berbuka puasa. Ada yang jalan-jalan ke mal, ada yang bermain layangan, atau membeli makanan untuk buka puasa.**
*That's because of the **ngabuburit** tradition, Danny. Approaching late afternoon, people like to fill in time as they wait to break the fast. Some go to the mall, some fly kites, or buy food for breaking the fast.*

DANNY:       **Kalau makanan ini apa ya?** *What's this food, then?*

PAK JOHAN:   **Itu kolak pisang. Kalau ini, bubur. Harga makanan seperti ini sangat murah.**
*That's a kind of banana pudding. This one is porridge. The price of food like this is very cheap.*

## New Words and Phrases

**ditunggu (menunggu)** *awaited, waited for (to wait)*
**setiap** *every, each*
**menjual** *to sell*
**berbéda** *different*
**biasanya** *usually*
**mempunyai** *to have, possess*
**murah** *cheap, inexpensive*
**sembako** *(one of nine) staple foods* (**sembilan bahan pokok**)
**mudah** *easy*

**datang** *come*
**mengapa** *why*
**soré hari** *in the afternoon*
**karena** *because*
**ngabuburit** *kill time before breaking the fast*
**menjelang** *to approach, approaching*
**buka puasa** *break the fast*
**tertarik** *interested*

**menghabiskan** *to finish off, finish up*
**saat** *moment, time*
**layangan** *kite*
**makanan** *food*
**kolak** *sweet traditional snack*
**pisang** *banana*
**bubur** *porridge*
**harga** *price*

**Exercise 3**

Reading comprehension: True or false? **Benar atau salah? (B / S)**

1. **Semua orang di dunia sangat senang saat bulan Ramadhan tiba.**       (B / S)

2. **Tidak ada banyak orang datang ke Pasar Murah karena cukup mahal.**   (B / S)

3. **Ngabuburit dilakukan di pagi hari.**       (B / S)

4. **Kolak pisang dan bubur termasuk makanan untuk buka puasa.**       (B / S)

5. **Pasar Murah diadakan selama bulan puasa.**       (B / S)

# 7.3  Angket Ramadhan   Ramadan survey

Adi is in charge of one of the local committees for special Ramadan events. He is trying to find out what teenagers want to make the program successful. He is sending a survey to every teenager in the neighbourhood, as below.

1. **Kegiatan apa yang paling kamu suka dari Ramadhan?**
   *What activity do you like most in Ramadan?*
   a. **Kuliah subuh**                  *dawn sermons*
   b. **Mengaji sore**                  *afternoon Koranic recitation*
   c. **Buka puasa bersama**            *breaking the fast together*
   d. **Membuat kartu Lebaran**         *making Lebaran greetings cards*

2. **Kegiatan apa yang kurang kamu suka?**
   *What activity do you least like?*
   a. **Kuliah subuh**                  *dawn sermons*
   b. **Mengaji sore**                  *afternoon Koranic recitation*
   c. **Buka puasa bersama**            *breaking the fast together*
   d. **Membuat kartu Lebaran**         *making Lebaran greetings cards*

3. **Di mana sebaiknya kegiatan buka puasa dilakukan?**
   *Where should breaking the fast be held?*
   a. **Di mesjid**                     *at the mosque*
   b. **Di alun-alun**                  *at the town square*
   c. **Dari rumah ke rumah**           *from house to house*

4. **Kapan sebaiknya sembako murah dijual?**
   *When should cheap staple foods be sold?*
   a. **Minggu pertama bulan Ramadan**  *the first week of Ramadan*
   b. **Minggu kedua bulan Ramadan**    *the second week of Ramadan*
   c. **Minggu ketiga bulan Ramadan**   *the third week of Ramadan*
   d. **Minggu keempat bulan Ramadan**  *the fourth week of Ramadan*

5. **Kirim komentar lainnya ke nomor yang di bawah ini: 08121426244**
   *Send other comments to this number below: 08121426244*

## New Words and Phrases

**kegiatan** *activity*
**subuh** *dawn (prayer) (in Islam)*
**mengaji** *to recite from the Koran*
**kartu** *card*

**Lebaran** *Eid-ul-Fitr (Idul Fitri), end-of-fasting celebration*
**kapan** *when?*

**sebaiknya** *should, it's best*
**mengajak** *to invite, ask along*

## 7.4 Ruang komentar  Comments

Adi is getting comments on his phone from many teenagers who would like to share their ideas. Here are some:

**Halo Adi,**
**Saya Zahra, dari Jalan Pelikan no. 5. Terima kasih atas angketnya. Saya ingin memberikan masukan. Kalau boleh, tolong diadakan acara mengaji Al-Quran di pagi hari setelah sholat subuh. Ini membantu saya dan kawan-kawan supaya kami bisa pandai membaca Al-Quran dengan lebih baik.**
**Terima kasih,**
**– Zahra, 08592257771**

*Hello Adi,*
*I'm Zahra, from Jalan Pelikan no. 5. Thanks for your survey. I want to give a suggestion. If possible, there should be reciting from the Koran in the morning after the dawn prayer. This would help me and my friends to be able to read the Koran well.*
*Thank you,*
*Zahra*

**Assalamu'alaikum Adi,**
**Saya menulis masukan ini untuk adik saya, Yoga, yang masih berumur 7 tahun. Dia malas berpuasa karena masih belum mengerti tujuan dari puasa. Tolong diadakan acara kuliah subuh, agar adik saya bisa belajar lebih banyak tentang artinya puasa.**
**– Suci, 081313472468**

*Peace be upon you, Adi,*
*I am writing this suggestion for my little brother Yoga, who is just 7 years old. He is lazy about fasting because he doesn't yet understand the goal of the fast. Please hold a dawn sermon, so that my brother can learn more about the meaning of fasting.*
*Suci*

**Selamat pagi Adi,**
**Tahun lalu saya ikut buka puasa bersama, tapi saya punya keluhan karena para pesertanya nakal! Makanan untuk buka puasa tidak dibagikan dengan benar. Ada beberapa peserta yang mendapat lebih dari satu paket makanan, sementara yang lainnya tidak mendapat. Saya berdoa agar ini tidak terjadi lagi. Terima kasih.**
**– Agridan, 02189012345**

*Good morning Adi,*
*Last year I joined a breaking of the fast, but I have a complaint because the people who came were naughty! Food for breaking the fast was not distributed properly. There were some participants who got more than one parcel of food, while others didn't get any. I am praying that this doesn't happen again.*
*Thank you,*
*Agridan*

## New Words and Phrases

**angkét** *survey*
**masukan** *feedback, suggestion*
**acara** *program, event*
**Al-Quran** *the Koran*
**setelah, sesudah** *after*

**Assalamu'alaikum** *Peace be upon you (Muslim greeting)*
**tentang** *about*
**arti** *meaning*
**malas** *lazy*
**keluhan** *complaint*

**peserta** *participant*
**nakal** *naughty*
**pakét** *packet, package*
**sementara** *while, meanwhile*
**berdoa** *to pray*

### Exercise 4

Quick comprehension questions

1. Who has a complaint about breaking the fast together? What is the problem?

2. Who is writing about her brother attending a morning sermon?

3. Who is writing about reading the Koran early in the morning?

## Grammar note: Conjunctions 1—*agar* and *supaya*

In this unit, we have seen the use of these two words as a conjunction or link word. **Agar** and **supaya** have a similar meaning, "in order to" and "so that," and they are used in similar ways.

> a. **Tolong diadakan acara kuliah subuh, supaya adik saya bisa belajar lebih banyak ...**
> *Please hold a dawn lecture, so my younger brother can learn more ...*

> b. **Sekolah meliburkan murid-muridnya selama Ramadhan, supaya mereka bisa beristirahat.**
> *Schools give their students a holiday during Ramadan, so that they (the students) can rest.*

> c. **Pasar Murah biasanya diadakan di alun-alun kota supaya warga bisa dengan mudah datang membeli.**
> *Bazaars are usually held in the town square so that locals can easily come to shop.*

> d. **Ini membantu saya dan kawan-kawan agar bisa pandai membaca Al-Quran dengan lebih baik.**
> *This helps me and my friends to be better able to read the Koran.*

Essentially, **supaya** should come before a noun, as it introduces a clause. In sentence a, the noun (or nominal group) is **adik saya** ("my younger brother"); in sentence b, the noun is **mereka** ("they" or "the students," as **mereka** is always for humans, not objects); and in sentence c the noun is **warga** ("locals").

Agar usually comes before a phrase and is not necessarily followed by a noun. In sentence d, **agar** is followed by **bisa pandai membaca Al-Quran** ("can be good at reading the Koran"), **bisa** being an auxiliary verb.

However, you may sometimes see exceptions to this, and even the use of **agar supaya** together!

### Exercise 5

Fill in the correct word, **agar** or **supaya**.

1. **Ayah membersihkan mushola keluarga _____ bersih untuk sholat taraweh.**

   *Father cleans the family prayer room _____ it is clean for the Ramadan evening prayers.*

2. **Sembako dijual di pasar murah _____ warga bisa membeli dengan mudah.**

   *Staple foods are sold at the bazaar _____ locals can buy them easily.*

3. **Belajar dengan rajin, _____ mendapat nilai baik.**

   *Study diligent, _____ get good grades.*

4. **Siti belajar dengan rajin, _____ dia mendapat nilai baik.**

   *Siti studies diligently, _____ she gets good grades.*

## Grammar note: Conjunctions 2—*karena* and *sementara*

You have just learned two conjunctions, **agar** and **supaya**. Another very useful conjunction or link work is **karena**, meaning "because." **Karena** is often used in tandem with **mengapa**, "why." You will find Indonesians often ask a (rhetorical) question before answering it themselves, using **mengapa** and **karena**. In formal language, you will also see **oleh karena** ("because") as well as **oleh karena itu** ("therefore").

> **Mengapa banyak orang keluar sore hari?**
> *Why do lots of people go out in the afternoon?*
>
> **Itu karena adanya ngabuburit.**
> *That's because of the* **ngabuburit** *(tradition).*
>
> **Mengapa sekolah diliburkan? Karena kita ingin anak-anak beristirahat selama bulan puasa.**
> *Why are schools on holiday? Because we want the children to rest during fasting month.*

**Mengapa** is a question word. Other question words already studied include:

| | |
|---|---|
| **apa** | *what?* |
| **berapa** | *how much? how many?* |
| **di mana** | *where?* |
| **kapan** | *when?* |
| **siapa** | *who?* |

We will learn **bagaimana** ("how") in Unit 8.

### Exercise 6

Match the questions and answers using **mengapa** and **karena**.

1. **Mengapa dia membuat kartu Lebaran?**
2. **Mengapa dia tidak nonton film itu?**
3. **Mengapa dia suka makan gudeg?**
4. **Mengapa Wina menjadi guru?**

a. **Karena dia suka anak-anak.**
b. **Karena besok sudah Idul Fitri.**
c. **Karena rasanya enak.**
d. **Karena tidak menarik.**

## 7.5 Meugang, menyambut Ramadhan dan Lebaran di Aceh
**Meugang**, welcoming Ramadan and Idul Fitri in Aceh

Adi's family driver, Pak Mur, has told Danny about Ramadan and Idul Fitri in Aceh, his home province. Danny finds a book in the library with some information.

## Reading

Aceh adalah salah satu provinsi di Indonesia. Aceh terletak di utara pulau Sumatera dan merupakan provinsi paling barat di Indonesia. Ibukotanya adalah Banda Aceh. Aceh adalah tempat agama Islam pertama kali masuk ke dalam kepulauan Indonesia. 99% dari penduduk Aceh adalah orang Muslim, yaitu persentase yang tertinggi di Indonesia.

*Aceh is a province in Indonesia. It lies in northern Sumatra and is the most westerly province in Indonesia. The capital is Banda Aceh. Aceh was where Islam first entered the Indonesian archipelago. Ninety-nine percent of the population there is Muslim, the highest percentage in Indonesia.*

Salah satu tradisi masyarakat Aceh saat Ramadhan dan Lebaran adalah Meugang, yaitu membeli dan memakan daging. Tradisi ini dilakukan pada hari istimewa, biasanya dua hari menjelang puasa dan dua hari menjelang Lebaran (Idul Fitri) atau Lebaran Haji (Idul Adha).

*An Acehnese tradition during Ramadan and Idul Fitri is **Meugang**, or buying and eating meat. This tradition is carried out on special days, usually two days before fasting and two days before Idul Fitri or Idul Adha (Feast of the Sacrifice).*

## New Words and Phrases

| | | |
|---|---|---|
| **terletak** *located in* | **perséntase** *percentage* | **haji** *man who has completed* |
| **kepulauan** *archipelago* | **istiméwa** *special* | *the pilgrimage to Mecca* |
| **Muslim** *Muslim, Moslem* | **menjelang** *to approach,* | |
| **yaitu** *that is, i.e.* | *approaching* | |

## Grammar note: *yaitu*

**Yaitu** is another useful conjunction, meaning "that is." It introduces further information on a topic, as seen in the sentences below.

> **99% dari penduduk Aceh adalah orang Muslim, yaitu persentase yang tertinggi di Indonesia.**
> *Ninety-nine percent of Aceh's population is Muslim, (that is) the highest percentage in Indonesia.*

Here, **yaitu** is not necessarily translated, but explains further information about the statistic.

> **Salah satu tradisi masyarakat Aceh saat Ramadhan dan Lebaran adalah Meugang, yaitu membeli dan memakan daging.**
> *An Acehnese tradition during Ramadan and Idul Fitri is **Meugang**, or buying and eating meat.*

In this sentence, **yaitu** explains the meaning of **Meugang**. You sometimes see **yakni** instead of **yaitu**, but the two words are used in the same way.

### Exercise 7

Fill in the missing words in these sentences showing the use of **yaitu**. Then translate them into English.

Missing words (not in order): **Idul Adha**      **Banda Aceh**      **Meugang**

1. _____, yaitu ibukotanya Aceh, adalah kota paling barat di Indonesia.

_____.

2. _____, yaitu tradisi pada Idul Fitri di Aceh, dilakukan dengan membeli dan memakan daging.

_____.

3. Lebaran Haji, yaitu _____, merayakan para haji pergi ke Mekkah.

_____.

## 7.6 Makanan dan minuman di bulan Ramadhan
Favorite food and drink during Ramadan

Ibu Ratna is a housewife who is trying to earn some money during Ramadan by selling some sweets and finger foods. Listen to a conversation between Ibu Ratna and Naufal, a customer.

Ibu Ratna has made a menu for her customers:

---

### *Makanan* / Food

**Kolak Pisang**
*A very sweet dessert made with brown sugar* (**gula merah**).

**Harga** / *Price: Rp. 10.000*

**Bubur Sumsum**
*A kind of sweet porridge made from rice flour, coconut cream* (**santan**) *and brown sugar.*

**Harga** / *Price: Rp. 15.000*

**Es Cendol**
*A green, red and white dessert-style drink. The green is from rice flour, the white from* **santan** *and the red from brown sugar.*

**Harga** / *Price: Rp. 7.000*

**Jus Kurma**
*Dates are blended into a smoothie-like juice. Whole dates are often used to break the fast, in the tradition of the Prophet Muhammad.*

**Harga** / *Price: Rp. 15.000*

**Siomay**
*These savory, steamed dim-sum style fish cakes are served with spicy peanut sauce* (**bumbu kacang**).

**Harga** / *Price: Rp. 20.000*

**Teh Manis**
*Sweet tea gives you a sugar rush after breaking the fast. Iced sweet tea* (**es teh manis**) *is also popular.*

**Harga** / *Price: Rp. 3.000*

**Pisang Goreng**
*Bananas are peeled, lightly dusted in flour and then fried.*

**Harga** / *Price: Rp. 5.000*

---

NAUFAL: **Selamat sore, Bu.** *Good afternoon.*

IBU RATNA: **Selamat sore, Naufal... silakan, mau beli apa?**
*Good afternoon, Naufal... what would you like to buy?*

NAUFAL: **Saya mau beli makanan untuk buka puasa nanti.**
*I would like to buy some food to break the fast.*

IBU RATNA: **Boleh, silakan pilih mau apa.** *Sure, what would you like to choose?*

NAUFAL:  **Ini apa, ya, Bu?** *What is this?*

IBU RATNA:  **Oh, itu kolak pisang. Harganya murah, hanya lima belas ribu rupiah. Rasanya enak!**
*Oh, it is **kolak pisang**. It is cheap, only fifteen thousand rupiah. It tastes good!*

NAUFAL:  **Makanan ini dibuat dari apa, ya, Bu?** *What is this food made from?*

IBU RATNA:  **Kolak dibuat dari pisang, gula merah, dan santan.**
**Kolak** *is made from banana, brown sugar, and coconut milk.*

## ▌New Words and Phrases

**minuman** *drink*
**pilih, memilih** *to choose*
**gula** *sugar*
**gula mérah** *brown sugar*
**santan** *coconut milk*
**bubur sumsum** *rice flour porridge*

**ubi** *sweet potato*
**és** *ice*
**céndol** *green, white and red drink*
**jus** *juice*
**kurma** *date*
**siomay** *type of dim sum*

**bumbu** *sauce, spice*
**kacang** *nut*
**téh** *tea*
**manis** *sweet*
**goréng** *fried*

### Exercise 8

Can you sort the vocabulary items above into different categories?

| Drink | Sweet food |
|---|---|
| *eg.* **minuman** <br> **es cendol** | *eg.* **bubur sumsum** <br> **kolak pisang** |
| | |

### Exercise 9

Change the words in the dialogue between Ibu Ratna and Naufal. See if you can change the time of day, food, price and what the food is made of.

 ## ▌Unit review: *Ramadhan datang*

Tompi is a very well-known singer in Indonesia. One of his popular songs, **Ramadhan Datang**, is often heard during the Muslim holy month, because the song explains the meaning of Ramadan.

Find the following song on the Internet and fill in the missing words. A translation follows the exercise.

**Ramadhan Datang**
*oleh: Tompi*

| | |
|---|---|
| **Ramadhan _____ alam pun riang** | *Ramadan has come, the world is joyful* |
| **menyambut bulan yang berkah** | *welcoming the month of blessings* |
| **_____ berdendang kumandang azan** | *The people sing the call to prayer* |
| **pertanda hati yang senang** | *Sign of a happy heart* |
| | |
| **ohhh...hati yang _____** | *Ohhh ... joyful heart* |
| **ohhh...penuh suka cita** | *Ohhh ... full of happiness* |
| | |
| **Sebulan kita kan _____** | *A month we have fasted* |
| **melawan lapar dahaga** | *fighting hunger and thirst* |
| **kalahkan nafsu rayuan syetan** | *Defeating the devil's temptations* |
| **_____ insan yang taqwa** | *Becoming believers* |
| | |
| **ohhh...hati yang gembira** | *Ohhh ... joyful heart* |
| **ohhh...penuh suka cita** | *Ohhh ... full of happiness* |
| | |
| **Ref:** | *Refrain:* |
| **Tarawih dan tadarus** | *Evening prayers and the Holy Koran* |
| **bersujud di tengah _____** | *Prostrating at midnight* |
| **berzikir dan berdoa** | *Saying prayers and blessings* |
| **menyebut asmaMu ALLAH** | *Saying your name, God* |
| **dan tak _____ berzakat** | *And not forgetting to pay alms* |
| **sempurnakan kewajiban** | *Perfecting our duties* |
| **mensucikan jiwa** | *Purifying our souls* |
| **_____ insan yang fitri** | *As humans reborn* |
| **Tarawih dan tadarus** | *Evening prayers and the Holy Koran* |
| **bersujud di tengah _____** | *Prostrating at midnight* |
| **berzikir dan berdoa** | *Saying prayers and blessings* |
| **menyebut asmaMu ALLAH** | *Saying your name, God* |
| **dan tak _____ berzakat** | *And not forgetting to pay alms* |
| **sempurnakan kewajiban** | *Perfecting our duties* |
| **mensucikan jiwa** | *Purifying our souls* |
| **sebagai makhluk ALLAH** | *As God's creations.* |

## Unit 7 End-of-unit vocabulary list

**acara** *program, event*
**agar** *in order to, so*
**Al-Quran** *the Koran*
**angkét** *survey*

**arti** *meaning*
**assalamu'alaikum** *peace be upon you (Muslim greeting)*
**bagian** *part, share*

**benar** *correct; true*
**berbéda** *different*
**berdoa** *to pray*
**beristirahat** *to rest*

**berpuasa** *to fast*
**biasa** *usual, ordinary*
**biasanya** *usually*
**biji** *seed*
**bubur** *porridge*
**bubur sumsum** *porridge made from fine rice flour*
**buka, membuka** *open*
**buka puasa** *break the fast*
**bumbu** *sauce, spice*
**cendol** *green, white and red drink*
**dalam** *in, inside*
**datang** *come*
**dekat** *close, near*
**ditunggu-tunggu** *long-awaited*
**és** *ice*
**goréng** *fried*
**gula** *sugar*
**gula mérah** *brown sugar*
**hadiah** *gift, prize*
**haji** *man who has performed the pilgrimage to Mecca*
**hal** *matter, thing*
**harga** *price*
**Idul Adha** *Feast of the Sacrifice, held during the haj season*
**Idul Fitri** *Eid-ul-Fitr, end-of-fasting celebration*
**istiméwa** *special*
**jus** *juice*
**kacang** *bean, nut, legume*
**kali** *time*
**kapan** *when?*
**karena** *because*
**kartu** *card*
**kegiatan** *activity*
**keluhan** *complaint*
**kepulauan** *archipelago*
**kirim, mengirim** *to send*
**kolak** *sweet traditional snack*
**kurma** *date (fruit)*

**layangan** *kite*
**Lebaran** *Idul Fitri*
**makanan** *food*
**malas** *lazy*
**manis** *sweet*
**masukan** *suggestion, feedback*
**meliburkan** *to give a holiday to someone*
**memakan** *to eat*
**membeli** *to buy*
**memberi** *to give*
**membentuk** *to form, shape*
**membersihkan** *to clean*
**mempunyai** *to have, possess*
**mengajak** *to invite, ask along*
**mengaji** *to recite from the Koran*
**mengapa** *why*
**menghabiskan** *to finish off, finish up*
**mengirim** *to send*
**menjelang** *to approach, approaching*
**menjual** *to sell*
**menulis** *to write*
**menunggu** *to wait*
**menurut** *according to*
**merata** *evenly*
**minuman** *drink*
**mudah** *easy*
**murah** *cheap, inexpensive*
**mushola** *small prayer room*
**Muslim** *Muslim, Moslem*
**nakal** *naughty*
**ngabuburit** *kill time before breaking the fast*
**Pak RW (Rukun Warga)** *local neighborhood head*
**pakét** *package, packet*
**panitia** *committee*
**perayaan** *celebration*
**perlu** *need*

**perséntase** *percentage*
**peserta** *participant*
**pilih, memilih** *to choose*
**pisang** *banana*
**saat** *moment, time*
**sahur** *pre-dawn meal*
**salah** *wrong; false*
**santan** *coconut milk*
**sebaiknya** *it's best*
**sembako** *(one of nine) staple food (sembilan bahan pokok)*
**sementara** *while, meanwhile*
**setelah, sesudah** *after*
**setiap** *each, every*
**sholat** *one of the five daily prayers*
**sholat tarawéh** *voluntary evening prayers during Ramadan*
**siomay** *kind of dim sum*
**sore hari ini** *this afternoon*
**spanduk** *poster, banner*
**subuh** *pre-dawn prayer (Islamic)*
**supaya** *so that*
**téh** *tea*
**tentang** *about, concerning*
**terbentuk** *formed, created, shaped*
**terdekat** *nearest, closest*
**terdiri** *consisting*
**terjadi** *to happen, occur*
**terletak** *to be located, lie*
**termasuk** *including*
**tertarik** *interested*
**tertulis** *written, inscribed*
**terutama** *especially, particularly*
**tolong** *help; please*
**tujuan** *aim, destination*
**tulis, menulis** *to write*
**ubi** *sweet potato*
**warga** *local, resident*
**yaitu** *that is, ie.*
**zakat** *(Islamic) alms*

*This dialogue appears on the facing page.*

# UNIT

# 8

# Idul Adha di Sumatera Barat
## Idul Adha in West Sumatra

In this unit, we will:

- Learn about another important Islamic festival, Idul Adha,
- Learn how to use the second person plural (**kalian** and **sekalian**),
- Expand our vocabulary to include the names of some common animals,
- Describe people and their work,
- Learn how to identify and use the imperative form of verbs,
- Learn how to use counters such as **sebuah**, **seorang**, **seekor**,
- Identify nouns that use the **-an** suffix.

## 8.1  Uda Amir, penjual nasi Padang  Amir, the Padang food seller

Adi and Danny are having lunch in their favorite traditional restaurant, a **warung Padang**. This time, they have the chance to have a long chat with the owner of the restaurant, Uda Amir. Listen to their conversation.

 **Listening to a dialogue**

| | |
|---|---|
| ADI: | **Uda Amir sudah berapa lama di Jakarta?** |
| | *How long have you been in Jakarta?* |
| UDA AMIR: | **Sudah 30 tahun yang lalu sejak saya pindah dari Padang.** |
| | *It's been 30 years since I moved from Padang.* |
| ADI: | **Selain kita yang murid-murid SMA 3, siapa saja yang suka makan di sini?** |
| | *Apart from SMA 3 high school students like us, who else likes to eat here?* |
| UDA AMIR: | **Tamunya bukan hanya pelajar seperti kalian, tapi juga pegawai negeri, pegawai toko, supir, dan siapa saja yang merasa lapar.** |
| | *The customers are not just school students like you, but also civil servants, shop workers, drivers, and anyone else who feels hungry.* |
| DANNY: | **Makanan apa yang khas di sini?**  *What special foods do you have here?* |
| UDA AMIR: | **Makanan Padang, seperti rendang, soto Padang, daun singkong dan ayam pop.** |
| | *Padang food, such as beef rendang, clear Padang soup, cassava leaves and skinless chicken.* |
| DANNY: | **Uda Amin masih suka pulang ke Padang?**  *Do you still often go home to Padang?* |

UDA AMIR: **Pada hari istimewa, saya selalu pulang kampung. Saat Idul Adha nanti, saya dan keluarga akan pergi ke Padang. Kami mau berkurban! Apa Danny dan Adi mau ikut?**

*On special days, I always go back to the village. When Idul Adha comes, the family and I will go to Padang. We want to make a sacrifice! Do you two want to come with us?*

ADI: **Wah, perayaan Idul Adha di Padang biasanya ramai! Katanya orang Padang sangat bersemangat dengan perayaan keagamaan. Mau, Danny?**

*Wow, the Idul Adha celebrations in Padang are usually noisy! It's said that people in Padang are very enthusiastic about religious celebrations. Do you want to go, Danny?*

DANNY: **Mau!** *Yes!*

ADI: **Saya minta izin ke orang tua dulu ya, Uda. Mudah-mudahan kami bisa ikut, agar belajar banyak tentang budaya orang Minang.**

*I'll have to ask my parents' permission first, Uda Amir. Hopefully we can go, so we can learn more about the Minang culture.*

DANNY: **Selain itu, saya juga penasaran, apa rasa nasi padang di tempat aslinya akan lebih enak?**

*Apart from that, I'm also curious, whether Padang rice in its hometown will be even more delicious.*

## Ι New Words and Phrases

| | | |
|---|---|---|
| **Uda** *Minangkabau term for older brother* | **merasa** *to feel* | **ramai** *noisy, eventful* |
| **penjual** *seller* | **lapar** *hungry* | **bersemangat** *enthusiastic, full of spirit* |
| **nasi padang** *Padang-style dishes with rice* | **khas** *special, typical* | **keagamaan** *religious* |
| **kalian** *you* (plural) | **daun singkong** *cassava leaves* | **izin** *permission* |
| **toko** *shop, store* | **ayam pop** *skinless chicken dish, a Padang specialty* | **mudah-mudahan** *hopefully* |
| **supir** *driver* | **pulang kampung** *go back to the village* | **budaya** *culture* |
| **siapa saja** *whoever* | **berkurban** *to make a sacrifice (of an animal)* | **selain** *apart from* |
| | | **penasaran** *curious* |

## Ι Cultural note: Idul Adha

Idul Adha is one of the biggest celebrations for Muslims. It is celebrated to remember the willingness of the prophet Abraham to sacrifice his son when God ordered him to, as in the tale of Ishmael. While the rich may be able to perform the hajj pilgrimage to Mecca in Saudi Arabia, those who cannot afford to do so may sacrifice a cow, sheep, or goat as a reminder of Abraham's obedience to Allah.

Many people go back to their village (**pulang kampung**) either on **Idul Adha** or **Idul Fitri**, or both. This way they can visit their ancestors' graves, gather with their extended family and maintain cultural links with their origins.

## Ι Cultural note: West Sumatra

West Sumatra (**Sumatera Barat**) is a province in Indonesia. Most of the population is Muslim, and are from the **Minangkabau** (**Minang**, for short) ethnic group. The celebration of Idul Adha in West Sumatra, especially in Padang, is always fascinating for domestic tourists and foreigners. **Nasi padang**, a famous local dish, is very well-known across Indonesia.

## Grammar note: Pronouns *kalian* and *sekalian*

In the conversation above, Uda Amin refers to both Adi and Danny as **kalian**. This is a useful word referring to the second person plural (i.e., more than one person), both informally as well as in a formal situation.

> **Tamunya bukan hanya pelajar seperti <u>kalian</u>.**
> *The customers are not just school students like you (two).*

The related word **sekalian** can be used in a similar way.

> **Saudara <u>sekalian</u>, selamat datang di Hotel Satria.**
> *Ladies and gentlemen, welcome to Hotel Satria.*

However, **sekalian** literally means "all (at once)" or "together," such as in this example:

> **Kita ke kota saja, <u>sekalian</u> beli makanan.**
> *Let's just go to town, and buy food at the same time.*

### Exercise 1

Write either **kalian** or **sekalian** as appropriate in the blank space.

1. **Ayo, Adi dan Danny! _____ mau ikut atau tidak?**
   *Come on, Adi and Danny! Do _____ want to come or not?*

2. **Mau lewat sekolah? Kami ikut _____ di mobil.**
   *Are you going past the school? We'll join _____ in the car.*

3. **Anak-anak, kapan _____ ada pelajaran bahasa Inggris?**
   *Children, when do _____ your English lesson?*

4. **Para bapak-bapak dan ibu-ibu _____, silakan masuk.**
   *Ladies and gentlemen, please come in.*

## 8.2 Siapa mereka? Who are they?

## Reading Comprehension

When they arrived in Padang, Adi and Danny met many people. Here is some information about them.

### Dahlan

**Dahlan seorang supir angkot. Dia sangat lucu! Setiap penumpang yang naik angkotnya selalu tertawa- tawa karena Dahlan selalu bercanda dengan mereka. Dia punya hobi menyanyi.**

*Dahlan is a public minibus driver. He's very funny! Every passenger on his minibus always laughs and laughs because Dahlan always jokes with them. His hobby is singing.*

### Salim

**Salim seorang pemandu wisata. Dia sangat pintar. Dia tahu banyak tentang sejarah dan budaya orang Padang. Salim sangat bangga akan sejarah dan budaya Padang.**

*Salim is a tour guide. He is very clever. He knows a lot about the history and culture of the Padang people. Salim is very proud of Padang's history and culture.*

**Bahri**

**Bahri penjaga mesjid. Dia tidak suka kalau ada orang yang membuang sampah dan membuat kotor di sekitar mesjid. Setiap hari dia melakukan adzan untuk memanggil orang-orang melakukan sholat.**

*Bahri is a guard at the mosque. He doesn't like people littering and making the mosque area dirty. Every day he does the prayer call, to call people to pray.*

**Aminah**

**Aminah teman Uda Amir sejak kecil. Dia seorang guru di sebuah sekolah dasar. Dia sangat penyayang. Setiap siswa suka dengan pelajaran dia. Hobi dia memasak. Setiap akhir minggu dia memasak masakan istimewa, seperti rendang, ayam pop, dan lain-lain.**

*Aminah has been Amir's friend since they were little. She is a teacher at an elementary school. She is very loving. All students like her lessons. Her hobby is cooking. Every weekend she cooks special food, such as beef rendang, skinless chicken, and so on.*

**Fauziah**

**Fauziah adalah anak Bahri. Dia seumur dengan Adi dan Danny. Dia seorang pelajar SMA. Cita-citanya menjadi seorang pegawai negeri. Dia sangat pintar dan pandai bergaul.**

*Fauziah is Bahri's daughter. She is the same age as Adi and Danny. She is a senior high school student. Her dream is to become a civil servant. She is very clever and mixes well with others.*

## New Words and Phrases

| | | |
|---|---|---|
| **angkot** *public minibus* (**angkutan kota**) | **penjaga** *guard, night watchman* | **penyayang** *loving* |
| **penumpang** *passenger* | **membuang** *to throw away* | **akhir** *end* |
| **tertawa-tawa** *to laugh* | **sampah** *rubbish, garbage, trash* | **dan lain-lain** *etc., et cetera* |
| **bercanda** *to joke around* | **kotor** *dirty* | **seumur** *the same age (lit., "one age")* |
| **pintar pandai**, *smart, clever* | **adzan** *the call to prayer* | **bergaul** *to mix with others, socialize* |
| **sejarah** *history* | **memanggil** *to call* | |
| **bangga akan** *proud of* | **teman, kawan** *friend* | |

## Exercise 2

Here are Adi's impressions of the people he met recorded on a video he is making to send to his family back in Jakarta. Write down the name of the person whom Adi is talking about.

EXAMPLE:

**"Wah, dia sangat baik, ya! Murid-muridnya semua suka dengan dia. Saya juga mau makan rendang yang dibuatnya. Pasti enak…"**

ANSWER:

<u>Aminah</u>

1. **"Saya suka dia. Dia murid SMA yang punya banyak kawan. Saya akan berteman dengan dia di Facebook."**

   _____

2. **"Dia sangat beragama. Setiap hari dia membuat mesjid bersih. Orang tidak mau membuang sampah di depan dia."**

   _____

3. **"Saya selalu dibuat tertawa oleh dia. Selain ramah, dia pandai menyanyi! Banyak lagi yang dia tahu."**

   _____

4. **Saya melihat dia berbahasa Inggris dengan wisatawan. Dia juga** _____
   **tahu banyak tentang Sumatera Barat dan Padang.**

## 8.3 Uda Amir berkurban    Amir offers a sacrifice

Early in the morning, Uda Amir leaves his house to go to a cattle market to buy a goat for Idul Adha. He meets a sheep seller and has a conversation with him.

| | |
|---|---|
| UDA AMIR: | **Selamat pagi, Pak! Ada kambing yang bagus untuk saya?** |
| | _Good morning! Do you have a good goat for me?_ |
| PENJUAL KAMBING: | **Selamat pagi. Ada, Pak. Saya punya banyak. Silakan lihat-lihat. Saya juga menjual sapi dan domba. Semuanya sehat.** |
| | _Good morning. Yes, Sir. I have lots. Please have a look. I'm also selling cows and sheep. All of them are healthy._ |
| UDA AMIR: | **Saya tidak akan membeli sapi. Terlalu mahal. Kambing yang hitam itu berapa harganya, ya?** |
| | _I'm not going to buy a cow. It's too expensive. How much is the black goat?_ |
| PENJUAL KAMBING: | **Aduh, maaf, Pak! Kambing itu sudah dibeli orang. Bagaimana dengan ini? Kambing ini sehat juga. Harganya dua juta seratus ribu rupiah. Saya beri diskon nanti.** |
| | _Oh, sorry, Sir! That goat has already been sold. What about this one? This goat is also healthy. Its price is two million one hundred thousand rupiah. I'll give you a discount._ |
| UDA AMIR: | **Apakah harganya sudah termasuk ongkos kirim? Rumah saya di Jalan Raya Ampang, dekat dari sini.** |
| | _Does the price include the delivery fee? My house is in Ampang Road, close to here._ |
| PENJUAL KAMBING: | **Boleh, Pak! Harganya sudah termasuk ongkos kirim.** |
| | _Sure, Sir! The price already includes the delivery fee._ |
| UDA AMIR: | **Baiklah. Saya ambil kambingnya, ya. Apakah saya bayar sekarang atau nanti?** |
| | _Fine. I'll take the goat. Should I pay now or later?_ |
| PENJUAL KAMBING: | **Sekarang juga boleh.** _Now is fine._ |
| UDA AMIR: | **Tolong antar kambingnya sebelum Hari Raya.** |
| | _Please deliver the goat before Idul Adha._ |
| PENJUAL KAMBING: | **Insya Allah.** _God willing._ |

## ▌New Words and Phrases

**lihat-lihat** _have a look_
**menjual** _to sell_
**sapi** _cow_
**domba** _sheep_
**séhat** _healthy_
**terlalu** _too (much, many)_
**mahal** _expensive_
**aduh!** _oh!_

**maaf** _sorry_
**lain** _other_
**bagaimana** _how (about)_
**ratus** _hundred_
**diskon** _discount_
**ongkos** _fee, charge (for a service)_

**bayar, membayar** _to pay_
**antar, mengantar** _to deliver_
**Hari Raya** _Idul Adha or Idul Fitri (lit., "holiday")_
**Insya Allah** _God willing,_ **insha Allah** _(from the Arabic)_

**Exercise 3**

## Comprehension check

Some of the statements below are false. Correct the underlined words to make the false statements true.

eg. **Penjual kambing <u>hanya menjual kambing</u>.**
  → **Penjual kambing <u>menjual kambing, sapi dan domba</u>.**

1. Uda Amir tidak mau membeli <u>domba</u> karena harganya mahal.
2. <u>Penjual nasi</u> memberi harga diskon kepada Uda Amir.
3. Rumah Uda Amir <u>sangat jauh</u> dari pasar.
4. Uda Amir tidak bisa membeli <u>kambing hitam</u>.
5. Harga kambing <u>tidak termasuk ongkos kirim</u>.
6. Penjual kambing <u>boleh datang kapan saja</u> untuk mengantar kambing ke rumah Uda Amir.

## Grammar note: *orang*

One of the first words learned in this book was **orang**, meaning "person." Usually **orang** is used, followed by a modifying word, such as **orang utan** (**orangutan**, literally, "person of the forest"), **orang Jawa** ("Javanese person"), **orang Tionghoa** ("Chinese person") and so on.

However, **orang** can also be used alone, as in the conversation above when the goat seller refuses to sell Uda Amir the black goat.

**Kambing itu sudah dibeli orang.**     *That goat has already been bought by someone (else).*

If we need to use the toilet, but the door is locked, then someone might say,

**Ada orang.**                          *There's someone (inside).*

If a child goes to take a ball in the swimming pool, his mother might say,

**Jangan, itu punya orang.**            *Don't, it belongs to someone (else).*

We can also say, of someone who has grown up and become an adult,

**Dia sudah menjadi orang.**            *She has become someone (adult and respected).*

**Orang** can also be used as a counter for people. This will be explained in the section below.

**Ada dua puluh orang di bis.**         *There are twenty people in the bus.*

## Grammar note: Counters *(sebuah, seorang, seekor)*

As with many Asian languages, Indonesian uses words known as "counters" when expressing amounts of something. In English, this is less common, only appearing in constructions such as "a pair of shoes," "a pair of scissors" or "ten head of cattle."

When there is only one item, the counter is still used, but **satu** ("one") is abbreviated to **se-** ("a").

### Buah

In Indonesian, the most useful and general counter is **buah** (literally, "fruit"), which can be used for almost any item, informally at least.

| | |
|---|---|
| **sebuah apel** | *an apple* |
| **dua buah apel** | *two apples* |
| **sebuah kursi** | *a chair* |

### Orang

For people, **orang** is used.

| | |
|---|---|
| **Seorang Muslim** | *a Muslim (person)* |
| **Tiga orang Sunda** | *three Sundanese (people)* |

For animals, **ékor** ("tail") is used.

| | |
|---|---|
| **seekor kambing** | *a goat* |
| **empat ekor kambing** | *four goats* |

Other common counters are **biji** ("seed") for small items, **ikat** ("bunch") and **potong** ("slice").

| | |
|---|---|
| **lima biji kacang** | *five nuts* |
| **seikat bunga** | *a bunch of flowers* |
| **beberapa potong kue** | *several slices of cake* |

### Exercise 4

Choose the correct number and counter from the following: **buah, orang, ekor, biji, ikat** or **potong**.

1. _____ **toko** *(a shop)*

2. _____ **supir** *(a driver)*

3. _____ **kurma** *(three dates)*

4. _____ **sapi** *(a hundred cows)*

5. _____ **sayuran** *(a bunch of vegetables)*

6. _____ **kue** *(two slices of cake)*

## ▌ Grammar note: Imperative verbs

So far, we have learned several different types of verbs:

| | EXAMPLES: |
|---|---|
| simple verbs | **makan, minum, buka, lihat** |
| active **meN-** verbs | **memakan, membuka, melihat** |
| passive **di-** verbs | **dimakan, diminum, dibuka, dilihat** |
| passive **ter-** verbs | **termakan, terbuka, terlihat** |

In the last dialogue, we saw an example of another kind of verb: an imperative verb or command. In Indonesian, this takes the simple, base form of the verb, plus any suffixes.

**Tolong <u>antar</u> kambingnya sebelum Hari Raya.**
*Please <u>deliver</u> the goat before Idul Adha.*

Other examples of imperatives already covered include:

**Lebih baik <u>bawa</u> sepatu sendal saja.**
*Better to just <u>bring</u> sandals.*

**<u>Kirim</u> komentar lainnya ke nomor yang di bawah ini: 08121426244.**
*<u>Send</u> other comments to the number below: 08121426244.*

**Exercise 5**

Can you write the following commands in Indonesian, using the imperative form?

1. Eat here! _____

2. Go home to Medan! _____

3. Cook beef rendang! _____

4. Pay now! _____

5. Buy seven fish! _____

6. Buy three slices of pizza! _____

## 8.4  Perayaan Idul Adha  Feast of the Sacrifice celebrations

Read Danny's diary entry below to find out what the festival of Idul Adha is like.

**Senin, tanggal 12 September 2017**

**Idul Adha jatuh pada hari ini. Adi, saya dan keluarga besar Uda Amir pergi ke lapangan mesjid sekitar jam 6.30 pagi. Ketika sampai di lapangan, banyak orang sudah berbaris bersiap-siap untuk melakukan sholat. Selesai sholat, semua orang saling bersalaman dan cepat pulang ke rumah, karena masih ada kegiatan lain, yaitu berkurban.**

**Kambing yang dibeli Uda Amir dibawa ke tempat pemotongan. Ada sekitar 15 ekor kambing, 5 ekor domba, dan 3 ekor sapi yang akan dipotong. Banyak orang berkumpul di sana. Adi berani nonton acara pemotongan, tapi saya tidak!**

**Sekitar jam 12 siang banyak orang miskin sudah datang. Mereka menunggu bagian dari daging kurban tersebut. Mereka sangat senang karena hari ini, mereka akan mempunyai makanan istimewa.**

*Monday, 12 September 2017*

*Today was the Feast of the Sacrifice. Adi, Amir's extended family and I went to the plain in front of the mosque at around 6.30 a.m. When we got there, lots of people had already lined up, getting ready to do the prayer. After the prayer, everyone greeted each other and quickly went home, because there was something else to do: offer a sacrifice.*

*The goat that Amir bought was taken to the slaughter place. There were around 15 goats, five sheep and three cows to be sacrificed. Many people were gathered there. Adi was brave enough to watch the slaughter, but I wasn't!*

*Around 12 noon, many poor people had arrived. They were waiting for portions of meat from the animals sacrificed. They were very happy because today they will have special food.*

## New Words and Phrases

| | | |
|---|---|---|
| **keluarga besar** *extended family* | **selesai** *finished, over* | **lain** *other* |
| **lapangan** *field* | **bersalaman** *to shake hands* | **pemotongan** *slaughtering* |
| **ketika** *when (in past)* | *with each other* | **berani** *brave* |
| **berbaris** *to line up* | **cepat** *fast, quick* | **daging** *meat* |
| **bersiap-siap** *to get ready* | | **kurban** *(animal) sacrifice* |

## Grammar note: Suffix *-an*

A number of words, especially nouns, end with **-an**. The **-an** suffix often refers to an object or noun related to another word. So far, we have encountered the following **-an** words. See how they relate to others:

| -an noun | | base word | |
|---|---|---|---|
| **sayur**an | *vegetables* | **sayur** | *vegetables* |
| **pakai**an | *clothing* | **pakai, memakai** | *to wear* |
| **makan**an | *food* | **makan, memakan** | *to eat* |
| **keluh**an | *complaint* | **mengeluh** | *to complain* |
| **potong**an | *slice* | **potong, memotong** | *to cut, slice* |
| **bagi**an | *part, portion* | **membagi(kan)** | *to hand out, share divide up* |

There are some words ending in **-an**, however, that are not related to a commonly used base word. Examples of these include **rombongan**, **Lebaran** and **selatan**.

### Exercise 6

Guess the missing words, using the underlined words as hints.

1. **Adi belum <u>makan</u> malam. Dia ingin beli _____ padang di warung.**

2. **Danny mau <u>pakai</u> baju baru. _____nya hadiah dari Ibu Maya.**

3. **Semua <u>dibagikan</u> daging. Anak-anak mendapat _____ paling kecil.**

4. **Ada _____ orang di angkot. Mungkin sekitar tiga <u>belas</u> sampai enam belas orang!**

## Unit review: "Idul Adha di Sumatera Barat"

Match the following sentences to the correct pictures.

1. **Adi sangat lapar. Dia harus pergi ke warung.**

| a. | b. | c. |

2. **Saat makan di warung Uda Amir, ada seorang supir yang sedang makan juga.**

a.

b.

c.

3. **Adi dan Danny ikut ke Padang karena mau melihat budaya di Sumatera Barat.**

a.

b.

c.

4. **Uda Amir membeli seékor kambing untuk berkurban pada hari Idul Adha.**

a.

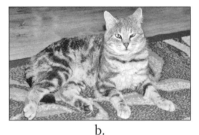

b.

c.

5. **Perayaan Idul Adha di Padang biasanya sangat ramai!**

a.

b.

c.

## Part 2

Reread the description of Salim below. Use this description as a model to write about yourself in the blanks provided.

Salim seorang <u>pemandu wisata</u>. Dia sangat pintar. Dia tahu banyak tentang <u>sejarah</u> dan <u>budaya orang Padang</u>. Dia bangga akan <u>sejarah</u> dan <u>budaya Padang</u>.

Your turn:

**Saya seorang** _____. **Saya sangat** _____. **Saya tahu banyak tentang** _____ **dan** _____. **Saya bangga akan** _____ **dan** _____.

Use the pattern above to describe three different people whom you are familiar with.

## Unit 8 End-of-unit vocabulary list

**aduh** *oh*

**adzan** *the call to prayer*

**akhir** *end, finish*

**Allah** *God*

**angkot (angkutan kota)** *public minibus*

**antar, mengantar** *to deliver*

**ayam pop** *skinless chicken*

**bagaimana** *how*

**bangga** *proud*

**bayar, membayar** *to pay*

**berani** *brave*

**berbaris** *to stand, line up*

**bercanda** *to joke around*

**bergaul** *to mix with others, socialise*

**berkurban** *to make a sacrifice (of an animal)*

**bersalaman** *to shake hands with each other*

**bersiap-siap** *to get ready*

**bersemangat** *enthusiastic*

**buah** *fruit; object (counter)*

**budaya** *culture*

**cepat** *fast, quick*

**daging** *meat*

**dan lain-lain (dll)** *etc., et cetera*

**daun singkong** *cassava leaves*

**diskon** *discount*

**domba** *sheep*

**ékor** *tail; counter for animals*

**hari raya** *holiday*

**hobi** *hobby*

**Insya Allah** *God willing (from the Arabic)*

**izin** *permission*

**kalian** *you (plural)*

**keagamaan** *religious*

**keluarga besar** *extended family*

**ketika** *when (in past)*

**khas** *special, typical*

**kotor** *dirty*

**kurban** *sacrifice (animal)*

**lain** *other*

**lapangan** *open space, field*

**lapar** *hungry*

**lihat-lihat** *have a look*

**maaf** *sorry*

**mahal** *expensive*

**memanggil** *to call*

**membayar** *to pay*

**membuang** *to throw away*

**mempunyai** *to have, own, possess*

**mengantar** *to sweep*

**menjual** *to sell*

**merasa** *to feel*

**mudah-mudahan** *hopefully*

**nasi padang** *Padang-style food with rice*

**ongkos** *fee, charge (for a service)*

**pemotongan** *slaughtering*

**penasaran** *curious*

**penjaga** *guard, night watchman*

**penjual** *seller, vendor*

**penumpang** *passenger*

**penyayang** *loving*

**pintar, pandai** *smart, clever*

**potong** *slice; to cut*

**potongan** *slice*

**pulang kampung** *to go back to the village*

**punya, mempunyai** *have, own, possess*

**ramai** *noisy, eventful*

**ratus** *hundred*

**rendang** *special Padang meat dish*

**saja** *just, only*

**sampah** *rubbish, trash*

**sapi** *cow*

**sebuah** *a, one (general counter)*

**séhat** *healthy*

**seikat** *a bunch*

**sejak** *since*

**sejarah** *history*

**sekalian** *all (at once)*

**selain** *apart from*

**selesai** *finished, over*

**seumur** *the same age*

**siapa saja** *whoever*

**soto** *clear meat soup*

**suasana** *atmosphere*

**supir** *driver*

**takut** *scared*

**teman, kawan** *friend*

**terlalu** *too (much, many)*

**tertawa** *to laugh*

**tertawa-tawa** *to laugh a lot*

**toko** *shop, store*

**Uda** *Minang term for older brother*

**Danny! Ada lomba panjat pinang hari Rabu nanti.**
*Danny! There's a greasy pole climbing competition on Wednesday.*

Pesta Kemerdekaan
HUT Republik Indonesia

Ikuti Lomba
Panjat Pinang!

Rabu 17 Agustus
di Lapangan Kelurahan
menangkan berbagai macam hadiah menarik

**Lomba apa itu, Adi?**
*What competition is that, Adi?*

**Lomba untuk mendapat hadiah di atas pohon.**
*A competition to get prizes on top of a tree.*

**Hadiahnya ada sepeda.**
*The prizes include a bicycle.*

**Wah, asyik! Ayo kita ikut bermain.**
*Wow, great! Let's join in.*

**Kita cari dua orang lain untuk menjadi tim kita.**
*We'll find two other people for our team.*

**Ayo. Pasti seru!**
*Let's. It's going to be great!*

**Pengen cepat main!**
*I can't wait to do it!*

*This dialogue appears on page 152.*

# UNIT
# 9

## Merdeka!
### Independence!

In this unit, we will:

- Learn about Indonesian independence and how this is celebrated,
- Know when to use **bukan** and when to use **tidak** to mean "no" or "not,"
- Use adjectives to describe events and opinions,
- Be able to describe different types of weather,
- Show understanding of place and time through the use of prepositions,
- Learn the differences between the **-kan** and **-i** verb endings,
- Be introduced to the **memper-** verb prefix.

## 9.1 Sukarno

### Reading

August 17, 1945 is a very special day for Indonesia since it was the date when the freedom fighters Sukarno and Hatta declared independence. Danny is reading a short paragraph about Sukarno from a book about Indonesian national heroes.

**Soekarno adalah pemimpin pemuda Indonesia waktu melawan Belanda. Soekarno adalah tokoh yang berhasil mempersatukan orang-orang yang berbeda budaya dan agama secara damai. Karena dianggap membahayakan, Soekarno pernah dipenjara oleh Belanda di penjara Sukamiskin, Bandung. Ibu Inggit, isteri pertamanya, membantu dia selama dipenjara.**

*Sukarno was an Indonesian youth leader fighting against the Dutch. He was a figure who succeeded in uniting people from different cultures and religions peacefully. Since he was considered dangerous, Sukarno was jailed by the Dutch in Sukamiskin prison, Bandung. Inggit, his first wife, helped him while he was in prison.*

**Setelah perjuangan yang panjang, Soekarno dan Hatta memproklamasikan kemerdekaan Indonesia pada tanggal 17 Agustus 1945. Besoknya, Soekarno dan Hatta dipilih sebagai Presiden dan Wakil Presiden Indonesia yang pertama.**

*After a long struggle, Sukarno and Hatta proclaimed Indonesian independence on August 17, 1945. The following day, Sukarno and Hatta were chosen as Indonesia's first President and Vice President.*

Pada tanggal 21 Juni 1970, Soekarno mening-gal dunia karena sakit. Walaupun pada saat itu dia sudah bukan seorang presiden lagi, tapi rakyat Indonesia sangat sedih. Pemerintah Indonesia memberikan gelar Pahlawan Prokla-masi kepadanya.

*On June 21, 1970, Sukarno died after an illness. Although at that time he was no longer a president, the Indonesian people were very sad. The Indonesian government gave him the title of Proclamation Hero.*

## New Words and Phrases

**pemimpin** *leader*
**pemuda** *youth*
**Belanda** *Dutch, the Netherlands*
**mempersatukan, menyatukan** *to unite*
**secara** *in a ... way*
**damai** *peaceful*
**dianggap, menganggap** *considered, to consider*

**membahayakan** *dangerous, to put in danger*
**memenjara** *to jail, imprison*
**isteri** *wife*
**perjuangan** *struggle*
**memproklamasikan** *to proclaim*
**kemerdékaan** *independence*
**wakil** *deputy, vice*

**meninggal dunia** *to die (lit., "to leave this world")*
**sakit** *ill, sick*
**walaupun** *although*
**sedih** *sad*
**pemerintah** *government*
**gelar** *title*
**proklamasi** *proclamation*

## Grammar note: The *memper-* affix

The affix **memper-** is a variant of the **meN-** prefix. **Memper-** is used in the same way as **meN-**, but in a sense of extending or taking something further.

| | | | | |
|---|---|---|---|---|
| **menyatukan** | *to make one* | vs | **mempersatukan** | *to unite many things* |
| **memanjang** | *to grow long* | vs | **memperpanjang** | *to extend, make longer* |

## Cultural note: *Soekarno* or *Sukarno*?

As you can see in the text above, in Indonesian we have spelt the first President's name as he spelled it, **S-O-E-K-A-R-N-O**. This is also the way it is spelled at Jakarta's airport, Soekarno-Hatta International Airport. In Dutch times, the sound **u** was spelled **oe**.

In the English translation, we have spelled his name **S-U-K-A-R-N-O**, as this follows modern Indonesian spelling and is less confusing for those beginning Indonesian. You will find a mix of spelling among names in Indonesia, particularly those of older people.

### Exercise 1

Match these questions to the answers below.

a. **Kapan Soekarno dan Hatta menjadi Presiden dan Wakil Presiden pertama?**
*When did Sukarno and Hatta become the first President and Vice President?*

b. **Kapan Soekarno dipenjara?**
*When was Sukarno jailed?*

c. **Mengapa Soekarno dipenjara oleh Belanda?**
*Why was Sukarno jailed by the Dutch?*

d. **Siapa itu Soekarno?**
   *Who was Sukarno?*

e. **Siapa yang memberi gelar "Pahlawan Proklamasi"?**
   *Who gave him the title of "Proclamation Hero"?*

1. _____?
   **Pada waktu rakyat Indonesia melawan Belanda.**

2. _____?
   **Dia adalah tokoh yang dapat mempersatukan orang-orang yang berbeda bangsa, budaya dan agama secara damai.**

3. _____?
   **Karena kegiatannya melawan Belanda dianggap sangat membahayakan.**

4. _____?
   **Besoknya, tanggal 18 Agustus 1945.**

5. _____?
   **Pemerintah Indonesia.**

## ▌Grammar note: *Kepada*

**Kepada** is used when we need to say "to" regarding a person.

> **Pemerintah Indonesia memberikan gelar Pahlawan Proklamasi <u>kepada</u>nya.**
> *The Indonesian government gave him the title of Proclamation Hero.*

However, **untuk** is still used in the sense of doing something "for" someone.

> **Saya punya hadiah <u>untuk</u> dia.**
> *I have a present for her.*

> **Saya akan beri hadiah itu <u>kepada</u>nya besok.**
> *I will give the present to her tomorrow.*

## ▌Grammar note: *Walaupun ... , tetapi...*

**Walaupun** (and its synonym, **meskipun**) is used similarly to "although" in English.

> <u>**Walaupun**</u> **pada saat itu dia sudah bukan seorang presiden lagi, <u>tapi</u> rakyat Indonesia sangat sedih.**
> *Although at that time he was no longer a president, [but] the Indonesian people were very sad.*

You will notice in the Indonesian sentence that the word **tapi** (short for **tetapi**) is then used as part of the main clause, to reinforce the fact that it contrasts with the first part of the sentence. Remember to use the **Walaupun ... , tapi ...** format in Indonesian, even though the structure differs from English.

### Exercise 2

Complete the sentences using the **Walaupun ... , tetapi ...** model.

1. **Walaupun sudah sore, tetapi** _____.
   *Although it was already late, he still wanted to play soccer.*

2. _____, **tetapi Soekarno masih berjuang agar Indonesia merdeka.**
   *Although he was put in prison, Sukarno still fought so that Indonesia could be free.*

3. **Walaupun** _____, **tetapi** _____.
   *Although Sukarno was jailed, his wife Inggit still helped him.*

## Grammar note: *Bukan atau tidak?* / "No" or "not"?

In previous units, we have seen the use of the word **tidak** as a negative, for example:

> **Program "Buka Puasa Bersama" bagus tapi tidak tertib.**
> *The "Breaking the Fast Together" program is good, but not orderly.*

> **Tidak ada yang menang.**
> *Nobody won.*

In the first sentence, **tidak** negates the adjective **tertib** ("orderly"). In the second sentence, **tidak** negates the verb **menang** ("won"). What if we want to negate a noun? In this case, we use the word **bukan**:

> **Pada saat itu dia sudah bukan seorang presiden lagi.**
> *At that time he was not President anymore.*

### Exercise 3

Negate the following sentences.

1. **Dia adalah pemimpin Indonesia.**
   *He was an Indonesian leader.*

   _____

2. **Dia adalah tokoh yang dapat mempersatukan banyak orang.**
   *He was a figure who could unite many people.*

   _____

3. **Ini tempat beragama orang Islam.**
   *This is a religious place for Muslims.*

   _____

4. **Juara umum Porseni adalah SMA 3.**
   *The winner of Porseni was SMA 3 high school.*

   _____

**Exercise 4**

Translate the following sentences into Indonesian.

1. Sukarno was not Dutch.

_____

2. Inggit was not Hatta's wife.

_____

## 9.2  Lomba tumpeng  The rice-cone competition

**Tumpeng** is a cone-shaped rice dish like a mountain served with side dishes. The cone shape of the rice is made by using a woven bamboo container. The rice itself is either plain steamed rice or yellow rice, colored with turmeric (**kuning**). Indonesians usually make a **tumpeng** to celebrate an important event. **Tumpeng** is a symbol of gratitude, and is an integral part of any thanksgiving ceremony (**syukuran**). After a short prayer, the top of the **tumpeng** is cut and delivered to the most important person. Then everyone enjoys the **tumpeng** together. On Independence Day, many people also participate in **tumpeng**-making competitions (**lomba tumpeng**). Here are the rules for a **tumpeng**-making competition.

**Tata Tertib Lomba Tumpeng**

1. **Setiap kelompok/tim terdiri atas 4 orang (ibu-ibu atau remaja putri).**

2. **Tumpeng dan hiasan disiapkan 30 menit sebelum lomba dimulai.**

3. **Tidak boleh menghias tumpeng sebelum lomba dimulai.**

4. **Tumpeng yang menang harus enak, kréatif, rapi dan bersih.**

5. **Tumpeng yang dibuat harus cukup untuk dimakan enam orang.**

*Rice-cone Competition Rules*

*Each group/team consists of 4 people (women or teenage girls).*

*The rice-cone and decorations are prepared 30 minutes before the competition begins.*

*You may not decorate the rice-cone before the competition begins.*

*The winning rice-cone should be tasty, creative, neat and clean.*

*The rice-cone should be made so that there is enough for six people to eat.*

## ▌New Words and Phrases

**tata tertib** *rules*
**kelompok** *group*
**remaja** *teenager, youth*

**hiasan** *decoration*
**disiapkan/menyiapkan** *is prepared/to prepare*

**menghias** *to decorate*
**rapi** *neat*
**kréatif** *creative*

## Exercise 5: Reading comprehension

Mark the following sentences as **Benar** (true) or **Salah** (false).

|  | B (✔) | S (✘) |
|---|---|---|
| 1. **Adi dan Danny boleh ikut lomba tumpeng.** | ___ | ___ |
| 2. **Tumpeng bisa dibuat 60 menit sebelum lomba dimulai.** | ___ | ___ |
| 3. **Tumpeng harus mempunyai rasa enak.** | ___ | ___ |
| 4. **Peserta lomba harus mengikuti tata tertib.** | ___ | ___ |
| 5. **Boleh membuat tumpeng yang besar atau tumpeng yang kecil.** | ___ | ___ |

## Exercise 6

Check your new vocabulary. Fill in the missing letters.

1. *decoration*       ___ ___ **a s a** ___
2. *cone-shaped rice dish*    **t** ___ **m p** ___ ___ ___
3. *must*      ___ **a** ___ ___ **s**
4. *creative*      **k** ___ **e a** ___ **i** ___
5. *teenager, youth*      ___ ___ ___ **a** ___ **a**

# 9.3 Melihat pengumuman   An announcement

While Adi and Danny were cycling around their neighborhood, they saw a newspaper on a wall (**majalah dinding**, or **mading** for short) in front of the **kelurahan** (sub-district) office. announcing that there would be a **panjat pinang** (greasy pole climbing) competition. Adi and Danny want to join in. Listen to their conversation.

## ▌ Listening to a dialogue

ADI: **Danny! Lihat pengumuman itu. Ada lomba Panjat Pinang hari Rabu nanti.**
*Danny! Look at that announcement. There's a greasy pole climbing competition on Wednesday.*

DANNY: **Lomba apa itu, Adi?** *What competition is that, Adi?*

ADI: **Lomba untuk mendapatkan banyak hadiah tergantung di atas pohon pinang. Hadiahnya ada sepeda, baju, payung, sepatu dan masih banyak lagi.**
*A competition to get lots of prizes hung on top of the areca palm. The prizes include a bicycle, clothes, umbrellas, shoes and lots more.*

DANNY: **Wah, asyik! Ayo kita ikut bermain. Kita cari dua orang lain untuk menjadi tim kita.**
*Wow, great! Let's join in. We'll find two other people for our team.*

ADI: **Ayo. Pasti seru!** *Let's. It's going to be great!*

DANNY: **Pengen cepat main!** *I can't wait to do it!*

## New Words and Phrases

**HUT (Hari Ulang Tahun)** *anniversary*
**republik** *republic*
**mengikuti** *to follow, take part in*
**pelaksanaan** *event, when something is held*
**kelurahan** *sub-district (office)*

**pengumuman** *announcement, notice*
**tergantung** *to be hung; to depend*
**pohon pinang** *areca palm*
**sepéda** *bicycle*

**payung** *umbrella*
**pasti** *must, surely*
**seru** *fun, exciting*
**péngén** *really want to (informal)*

## Cultural note

**Panjat pinang** is a traditional Indonesian game usually played around August 17 to coincide with Independence Day. It requires chopping down a tall areca nut tree and mounting it as a pole. A large, circular wheel is then attached to the top of it. Prizes are then hung up from this wheel. These prizes can include food, drink, clothing, electronics, and other useful items or small appliances, such as rice cookers. Often the prizes are wrapped or bagged so that they remain a mystery. Of course, this also means people usually try to grab the biggest one. To combat this, sometimes the game is played with pieces of paper hung from the wheel, each containing a number which corresponds to a particular prize.

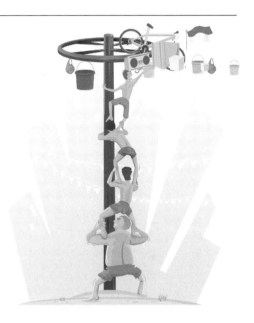

### Exercise 7

Match the expressions below.

1. **Pasti seru!**
2. **Ayo ikut bermain!**
3. **Wah, asyik!**
4. **Pengen cepat main!**
5. **Lihat pengumuman itu!**
6. **Kita cari dua orang lain!**

a. Look at the announcement!
b. Great!
c. Let's join in!
d. Can't wait!
e. It must be fun!
f. Let's find two more people!

## 9.4 Cuaca hari ini   Today's weather

### Reading

It is Wednesday. Adi and Danny are getting ready to attend the **panjat pinang** competition. Before leaving the house, Adi checks the newspaper to see what the weather will be like today.

**"Hari ini cuaca akan cerah di pagi hari sampai siang hari, tetapi hujan akan turun di sore hari. Untuk Anda yang akan beraktifitas di luar, disarankan untuk membawa payung atau jas hujan supaya kegiatan Anda tidak terganggu. Sebaiknya Anda melakukan kegiatan di dalam ruangan karena akan mendung dan hujan sampai malam."**

*"Today the weather will be fine in the morning until middle of the day, but rain will fall in the late afternoon. For those doing activities out-side, it is recommended to bring an umbrella or raincoat so that your activities are not disrupted. It is better to do indoor activities as it will be cloudy and there will be rain until evening."*

## ▌New Words and Phrases

**hari ini** *today*
**cuaca** *weather*
**cerah** *bright*
**turun** *fall*

**beraktifitas** *to do an activity, be busy*
**di luar** *outside*
**disarankan / menyarankan** *recommended, to recommend*

**jas** *coat, jacket*
**terganggu** *disturbed*
**di dalam ruangan** *indoor*
**mendung** *cloudy*

## ▌Cultural note: Weather in Indonesia

Weather in Indonesia is fairly constant, making weather forecasts not as important as they are in countries with four seasons. Interest in the weather mainly revolves around whether or not it will rain, rather than what the actual temperature will be. On the coast, the average tempera-ture is around 30 degrees Celsius, while up in the highlands it might fall to 24 degrees or so during the day.

### Exercise 8

Can you write the Indonesian sentences in the boxes below the English? Use or adapt phrases from the text.

| Today it will be sunny. |
| --- |
| |

| The weather will be cloudy. |
| --- |
| |

| It will rain this afternoon. |
| --- |
| |

| You should bring a raincoat. |
| --- |
| |

| It is recommended to bring an umbrella. |
| --- |
| |

## ▌Indonesian and me

**Exercise 9**

Answer the following questions.

1. **Lebih suka cuaca panas, atau cuaca dingin?**
2. **Sekarang sedang cuaca apa?**
3. **Besok cuaca akan bagaimana?**

## 9.5 Lomba panjat pinang   Climbing a greasy pole

Read Adi's blog post about the greasy pole climbing contest on Independence Day.

**BLOG ADI**

 RUMAH   TENTANG SAYA   KOMENTAR

 **17 Agustus**  # Lomba Panjat Pinang

**Teman-teman,**

**Pagi-pagi sekali, aku, Danny dan dua teman lain sudah ada di lapangan kelurahan. Kami sudah siap untuk ikut lomba panjat pinang. Kami memakai pakaian dengan warna yang sama, merah. Kami adalah satu tim!**

**Lawan kami pun sudah siap. Mereka memakai pakaian seragam juga. Badan mereka tinggi besar. Mereka datang dari daerah berbeda-beda. Kami tidak kenal mereka.**

**Tim lawan yang pertama untuk melakukan panjat pinang. Satu orang yang paling besar berdiri paling bawah. Dua teman lainnya menaiki badan dia sambil memegang pohon pinang yang sudah diolesi minyak, sehingga warnanya menjadi hitam dan licin. Selama 15 menit mereka mencoba untuk memanjat pinang supaya mendapatkan hadiah yang tergantung di atasnya, tapi mereka tidak berhasil sampai waktu sudah habis.**

**Sekarang saatnya tim aku melakukan panjat pinang. Kami sudah banyak belajar bagaimana bisa memanjat sampai atas dari tim sebelumnya. Akhirnya Danny yang berhasil memanjat ke bagian paling atas dari pohon pinang sehingga bisa mencapai banyak hadiah yang tergantung! Para penonton menyambut dengan gembira.**

**Hadiah yang kami dapatkan adalah: satu buah sepeda, kaos-kaos, payung, dan masih banyak lagi. Asyik!**

*Friends,*

*Early in the morning, Danny, two other friends and I went to the plain by the sub-district office. We were ready to join the greasy pole climbing contest. We wore clothes in the same color, red. We were a team!*

*Our opponents were also ready. They also wore a uniform. They were big and tall. They came from different areas. We didn't know them.*

*Our opponents did the greasy pole climb first. The biggest person stood at the bottom. Two others climbed onto his body while holding the areca-nut palm which had already been greased with oil, making it black and slippery. For 15 minutes they tried to climb the pole to get the prizes hung at the top, but they were unsuccessful and time ran out.*

*Now was the moment for my team to climb up the greasy pole. We had learned a lot about how to climb to the top from the team before us. Finally, Danny was able to climb and reach all the prizes that were hanging from the top of the pole! The spectators greeted us excitedly.*

*The prizes we got were: a bike, T-shirts, umbrellas and lots more. Fantastic!*

## New Words and Phrases

**pagi-pagi** *early in the morning*
**sekali** *very (after word)*
**lawan** *opponent*
**pun** *also, even*
**berbéda-béda** *different (of many things, a variety)*

**berdiri** *to stand (up)*
**menaiki** *to climb*
**pégang, memégang** *to hold*
**diolési (mengolési)** *smeared*
**minyak** *oil*
**licin** *slippery*

**coba, mencoba** *to try*
**habis** *finished*
**sebelumnya** *previous, previously*
**mencapai** *to reach*
**menyambut** *to welcome*

## Grammar note: Prepositions

In the above reading we saw a number of prepositions:

**Mereka datang <u>dari</u> daerah berbeda-beda.**
*They came from different areas.*

**Selama 15 menit mereka mencoba <u>untuk</u> memanjat pinang.**
*For 15 minutes they tried to climb the greasy pole.*

**Akhirnya Danny yang berhasil memanjat <u>ke</u> bagian paling atas.**
*Finally, Danny succeeded in climbing to the topmost part.*

Meanwhile, in Unit 7, we had:

**Panitia Zakat Fitrah terdiri dari warga setempat.**
*The alms committee consists of local residents.*

Both **terdiri atas** and **terdiri dari** mean "consists of" and are equally correct. **Terdiri atas** is perhaps more formal.

Here are the prepositions that have been introduced so far:

| Prepositions of time | Prepositions of time and place | Prepositions of place | Prepositions of manner |
|---|---|---|---|
| **sebelum** *before* <br> **sesudah** *after* <br> **setelah** *after* | **dalam** *in, inside* <br> **di** *at, on, in* <br> **dari** *from, of* <br> **pada** *on, at* <br> **sampai** *until, at* | **atas** *above, over* <br> **belakang** *behind* <br> **bawah** *below, under* <br> **dekat** *near* <br> **depan** *front, before* <br> **ke** *to* <br> **keluar** *out of* <br> **kepada** *to (a person)* <br> **luar** *out, outside* <br> **sebelah** *beside* | **oleh** *by* <br> **dengan** *with, by* <br> **sambil** *while* <br> **untuk** *for, to* |

## Exercise 10

Using the table on page 156, write down the opposites of the following words.

sebelum       ✂       _____          atas          ✂       _____

dalam         ✂       _____          belakang      ✂       _____

dari          ✂       _____

## Exercise 11

Choose the correct preposition.

1. **Danny berdiri di paling atas / bawah.**
2. **Tim Adi bermain sebelum / sesudah tim lawan.**
3. **Orang yang paling besar berdiri paling atas / bawah.**
4. **Sambil / Sesudah nonton, tim Adi belajar bagaimana memanjat pinang.**

## Grammar note: The verb suffix -i

It is now time to talk about one of the different suffixes used with **meN-** verbs, as they help us to understand Indonesian better.

### Verbs with the -i suffix

The **-i** suffix can signify a number of things. It can suggest that

• the object that follows the verb is a person,
• that the verb has a multiple number of objects,
• the object is a physical place,
• the action happens a number of times.

Occasionally, this suffix has a negative connotation.

In this unit, we encountered these two **-i** verbs: **menaiki** and **mengolesi**.

> **Dua teman lainnya menaiki badan dia.**
> *Two other friends climbed onto his body.*

> **Pohon pinang yang sudah diolesi minyak.**
> *An areca-nut palm which had been greased with oil*

In both these examples, the **-i** ending indicates a location (someone's body, and an areca-nut palm) as the object of the sentence.

## Unit review

### Part 1

Make these sentences negative by writing in the correct word.

1. **Hari ini _____ mendung.** *Today is not cloudy.*
2. **Dimas _____ kawannya Adi.** *Dimas is not Adi's friend.*

## Part 2

Circle the correct form of the verbs below.

1. **Pohon pinang dioles / dioleskan / diolesi dengan minyak supaya licin.**
2. **Lawannya sangat membahaya / membahayai / membahayakan.**
3. **Badan-badannya tim lain cukup berotot / mengotot.**

## Part 3

Danny's Indonesian teacher back in Australia, Pak Yusep, has written to Danny asking for his news. Read his postcard below.

Now write a postcard from Danny to his Indonesian teacher in Australia, Pak Yusep, about his 17 August experience, and answering his questions.

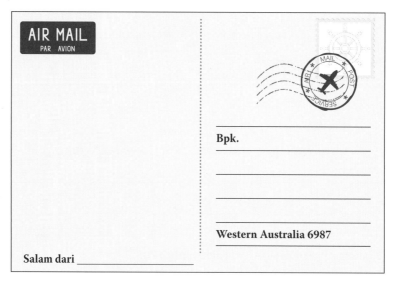

## Unit 9 End-of-unit vocabulary list

**apabila** *if, when (future)*
**asyik** *fun*
**bawah** *below, beneath*
**Belanda** *Dutch, the Netherlands*
**beraktifitas** *to do an activity, be busy*
**berbéda-béda** *different (of many things)*
**berdiri** *to stand*
**berhasil** *to succeed*
**bila** *if, when (future)*
**budaya** *culture*
**cepat** *fast, quick*
**cerah** *sunny*
**coba** *try*
**cuaca** *weather*
**damai** *peaceful*
**di luar** *out, outside*
**gelar** *title*
**habis** *finished*
**hari ini** *today*
**hiasan** *decoration*
**HUT (hari ulang tahun)** *anniversary; birthday*
**isteri** *wife*
**jaman** *era, time*
**jas** *jacket, coat*
**jauh** *far*
**kelompok** *group*
**kelurahan** *sub-district*
**kemerdékaan** *independence*
**ketika** *when (in past)*
**kréatif** *creative*
**lawan** *opponent*
**licin** *slippery*
**luar** *outside*

**mading** *wall newspaper* (**majalah dinding**)
**membahayakan** *dangerous, to put in danger*
**memégang, pégang** *to hold*
**memenjara** *to jail, imprison*
**memperhatikan** *to watch closely, take notice of*
**mempersatukan** *to unite*
**memproklamasikan** *to proclaim*
**memukuli** *to hit repeatedly, batter*
**menaiki** *to climb*
**menanjat** *to climb*
**mencapai** *to reach*
**mencoba, coba** *to try*
**mendapatkan** *to get, obtain*
**mendung** *cloudy*
**menganggap** *to consider*
**menghias** *to decorate*
**mengikuti** *to follow, attend, go to*
**mengolési** *to smear, grease, oil*
**meninggal dunia** *to die*
**menyambut** *to welcome*
**menyarankan** *to recommend*
**menyiapkan** *to prepare, get ready*
**minyak** *oil*
**pagi-pagi** *early in the morning*
**pahlawan** *hero*
**panjat pinang** *greasy pole climb*
**parah** *severe, grave*
**pasti** *must, definitely*
**payung** *umbrella*
**pégang, memégang** *to hold*
**pelaksanaan** *event, when something is held*
**pemerintah** *government*

**pemimpin** *leader*
**pemuda** *youth*
**péngén** *really want to (informal)*
**pengumuman** *announcement, notice*
**penuh** *full*
**perjuangan** *struggle*
**pohon pinang** *areca palm*
**Présidén** *President*
**proklamasi** *proclamation*
**pun** *also, even*
**rapi** *neat*
**remaja** *teenager, youth, young adult*
**républik** *republic*
**ruang** *room*
**ruangan** *room, indoor space*
**sakit** *ill, sick*
**sebelumnya** *previous(ly)*
**secara** *in a ... way*
**sedih** *sad*
**seharian** *all day*
**sejuk** *cool*
**sekali** *once; very*
**sepéda** *bicycle*
**seru** *fun, exciting*
**syukuran** *thanksgiving ceremony*
**tata tertib** *rules*
**terganggu** *disturbed*
**tergantung** *to be hung; to depend*
**tokoh** *figure*
**tumpeng** *ceremonial rice-cone*
**turun** *fall; go down*
**wah!** *wow!*
**wakil** *deputy, vice*
**walaupun** *although*

**Selamat siang, Danny!**
*Good afternoon, Danny!*

**Selamat siang, Bu. Bu Ratih, saya mau tanya tentang Sumpah Pemuda tadi.**
*Good afternoon. Miss, I want to ask about the Youth Pledge just now.*

**Silakan.**
*Go ahead.*

**Bu, saya mau tanya apakah Soekarno juga mempunyai peran penting.**
*Miss, I want to ask whether Sukarno also played an important role.*

**Pertanyaan yang bagus. Sepertinya Soekarno tidak ikut dalam Kongres Pemuda itu.**
*A good question. It seems that Sukarno didn't join the Youth Congress.*

**Apakah beliau pernah menjadi anggota Jong Java?**
*Was he ever a member of Jong Java?*

**Ya, tapi pada waktu Kongres Pemuda, sudah pindah ke organisasi lain.**
*Yes, but at the time of the Youth Congress, he had moved to another organization.*

*This dialogue appears on pages 167 and 168.*

# UNIT

# 10

# Satu Nusa, Satu Bangsa, Satu Bahasa
One Island, One Nation, One Language

In this unit, we will:

- Learn about the relevance of the Youth Pledge to Indonesian independence,
- Be able to both read and write a mini-biography of our own,
- Learn about a national hero,
- Listen to and learn about two nationalist songs,
- Be able to use **sangat** and **sekali** as intensifiers,
- Be able to use **-lah** as a softener,
- Learn how to use counters when discussing food,
- Understand how the **-kan** suffix of verbs works.

## 10.1 **Sumpah Pemuda** Youth Pledge

At Adi and Danny's school, there is a ceremony commemorating the Youth Pledge made on October 28, 1928, which was a milestone in Indonesia's path towards independence from the Dutch. A large banner stating the Youth Pledge has been displayed at the entrance to the school:

## ▌Basic Sentences

1. **Kami, putra dan putri Indonesia, mengaku bertumpah darah yang satu, Tanah Air Indonesia.**

   *We the sons and daughters of Indonesia, acknowledge one motherland, Indonesia.*

2. **Kami, putra dan putri Indonesia, mengaku bangsa yang satu, Bangsa Indonesia.**

   *We the sons and daughters of Indonesia, acknowledge one nation, the nation of Indonesia.*

3. **Kami, putra dan putri Indonesia, menjunjung bahasa persatuan, Bahasa Indonesia.**

   *We the sons and daughters of Indonesia, respect the language of unity, Indonesian.*

## New Words and Phrases

**mengaku** *to declare, claim*
**bertumpah darah** *to spill blood*
**tanah air** *homeland (lit., earth and water)*

**berbangsa** *to have a nationality or nation*
**menjunjung** *to hold in high esteem*

**persatuan** *unity*

 ## Reading: Lecture

Adi and Dani's civics teacher is now talking about the Youth Pledge. Listen to the lecture.

"Sumpah Pemuda adalah hasil dari kongres gerakan pemuda dari berbagai pulau di Indonesia. Para pemuda itu yang pertama bilang, Indonesia adalah satu nusa atau negara, satu bangsa dan satu bahasa. Itu yang mereka katakan pada tanggal 28 Oktober 1928, di Kongres Pemuda. Makanya, kita memperingati hari yang sama sebagai Hari Sumpah Pemuda. Pada hari itu juga, lagu kebangsaan "Indonesia Raya" juga pertama kali diperkenalkan.

*The Youth Pledge was the result of a congress of youth movements from various islands in Indonesia. Those youth were the first to say that Indonesia was one island or nation, one people and one language. That is what they said on 28 October, 1928, at the Youth Congress. Therefore, we commemorate the same day as Youth Pledge Day. On that day too, the national anthem "Great Indonesia" was also introduced for the first time.*

"Pada tahun 1928, Indonesia masih menjadi jajahan Belanda, dan dikenal dengan nama Hindia Belanda. Meskipun begitu, banyak gerakan pemuda yang sudah mulai muncul di pulau-pulau besar. Oleh karena waktu itu semua sekolah memakai bahasa Belanda, nama-nama gerakan pemuda itu pun bernama Jong Java, Jong Soematra, Jong Celebes dan Jong Ambon, karena kata jong itu berarti 'muda' dalam bahasa Belanda.

*In 1928, Indonesia was still a Dutch colony, and was known as the Dutch East Indies. Despite that, many youth movements had already started to appear in the larger islands. Because all schools at that time used Dutch, the names of the youth movements were also Jong Java, Jong Sumatra, Jong Celebes and Jong Ambon, because the word* **jong** *meant "young" in Dutch.*

"Anak-anak, sangat penting bagi kita untuk terus memperingati Hari Sumpah Pemuda, supaya rasa persatuan tetap dijunjung. Kita di Indonesia terdiri dari puluhan kelompok etnik di berbagai pulau yang memakai bahasa daerah yang berbeda-beda.

*Children, it is very important for us to keep commemorating Youth Pledge Day, so that we still foster a sense of unity. We in Indonesia consist of dozens of ethnic groups across many islands using different regional languages.*

"Salah satu hasil penting dari Kongres Pemuda adalah Bahasa Indonesia diakui sebagai bahasa persatuan dan kemerdekaan. Waktu itu, orang Bali pakai bahasa Bali, orang Aceh pakai bahasa Aceh, dan seterusnya. Tetapi, bahasa Melayu dipakai di pasar di seluruh Hindia Belanda sebagai bahasa dagang. Bahasa Melayu yang dianggap demokratis dan asli pun mulai disebut dengan 'Bahasa Indonesia.'"

*One important result of the Youth Congress was Indonesia being recognized as the language of unity and independence. At that time, the Balinese spoke Balinese, the Acehnese spoke Acehnese, and so on. But, Malay was used in markets throughout the Dutch East Indies as a trade language. Malay was considered democratic and indigenous, so it began to be known as "Indonesian."*

## New Words and Phrases

| | | |
|---|---|---|
| **hasil** *result* | **Hindia Belanda** *Dutch East Indies* | **puluhan** *tens, dozens* |
| **kongrés** *congress* | | **étnik** *ethnic* |
| **gerakan** *movement* | **meskipun, walaupun** *although* | **seluruh** *all, entire* |
| **berbagai** *various* | **begitu** *like that* | **dagang** *trade* |
| **maka, makanya** *therefore* | **muncul** *appear* | **démokratis** *democratic* |
| **jajahan** *colony* | **berarti** *to mean* | |
| **dikenal, mengenal** *to be known, recognized, to know* | **penting** *important* | |

## Grammar note: *Maka dan makanya*

The word **maka**, and the more informal **makanya**, are important words in written and spoken Indonesian respectively.

**Maka** is used at the start of a clause, either beginning the sentence, or halfway through, to show a logical development.

> **Makanya, kita memperingati hari yang sama sebagai Hari Sumpah Pemuda.**
> *That's why we commemorate the same day as Youth Pledge Day.*

As the teacher is speaking aloud to the class, she uses the more informal **makanya**. In written form, this sentence would have used the more formal **maka** instead, which tends to appear in the middle of sentences.

> **Itu yang mereka katakan pada tanggal 28 Oktober 1928, di Kongres Pemuda, maka kita memperingati hari yang sama sebagai Hari Sumpah Pemuda.**
> *That's what they said on 28 October, 1928, at the Youth Congress, therefore we commemorate the same day as Youth Pledge Day.*

## Grammar note: *Begini, begitu*

These are two very useful and common words that are aligned with **ini** ("this") and **itu** ("that").

| **begini** | *like this* |
|---|---|
| **begitu** | *like that* |

They act mostly as adverbs, describing how something is done.

| | |
|---|---|
| **Meskipun begitu ...** | *Despite (being like) that, ...* |
| **Begini caranya.** | *This is how you do it.* |
| **O, begitu!** | *Oh, it's like that!* |

**Begini** and **begitu** are often shortened to **gini** and **gitu** in informal speech.

## Exercise 1

Can you match up the appropriate heading (a–d) for each section of the lecture (1–4)?

1. **"Sumpah Pemuda adalah hasil ..."**
2. **"Pada tahun 1928 ... "**
3. **"Anak-anak, sangat penting ..."**
4. **"Salah satu hasil penting ..."**

a. **Munculnya Gerakan Pemuda**
b. **Bahasa Melayu dan Bahasa Indonesia**
c. **Kongres Pemuda**
d. **Mengapa Sumpah Pemuda?**

## Exercise 2

Answer the questions below in complete sentences. Use the words and phrases in the box to help you. One phrase is used twice.

| |
|---|
| **orang Indonesia    pemuda dan pemudi    Bahasa Indonesia    dengan Sumpah Pemuda** |

1. **Siapa yang bersumpah?** _____
   *Who took the pledge?*

2. **Siapa yang bertumpah darah satu?**_____
   *Who spilled blood as one?*

3. **Apa bahasa mereka?**_____
   *What was their language?*

4. **Apa bangsa mereka?**_____
   *What was their nation?*

5. **Bagaimana mereka bersatu?**_____
   *How did they unite?*

# 10.2  "Satu Nusa Satu Bangsa"

 Listen to this popular song that commemorates **Sumpah Pemuda**.

**Satu Nusa Satu Bangsa**
*(L. Manik)*

| | | | |
|---|---|---|---|
| **Satu nusa** | *One island* | **Indonesia pusaka** | *Indonesian heritage* |
| **Satu bangsa** | *One people* | **Indonesia tercinta** | *Indonesia, beloved,* |
| **Satu bahasa kita** | *One language are we.* | **Nusa, bangsa** | *Islands, people* |
| **Tanah air** | *Our homeland* | **dan bahasa** | *and language* |
| **Pasti jaya** | *Will be victorious* | **Kita bela bersama** | *we will defend together.* |
| **Untuk selama-lamanya** | *forever more.* | | |

## New Words and Phrases

**jaya** *victorious*
**selama-lamanya** *forever*

**pusaka** *heirloom, something of great value*

**tercinta** *beloved*
**béla, membéla** *to protect*

# 10.3  Wahidin Sudirohusodo

Danny is very interested in Indonesian schools. On his trip to Jogja, he was very excited to see the Taman Siswa school. He is also curious about the Budi Utomo schools, which one of his friends used to attend. Here he is reading a short biography about the school's founder on a brochure about Budi Utomo.

## Reading: Brochure

**Wahidin Sudirohusodo lahir di Yogyakarta pada tanggal 7 Januari 1852. Dia belajar di STOVIA, yaitu sekolah kedokteran di pulau Jawa.**

**Sebagai dokter, dia membantu orang miskin agar bisa berobat gratis. Menurut Wahidin, pendidikan adalah cara untuk membebaskan Hindia Belanda dari negara penjajah, yaitu Belanda. Maka dia sering memberikan sumbangan kepada pemuda yang berbakat supaya mereka bisa terus belajar. Di samping itu, di waktu senggang dia suka main gamelan.**

**Pada tanggal 20 Mei 1908, bersama kawan-kawannya, dia mendirikan Budi Utomo, yang merupakan organisasi sosial pertama di Indonesia dan mendirikan kongres yang kemudian memperkenalkan Sumpah Pemuda.**

*Wahidin Sudirohusodo was born in Jogjakarta on January 7, 1852. He studied at STOVIA, a medical school in Java.*

*As a doctor, he helped poor people receive free medical treatment. Wahidin believed that education was very important for liberating the country from the occupying power, the Netherlands, so he often gave donations to talented young people so they could continue their study. In his free time, he liked to play in a gamelan (a Javanese traditional orchestra).*

*On May 20, 1908, accompanied by his colleagues, he set up Budi Utomo. It was the first modern social organization in Indonesia, and it organized the congress that originally promoted Sumpah Pemuda.*

## New Words and Phrases

**kedokteran** *medical, medicine*
**miskin** *poor, underprivileged*
**berobat** *to seek medical advice*
**gratis** *free (of charge)*
**menurut** *according to*
**pendidikan** *education*
**cara** *way; method*

**membébaskan** *to free something*
**sering** *often*
**sumbangan** *donation*
**berbakat** *talented*
**di samping itu** *aside from that*

**senggang** *free, spare*
**gamelan** *traditional orchestra*
**mendirikan** *to establish, found, set up*

## Grammar note: The *-kan* verb affix

### Verbs with the *-kan* suffix

The **-kan** affix is mostly found at the end of **meN-** verbs (and their passive **di-** forms), though it sometimes occurs at the end of **ber-** or **ter-** verbs. The **-kan** suffix shows that the verb has a direct object. Here are some examples of such verbs learned in this unit (the direct objects are underlined).

**Kongres ini yang kemudian memperkenalkan Sumpah Pemuda.**
*This congress later introduced the Youth Pledge.*

**Soekarno-Hatta memproklamasikan kemerdekaan Indonesia.**
*Sukarno and Hatta proclaimed Indonesian Independence.*

These last two sentences can easily be transformed into the passive voice, focusing on the action and the object:

**Sumpah Pemuda kemudian diperkenalkan kongres ini.**
*The Youth Pledge was later introduced by this congress.*

**Kemerdekaan Indonesia diproklamasikan (oleh) Soekarno-Hatta.**
*Sukarno and Hatta proclaimed Indonesian independence.*

While the **-kan** suffix sometimes signifies that the verb takes an object, it may also mean that someone has done something for someone else.

**Maka dia sering memberikan sumbangan kepada pemuda yang berbakat.**
*Therefore he often gave donations to talented young people.*

**Danny membukakan pintu untuk Adi.**
*Danny opened the door for Adi.*

The same sentence without the **-kan** suffix—**Danny membuka pintu untuk Adi**—is not wrong. However, the use of **-kan** shows that Danny was opening the door because Adi needed help doing so (because Adi had his hands full, perhaps).

The affix **-kan** can also be used in imperatives:

**Tolong tuliskan nama!**
*Please write your name!*

The word **tolong** ("help," "please," the imperative form of **menolong**) shows us that the person speaking is asking for help.

### The *-kan* verb as an adjective

Sometimes, the object is understood, and therefore missing. In this case, the **-kan** verb works more like an adjective.

> **Oleh karena pergerakannya membahayakan, Soekarno dipenjara oleh Belanda.**
> *Since his (political) movement was dangerous, Sukarno was jailed by the Dutch.*

Here, there is no clear object, but we can assume it was the Dutch government that felt in danger.

> **Oleh karena pergerakannya membahayakan (Belanda), Soekarno dipenjara.**
> *Since his movement endangered (the Dutch), Sukarno was jailed.*

Other verbs you know that work like this include **menarik** ("interesting, attractive"), **membosankan** ("boring"), and **menyenangkan** ("pleasing, pleasant"). Note that all of them can be translated into -ing words in English.

## Indonesian and me

### Exercise 3

Using the sample above, create a mini-biography of your own. You can write about anyone you like. Here are some useful sentence starters:

**X lahir di ... pada tanggal ....**
**Dia belajar di ...**
**Sebagai ...., dia ...**
**Menurut X, ...**
**Di samping itu, di waktu senggang dia suka ...**

_____

_____

_____

_____

_____

_____

_____

_____

# 10.4 Pentingnya Sumpah Pemuda The importance of the Youth Pledge

 ## Listening to a dialogue

Danny still has some questions about **Sumpah Pemuda**. He finds his teacher, Ibu Ratih, after class.

IBU RATIH: **Selamat siang, Danny!** *Good afternoon, Danny!*
DANNY: **Selamat siang, Bu. Bu Ratih, saya mau tanya tentang Sumpah Pemuda tadi.**
*Good afternoon. Miss, I want to ask about the Youth Pledge just now.*

IBU RATIH:   **Silakan.** *Go ahead.*

DANNY:   **Bu, saya mau tanya apakah Soekarno juga mempunyai peran penting dalam sumpah tersebut.**
*Miss, I want to ask whether Sukarno also played an important role in the pledge.*

IBU RATIH:   **Pertanyaan yang bagus. Sepertinya Soekarno tidak ikut dalam Kongres Pemuda itu.**
*A good question. It seems that Sukarno didn't join the Youth Congress.*

DANNY:   **Apakah beliau pernah menjadi anggota Jong Java?** *Was he ever a member of Jong Java?*

IBU RATIH:   **Tepat sekali. Dia pernah menjadi anggota, tetapi pada waktu Kongres Pemuda, sudah pindah ke organisasi lain yang lebih bersifat nasional.**
*Absolutely correct. He was once a member, but at the time of the Youth Congress, he had moved to another organization, which was more nationalist.*

## New Words and Phrases

**tanya** *ask*
**peran** *role*
**tersebut** *that (one), the (aforementioned)*
**pertanyaan** *question*

**sepertinya** *it seems*
**tepat sekali** *exactly (lit., very exact)*
**bersifat** *to have a nature or characteristic*

### Exercise 4: True or false? *Benar atau salah?*

|  | B (✓) | S (✗) |
|---|---|---|
| 1. **Menurut Bu Ratih, apa pertanyaan Danny bagus?** | _____ | _____ |
| 2. **Apakah Soekarno pernah menjadi anggota Jong Java?** | _____ | _____ |
| 3. **Apakah Soekarno ikut Kongres Pemuda tahun 1928?** | _____ | _____ |

## Grammar note: Adverbs *sangat / sekali*

**Sangat** and **sekali** are adverbs used to intensify an adjective. Their meanings are identical. The only difference lies in that **sangat** precedes the word it intensifies, while **sekali** follows it.

> **sangat panas** *(very hot)*
> **panas sekali** *(very hot)*

In some parts of Indonesia, you will hear **sangat** used more. In other parts, you might hear **sekali** (especially in Sumatra).

### Exercise 5

Translate the following using **sekali**.

1. very exact _____
2. very poor _____
3. very important _____
4. very often _____

### Exercise 6

Translate the following using **sangat**.

1. very exact _____
2. very cool _____
3. very sad _____
4. very sick _____

# 10.5 Indonesia Raya  The Indonesian National Anthem

## | Listening: Song

Below is the Indonesian national anthem. You can find a recording of this easily on the Internet.

**Indonesia Raya**

*(W.R. Supratman)*

| | |
|---|---|
| **Indonesia tanah airku,** | *Indonesia, my country,* |
| **Tanah tumpah darahku,** | *Place where my blood falls,* |
| **Di sanalah aku berdiri,** | *There, I stand,* |
| **Jadi pandu ibuku.** | *As my mother's guide.* |
| | |
| **Indonesia kebangsaanku,** | *Indonesia, my nationality* |
| **Bangsa dan tanah airku,** | *My nation and homeland,* |
| **Marilah kita berseru,** | *Let us shout out* |
| **Indonesia bersatu.** | *Indonesia unite as one!* |
| | |
| **Hiduplah tanahku, hiduplah negeriku,** | *Long live my land, long live my country,* |
| **Bangsaku, rakyatku, semuanya,** | *My nation, my people, all of them,* |
| **Bangunlah jiwanya, bangunlah badannya,** | *Rise up in spirit, rise up in body,* |
| **Untuk Indonesia Raya.** | *For Indonesia the Great.* |
| | |
| **Indonesia Raya,** | *Indonesia the Great* |
| **Merdeka, merdeka,** | *Freedom, freedom* |
| **Tanahku, negeriku yang kucinta!** | *My land, my country that I love!* |
| **Indonesia Raya,** | *Indonesia the Great* |
| **Merdeka, merdeka,** | *Freedom, freedom* |
| **Hiduplah Indonesia Raya.** | *Long live Indonesia the Great.* |

## | New Words and Phrases

| | | |
|---|---|---|
| **tanah air** *homeland (lit., land and water)* | **-lah** *(added after words to be more polite)* | **bersatu** *to unite* |
| **tanah** *land, earth, soil* | **pandu** *guide* | **hidup** *to live* |
| **air** *water* | **kebangsaan** *nationality* | **negeri** *land, country* |
| **tumpah** *to spill, fall* | **mari** *let's* | **bangun** *arise, wake up, get up* |
| **darah** *blood* | **berseru** *to shout out* | **jiwa** *soul* |
| | | **raya** *great, greater* |

## | Grammar note: -lah

In the national anthem above, you will notice the ending **-lah** is used a number of times.

**Di sanalah aku berdiri**
*There, I stand*

**Marilah kita berseru**
*Let us shout out*

**Hiduplah tanahku, hiduplah negeriku**
*Long live my land, long live my country*

**Bangunlah jiwanya, bangunlah badannya**
*Rise up in spirit, rise up in body*

Leaving the **-lah** out would have the same meaning. **Di sana aku berdiri** still means "There I stand" or "I stand there." But the **-lah** adds a softening syllable, that lengthens the utterance. In a song, such as this, **-lah** can be useful as a filler for getting the right number of syllables in a line to maintain rhythm. However, it also has a stylistic function of making the nationalist message more poetic. (Most Indonesian songs have no **-lah** in their lyrics at all!)

Compare the difference between:

| | | | |
|---|---|---|---|
| **Mari!** | *Please! Let's go!* | **Marilah!** | *Let us go.* |
| **Makan!** | *Eat!* | **Makanlah!** | *Go on, eat!* |

## 10.6 Membuat gado-gado  Making a vegetarian dish

A number of Indonesian dishes are starting to achieve international fame, thanks to the Indonesian diaspora opening up restaurants around the world. Aside from **satay** (saté) and **nasi goreng** (fried rice), one of the most well-known Indonesian dishes is **gado-gado**. Gado-gado is a vegetarian dish, and the exact ingredients used varies around the country. Here is one recipe for the dish.

### ▍Reading: *Resep membuat gado-gado*

**Bahan:**

- bumbu kacang
- 100 g kol, dipotong tipis
- kacang panjang, potong 4 cm
- seikat bayam
- taoge
- 1 buah selada, potong
- 1 buah timun, potong
- telur
- kentang
- tahu goreng
- tempe goreng

**Cara:** Rebus sayuran sampai matang. Potong tipis tahu, tempe dan telur. Potong kol, kacang panjang, bayam, mentimun dan selada. Susun semua bahan di piring, kemudian tuang bumbu kacang di atas. Makan dengan nasi atau lontong.

*Method: Boil the vegetables until cooked. Slice the tofu, **tempé** and egg thinly. Slice the cabbage, string beans, spinach, cucumber and lettuce. Arrange all ingredients on a plate, then pour peanut sauce on top. Eat with rice or lontong.*

### ▍New Words and Phrases

**resép** *recipe; prescription*
**bahan** *ingredients; materials*
**bumbu** *spice, seasoning*
**kol** *cabbage*
**tipis** *thin, narrow*
**kacang panjang** *string beans*
**bayam** *spinach*
**taogé** *bean sprouts*
**selada** *lettuce*

**timun** *cucumber*
**telur** *eggs*
**rebus, merebus** *to boil*
**matang** *cooked, ripe, done*
**kentang** *potatoes*
**tahu** *tofu*
**témpé** *tempeh, soybean curd cakes*

**susun, menyusun** *to arrange, pile up*
**piring** *plate*
**tuang, menuang** *to pour*
**sajikan, menyajikan** *to serve*
**lontong** *rice cake*

## ▌Language note

In many ways, Indonesia can be considered a **gado-gado** nation, made up of many different and various parts. **Bahasa gado-gado** is also an expression for when two people have trouble communicating, so both use elements of their own languages.

## ▌Grammar review: *Se-* and counters

You will see that cooking food (as well as shopping for the ingredients) requires use of the counters learnt in Unit 8.  Here we see **sebuah** (generic counter for fruit and vegetables) and **seikat** ("a bunch").

So if you want to buy one head of lettuce, one head of cabbage, and three potatoes, you would say, "**Minta sebuah selada, sebuah kol dan tiga buah kentang.**" Or, if you want to buy one head of cabbage, two cucumbers and five eggs, you would say, "**Minta sebuah kol, dua buah mentimun dan lima butir telur.**" (Eggs use **butir** as a counter, although people will still understand if you say **buah**.)

For uncountable items, such as the spinach, bean sprouts, and string beans, you should ask for their weight in grams. Sometimes they are sold by the bunch (**seikat**). So, if you want to buy a bunch of spinach and three potatoes, you would say, "**Minta seikat bayam dan tiga buah kentang.**" Or, if you want to buy an egg, 100 g of bean sprouts and 200 g of string beans, you would say, "**Minta sebuah/sebutir telur, seratus gram taoge dan dua ratus gram kacang panjang.**"

The counter for chunks of food is **potong**. It is used for foods such as tofu or **tempe** (a protein-rich food made from unprocessed soybeans). So, if you want to buy six blocks of tofu and four chunks of **tempe**, you would say, "**Minta enam potong tahu dan empat potong tempe.**"

However, **se-** is not only used with counters or to mean "a" or "one."  It is also a common Indonesian prefix with various other meanings, including:

• as (**setinggi gunung**, "as high as a mountain")
• all (**seIndonesia**, "across Indonesia")

## ▌Grammar review: Imperatives

As in English, the imperative form of the verb in Indonesian is the plain form, based on the root word, and it always comes at the beginning of the sentence. For example, from the recipe, we have the following uses of the imperative:

**Rebus sayuran sampai matang.**
*Boil the vegetables until cooked.*

**Potong tipis tahu, tempe dan telur.**
*Slice thinly tofu, tempeh, and egg.*

**Susun semua bahan di piring ...**
*Arrange all ingredients on the plate ...*

**... tuang bumbu kacang di atas.**
*... pour peanut sauce on top.*

**Makan dengan nasi atau lontong.**
*Eat with rice or lontong.*

In instructions (such as recipes, manuals, etc.) we always use this form of the verb.

## Exercise 7

Adi's family is cooking in the kitchen at home. His mother, Ibu Maya, is asking Adi, Danny and Nina to help. Give instructions in Indonesian, using the imperative form of the verb. Use the vocabulary and sentences from the recipe to help you.

1. Ibu Maya wants the vegetables boiled until cooked. She says to Danny:

   **"Danny, tolong** _____

2. Ibu Maya wants the tofu, tempeh, and egg to be thinly sliced. She says to Adi:

   **"Adi,** _____

3. Ibu Maya wants Nina to slice the cabbage, beans and spinach. She says to Nina:

   **"Nina,** _____

## Unit Review

### Part 1

Match the Indonesian with the English equivalents. All the words or phrases are taken from this unit.

| a slice of tempeh | youth pledge | a bunch of spinach | very poor | very important |

1. **sepotong tempe** _____

2. **sangat miskin** _____

3. **Sumpah Pemuda** _____

4. **penting sekali** _____

5. **seikat bayam** _____

### Part 2

Translate the following sentences using **meN-kan** verbs into English. Use the knowledge of this structure that you have gained in this unit.

> EXAMPLE: **Dr Wahidin mendirikan sebuah organisasi modern.**
> _Dr Wahidin established a modern organization._

1. **Danny membelikan Riri seikat bunga putih.**

   _____

2. **Pendidikan bisa membebaskan sebuah negara jajahan.**

   _____

3. **Orang yang dipenjara tidak selalu membahayakan.**

   _____

4. **Gado-gado mau dimakan dengan nasi atau lontong?**

   _____

# Unit 10 End-of-unit vocabulary list

**bahan** *ingredient, material*
**bangun** *wake up, get up*
**bayam** *spinach*
**begini** *like this*
**begitu** *like that*
**béla, membéla** *to defend*
**berarti** *to mean*
**berbagai** *various*
**berbakat** *talented*
**berbangsa** *to have a nationality or nation*
**berobat** *to seek medical advice*
**bersatu** *to unite*
**berseru** *to shout out*
**bersifat** *to have a nature or characteristic*
**bertumpah** *to spill*
**bilang** *to say (informal)*
**bumbu** *sauce, spice*
**butir** *counter for eggs*
**cara** *way; method*
**dagang** *trade*
**darah** *blood*
**démokratis** *democratic*
**di samping itu** *aside from that*
**étnik** *ethnic*
**gado-gado** *Indonesian salad with peanut sauce*
**gamelan** *traditional Javanese orchestra*
**gerakan** *movement*
**gratis** *free (of charge)*
**hasil** *result*
**hidup** *to live*
**Hindia Belanda** *Dutch East Indies*
**jajahan** *colony*
**jaya** *victorious*
**jiwa** *soul*
**kacang panjang** *string beans*

**kebangsaan** *nationality*
**kedokteran** *medical, medicine*
**kemudian** *then*
**kentang** *potato*
**kol** *cabbage*
**kongrés** *congress*
**-lah** *(polite ending)*
**lontong** *rice cake*
**maka** *therefore, thus*
**makanya** *that's why*
**mari** *let's, come on*
**matang** *cooked*
**membébaskan** *to free something*
**memperingati** *to commemorate*
**mendirikan** *to establish, found, set up*
**mengaku, mengakui** *to declare, claim*
**mengenal** *to know, recognize*
**menjunjung** *to hold in high esteem*
**menuang** *to pour (out)*
**menurut** *according to*
**menyajikan** *to serve up*
**menyusun** *to arrange, pile up*
**meskipun** *although*
**miskin** *poor*
**muncul** *appear*
**negara** *country, state*
**negeri** *country, nation*
**nusa** *island, archipelago*
**organisasi** *(social) organization*
**pandu** *guide*
**pasti** *must, definitely*
**pemuda** *youth*
**pendidikan** *education*
**penting** *important*
**peran** *role*
**persatuan** *unity*
**pertanyaan** *question*

**pindah** *to move*
**piring** *plate, dish*
**puluhan** *tens, dozens*
**pusaka** *heirloom, something of great value*
**raya** *great, greater*
**rebus** *boil*
**resép** *recipe; prescription*
**samping** *side*
**saté** *satay*
**sekali** *very (after a word)*
**selada** *lettuce; salad*
**selama-lamanya** *forever*
**seluruh** *all, entire*
**senggang** *free, spare*
**sepertinya** *it seems*
**sepotong** *a slice*
**sering** *often*
**sumbangan** *donation*
**sumpah** *oath, pledge; swear*
**susun, menyusun** *to arrange, pile up*
**tahu** *tofu*
**tanah air** *homeland (lit., earth and water)*
**tanya** *ask*
**taogé** *bean sprouts*
**telur** *egg*
**témpé** *tempeh (unprocessed soybean cake)*
**tepat** *correct*
**tercinta** *beloved*
**tersebut** *that (one), the (aforementioned)*
**timun** *cucumber*
**tipis** *thin, narrow*
**tonggak** *moment, milestone*
**tuang** *pour*
**tumpah** *to spill, fall*

**Walikota Surabaya**
8 hrs

Untuk masyarakat Surabaya, kita sudah punya taman kota lagi! Namanya Taman Bungur. Silakan gunakan dengan baik. Ada fasilitas untuk berolahraga dan bersantai dengan keluarga.

*For the people of Surabaya, we have a new city park! It's called Bungur Park. Please use it well. There are facilities for doing sport and relaxing with family.*

**Agus Suyitno** Terima kasih banyak atas usahanya membuat Surabaya lebih ramah. Saya akan menjadi lebih betah lagi tinggal di sini.
*Thank you very much for your efforts at making Surabaya more friendly. I will feel even more at home living here.*

**Walikota Surabaya** Pak Agus.. terima kasih. Ajak keluarganya untuk datang ke taman, ya!
*Agus, thank you. Invite your family to come to the park, won't you?*

**Agus Suyitno** Pasti! Semoga sukses, ya!
*Definitely! Good luck!*

**Laras Wasito** Saya sangat bangga. Sejak menjadi walikota, Surabaya semakin indah! Terima kasih, ya.
*I am very proud. Since you have been mayor, Surabaya has become increasingly more beautiful! Thank you.*

**Walikota Surabaya** Terima kasih, Mbak Laras. Bantu jaga tamannya, ya!
*Thank you, Laras. Help to look after the parks, won't you?*

**Wahyu** Selamat pagi. Kemarin saya mengunjungi Taman Bungur. Ada banyak sampah di mana-mana. Mohon para pedagang diatur!
*Good morning. Yesterday I visited Bungur Park. There was lots of rubbish everywhere. Please regulate the traders!*

**Walikota Surabaya** Mas Wahyu, terima kasih atas laporannya. Saya akan segera meminta petugas yang ada di tempat untuk bertindak.
*Wahyu, thank you for your report. I will immediately ask the officer there to take action.*

*This social media posting appears on pages 175 and 176.*

# 11

## Ayo, Bung!
### Let's Go, Bro!

In this unit, we will:

- Learn how to read and respond to posts on social media,
- Learn about Indonesia's struggle for independence in East Java,
- Study **ke-an** nouns,
- Understand the importance of cemeteries in Indonesian society,
- Be able to recognize some common proverbs or sayings,
- Learn the difference between **per-an** and **peN-an** nouns.

Surabaya is the capital of **Jawa Timur** (East Java), located on the northeastern coast of Java next to the Madura Strait. It is the second-largest city in Indonesia. The city is known as **Kota Pahlawan**, "City of Heroes," due to the importance of the Battle of Surabaya in galvanizing Indonesian and international support for Indonesian independence during the Indonesian National Revolution. The term **Ayo, Bung** was used to invite the youth to struggle for independence.

## 11.1 Taman kota  City parks

Adi is reading about how the Mayor of Surabaya interacts with the community through social media to gain feedback. He is reading through conversations between the mayor and constituents on a social media site.

### ▎Reading: Social Media

*Walikota Surabaya*: Untuk masyarakat Surabaya, kita sudah punya taman kota lagi! Namanya Taman Bungur. Silakan gunakan dengan baik. Ada fasilitas untuk berolahraga dan bersantai dengan keluarga.

*Mayor of Surabaya: For the people of Surabaya, we have a new city park! It's called Bungur Park. Please use it well. There are facilities for doing sport and relaxing with family.*

*Agus Suyitno*: **Terima kasih banyak atas usaha-nya membuat Surabaya lebih ramah. Saya akan menjadi lebih betah lagi tinggal di sini.**

*Agus Suyitno*: *Thank you very much for your efforts at making Surabaya more friendly. I will feel even more at home living here.*

*Walikota Surabaya*: **Pak Agus.. terima kasih. Ajak keluarganya untuk datang ke taman, ya!**

*Mayor of Surabaya*: *Agus, thank you. Invite your family to come to the park, won't you?*

*Agus Suyitno*: **Pasti! Semoga sukses, ya!**

*Agus Suyitno*: *Definitely! Good luck!*

*Laras Wasito*: **Saya sangat bangga. Sejak menjadi walikota, Surabaya semakin indah! Terima kasih, ya.**

*Laras Wasito*: *I am very proud. Since you became mayor, Surabaya has become increasingly more beautiful! Thank you.*

*Walikota Surabaya*: **Terima kasih, Mbak Laras. Bantu jaga tamannya, ya!**

*Mayor of Surabaya*: *Thank you, Laras. Help to look after the parks, won't you?*

*Wahyu*: **Selamat pagi. Kemarin saya mengunjungi Taman Bungur. Saya sedikit kecewa karena terlalu banyak pengunjung dan pedagang kaki lima. Ada banyak sampah di mana-mana. Mohon para pedagang diatur!**

*Wahyu*: *Good morning. Yesterday I visited Bungur Park. I was a bit disappointed because there were too many visitors and street vendors. There was lots of rubbish everywhere. Please regulate the traders!*

*Walikota Surabaya*: **Mas Wahyu, terima kasih atas laporannya. Saya akan segera meminta petugas yang ada di tempat untuk bertindak.**

*Mayor of Surabaya*: *Wahyu, thank you for your report. I will immediately ask the officer there to take action.*

## ▌New Words and Phrases

**masyarakat** *community*
**fasilitas** *facilities*
**berolahraga** *to do sport*
**bersantai** *to relax*
**usaha** *effort*
**betah** *feel at home*
**semoga** *may; hopefully*
**suksés** *success*
**semakin** *increasingly*

**indah** *beautiful (of an object, scene)*
**jaga, menjaga** *to take care of, look after*
**kecéwa** *disappointed*
**pengunjung** *visitor*
**pedagang kaki lima** *street vendor*
**mana-mana** *everywhere*

**mohon** *to request*
**diatur / mengatur** *to regulate, bring under control*
**laporan** *report*
**segera** *immediately*
**petugas** *officer*
**bertindak** *to take action*

## ▌Grammar note: *Atas*

We have already seen the use of **atas** in the construction **terdiri atas**, a variant of **terdiri dari**, meaning "to consist of." In the social media posts above, **atas** is also used with **terima kasih**, as in "thank you for ..."

You will sometimes see **terima kasih untuk ...**, which is influenced from English. The correct form is **terima kasih atas ...** .

## Grammar note: *Mohon*

**Mohon** is a polite form of **minta** (previously covered in Unit 4), meaning "to ask." **Mohon** could therefore be properly translated as "to request." As it is a polite form, **mohon** generally is followed by a passive (**di-**) form of the verb.

| | |
|---|---|
| **Mohon diatur!** | *Please see that it is regulated!* |
| **Mohon dibantu!** | *Please help out.* |
| **Mohon dijaga.** | *Please take care of it.* |

### Exercise 1

How would you say the following in Indonesian? Use **mohon** and a verb (in the **di-** form if you are using a **meN-** verb). All relevant verbs have been studied in either this unit or the previous one.

1. Please pour it out.

2. Please pile it up.

3. Please try.

4. Please stand up.

## 11.2  Tri Rismaharini

## Reading

In Unit 4, we read about a real-life mayor of Surabaya, Tri Rismaharini. Adi is interested in her work and wants to find out more about her. He is reading a short profile in a news magazine.

A. Tri Rismaharini lahir pada tanggal 20 November 1961. Dia adalah Walikota Surabaya. Tri mendapatkan gelar sarjana di bidang arsitektur dari Institut Teknologi Sepuluh November.

*Tri Rismaharini was born on 20 November, 1961. She is the mayor of Surabaya. Tri gained a bachelor's degree in architecure from the 10 November Institute of Technology.*

B. Tri Rismaharini sangat dicintai oleh masyarakatnya karena dia berhasil membuat Kota Surabaya lebih maju. Selama menjadi walikota, dia mendapatkan sejumlah penghargaan, baik dari dalam negeri maupun dari luar negeri. Dia dipilih sebagai salah satu dari sepuluh wanita paling inspiratif di dunia oleh majalah Forbes.

*Tri Rismaharini is much loved by her community because she has successfully made Surabaya more developed. During her term as mayor, she has received a number of awards, both domestic and international. She was chosen as one of the ten most inspirational women in the world by Forbes magazine.*

C. Tri Rismaharini sangat mencintai kotanya, Surabaya. Dia ingin setiap orang di Indonesia mengenal Surabaya sebagai kota pahlawan yang modern dan maju. Tri akan memelihara gedung-gedung tua peninggalan Belanda serta membangun gedung modern untuk menambah fasilitas kota. Tri berharap setiap orang yang datang ke Surabaya akan bisa belajar sejarah dan tahu keadaan kini.

*Tri Rismaharini loves her city, Surabaya, very much. She wants all Indonesians to know Surabaya as a city of heroes that is both modern and developed. Tri will maintain old Dutch buildings as well as build modern buildings to enhance city facilities. Tri hopes that everyone who comes to Surabaya will be able to study both history as well as the current situation.*

## New Words and Phrases

**sarjana** *undergraduate, bachelor*
**arsitéktur** *architecture*
**institut téknologi** *institute of technology*
**préstasi** *achievement*
**dicintai / mencintai** *to be loved / to love*

**maju** *developed; move ahead*
**penghargaan** *award, appreciation*
**baik ... maupun** *... both ... and ...*
**dalam negeri** *local, domestic*
**luar negeri** *international*
**inspiratif** *inspirational*

**memelihara** *to maintain*
**peninggalan** *heritage*
**serta** *as well as*
**menambah** *to increase*
**kini, sekarang** *now, present*

### Exercise 2

Can you match the headings to the correct paragraphs (A, B or C) above?

1. **Apa prestasi dia?**
   *What are her achievements?*

2. **Mengapa Surabaya penting?**
   *Why is Surabaya important?*

3. **Siapa dia?**
   *Who is she?*

## Grammar note: *Baik ... maupun ...* "both ... and"/"neither ... nor"

The above text uses the structure **baik ... maupun ...**, which means "both ... and ..." in English. This structure is used when talking about two things which are similarly important.

**Dia mendapatkan sejumlah penghargaan, baik dari dalam negeri maupun dari luar negeri.**
*She has received a number of awards, both domestic and international.*

Sometimes, in English, **baik ... maupun ...** can be translated as "neither ... nor ..." when talking about something negative.

**Baik Adi maupun Danny belum pernah ke Surabaya.**
*Both Adi and Danny have never been to Surabaya.*
*(Neither Adi nor Danny has ever been to Surabaya.)*

### Exercise 3

Fill in the blanks using **baik ... maupun** in the correct places. Then translate into English.

1. _____ **wisatawan domestik** _____ **yang internasional suka kota Surabaya yang modern.**

2. **Tri Rismaharini berusaha untuk memelihara gedung,** _____ **yang peninggalan Belanda** _____ **yang lebih baru.**

3. _____ **Hotel Majapahit** _____ **setasiun Gubeng bukan bangunan baru.**

# 11.3 Bung Tomo dan Surabaya  Bung Tomo and the Battle of Surabaya

## Reading

Danny is reading a short biography of Bung Tomo at the museum.

Sutomo (**Bung Tomo**) is an Indonesian national hero strongly associated with the Battle of Surabaya, when local resistance forces fought against returning colonial troops backed up by the British.

**Bung Tomo adalah pahlawan yang lahir di Surabaya. Dia menjadi tokoh penting dalam pertempuran 10 November 1945 yang diperingati sebagai Hari Pahlawan.**

*Sutomo was a hero who was born in Surabaya. He was an important figure in the battle of November 10, 1945, which is commemorated as Heroes' Day.*

### Masa Kecil
**Bung Tomo lahir dan dibesarkan dalam keluarga kelas menengah yang menghargai pendidikan. Dia aktif dalam organisasi pramuka (dulu bernama kepanduan). Dia tertarik pada dunia kewartawanan dan pernah bekerja sebagai wartawan di sebuah surat kabar.**

### Childhood
*Sutomo was born and raised in a middle-class family that valued education. He was active in the scouting organization (formerly known as Guides). He was interested in journalism and once worked as a reporter for a newspaper.*

*Pertempuran Surabaya 10 November 1945*

Pada tanggal 10 November 1945 sebuah kejadian terjadi di Hotel Yamato (kini Hotel Majapahit). Sekelompok orang Belanda menaikkan bendera mereka di atas hotel itu. Rakyat pun marah lalu menurunkan bendera itu. Bagian biru dirobek oleh pemuda Indonesia, tinggal merah putih, dan dikibarkan kembali. Itu adalah warna bendera Indonesia.

Dalam pertempuan ini, Bung Tomo menjadi orator yang memberi semangat untuk berjuang melawan tentara Inggris dan Belanda.

### Gelar Pahlawan

Gelar pahlawan nasional diberikan untuk Bung Tomo pada Hari Pahlawan tahun 2008. Perjuangan rakyat Indonesia di Surabaya sangat dahsyat. Tidak ada rasa takut!

*The Battle of Surabaya, 10 November, 1945*

*On 10 November, 1945, there was an incident that occurred at the Hotel Yamato (now Hotel Majapahit). A group of Dutch raised their flag above the hotel. Local people were angry so they took the flag down. The blue section was torn off by an Indonesian youth, leaving the red and white, and flown again. These were the colors of the Indonesian flag.*

*In this battle, Sutomo stood out as an orator who provided much spirit to fight against the English and Dutch soldiers.*

### Hero Award

*The title of National Hero was given to Sutomo on Heroes' Day in 2008. The struggle of the Indonesian people in Surabaya was very powerful. There was no fear!*

## ▌New Words and Phrases

**Bung** (elder) Brother
**tokoh** figure
**pertempuran** battle
**dibesarkan / membesarkan**
  raised, brought up / to raise,
  bring up
**kelas menengah** middle class
**aktif** active
**pramuka, kepanduan** (Boy)
  Scouts, Guides
**kewartawanan** journalism

**wartawan** reporter, journalist
**surat kabar** newspaper
**kejadian** incident, happening
**menaikkan** to put up, raise
**bendéra** flag
**lalu** then
**menurunkan** to lower, bring
  down
**dirobék / merobék** torn,
  ripped / to tear, rip

**dikibarkan / mengibarkan**
  raised, hoisted, flown / to raise,
  hoist, fly
**tentara** army, soldier
**semangat** spirit
**berjuang** to struggle
**dahsyat** powerful

## ▌Grammar note: *Ke-an* nouns

There are several vocabulary words in this unit that use the **ke-an** form. The **ke-an** form indicates a noun form, with the base word enclosed by the prefix **ke-** and the suffix **-an**. Generally speaking, **ke-an** nouns have general, abstract meanings. If we compare the base words with their **ke-an** derivation, we get an idea of how **ke-an** is used.

| | |
|---|---|
| **pandu** guide | **kepanduan** an old name for Scouts |
| **wartawan** journalist, reporter | **kewartawanan** journalism |
| **jadi** happen, occur | **kejadian** happening, occurrence, incident |
| **merdeka** free, independent | **kemerdekaan** freedom, independence |

Other **ke-an** words we have met in this course include:

| | | | |
|---|---|---|---|
| **keadaan** *situation, condition* | | **ada** *to exist; to have* | |
| **kebangsaan** *nationality* | | **bangsa** *nation* | |
| **kebersihan** *cleanliness, hygiene* | | **bersih** *clean* | |
| **kedokteran** *medical, medicine* | | **dokter** *doctor* | |
| **kelautan** *maritime* | | **laut** *sea* | |
| **kelurahan** *sub-district (office)* | | **lurah** *sub-district head* | |
| **kepulauan** *archipelago* | | **pulau** *island* | |
| **kesebelasan** *eleven, team* | | **sebelas** *eleven* | |
| **keturunan** *descent* | | **turun** *go down* | |
| **kewarganegaraan** *citizenship* | | **warganegara** *citizen, national* | |

## Exercise 4

Using your new knowledge of Indonesian grammar, choose the correct word to complete the sentences. All the words are taken from the two lists of fourteen word pairs directly above.

1. _____ **Indonesia terdiri dari 17.000** _____ **.**
   *The Indonesian archipelago consists of 17,000 islands.*

2. **Negara yang belum** _____ **selalu ingin** _____ **.**
   *A country that is not yet independent always wishes for independence.*

3. **Seorang** _____ **bekerja di kantor** _____ **.**
   *A sub-district head works at the sub-district office.*

4. _____ **orang main di** _____ **sepak bola.**
   *Eleven people play in a soccer team (eleven).*

5. **Seorang** _____ **menjadi kepala negara** _____ **.**
   *A king is the head of a kingdom.*

6. **Menteri** _____ **mengatur hal-hal tentang** _____ **dan samudera.**
   *The Minister for Maritime Affairs deals with matters relating to the seas and oceans.*

A few **ke-an** words do not have a general, abstract meaning. Some **ke-an** words suggest a condition of suffering:

| | |
|---|---|
| **kedinginan** | *suffering from the cold/too cold (from* **dingin**, *cold)* |
| **kepanasan** | *suffering from the heat/too hot (from* **panas**, *hot)* |
| **kehujanan** | *getting caught in the rain (from* **hujan**, *rain)* |

Finally, there are also a few words where the **ke-an** form indicates something accidental, for example,

| | |
|---|---|
| **ketiduran** | *to fall asleep unintentionally (from* **tidur**, *sleep)* |
| **kejatuhan** | *to accidentally have something fall on you (from* **jatuh**, *fall)* |

## 11.4 Berkunjung ke Taman Pahlawan Visiting the heroes' cemetery

Adi's grandfather is buried in the heroes' cemetery. This is a sign of respect for former soldiers and those who have served the Indonesian nation. When Adi is in the town where his grandfather is buried, especially before Ramadan and at Idul Fitri, he and his family will visit the grave to pay their respects.

Danny goes with Adi to the cemetery this year. He then writes a letter to Pak Yusep back in Australia about visiting the heroes' cemetery on Heroes' Day.

## ▋ Reading a Letter

**11 November 2017**

**Pak Yusep yang baik,**
**Apa kabar? Saya sangat senang bisa melihat perayaan Hari Pahlawan pada 10 November kemarin. Salah satu kegiatan adalah berkunjung ke Taman Pahlawan, tempat para pahlawan dikuburkan. Banyak warung menjual bunga-bunga untuk dibeli oleh pengunjung lalu ditaburkan di atas kuburan.**

**Acara itu dimulai dengan upacara bendera. Polisi, tentara, pegawai negeri dan pelajar berbaris di depan tiang bendera. Ketika bendera berkibar di atas tiangnya, semua peserta memberikan hormat kepada bendera. Pemimpin upacara juga memberikan pidato tentang betapa pentingnya peran pahlawan dalam kehidupan masa kini. "Kita harus meneruskan cita-cita mereka," katanya.**

**Acara diakhiri dengan kegiatan menaburkan bunga pada masing-masing kuburan pahlawan. Kegiatan ini dilakukan setiap tahun di seluruh Indonesia. Orang Indonesia sangat menghormati jasa para pahlawan.**

**Salam saya untuk semua teman-teman,**
**Danny**

*11 November, 2017*

*Dear Yusep,*
*How are you? I was very pleased to be able to see the Heroes' Day celebrations yesterday on 10 November. One activity was visiting the Heroes' Cemetery, where heroes are buried. Lots of stalls were selling flowers for visitors to buy, and then scatter on the graves.*

*The commemoration began with a flag ceremony. Police, army, civil servants and students lined up in front of a flagpole. When the flag fluttered on top of the pole, all participants saluted it. The commandant also gave a speech about how important the role of heroes is in life nowadays. "We must continue their dreams," he said.*

*The commemoration ended with the scattering of flowers on the heroes' graves. This is done annually throughout Indonesia. Indonesians greatly respect their heroes.*

*My regards to all our friends,*
*Danny*

## New Words and Phrases

**berkunjung** *to (pay a) visit*
**dikuburkan / menguburkan** *to be buried / to bury*
**bunga** *flowers*
**ditaburkan / menaburkan** *scattered, strewn / to scatter, strew*

**kuburan** *grave; graveyard*
**polisi** *police*
**tiang** *pole*
**memberikan hormat** *to salute (lit., to give respect)*
**pidato** *speech*
**tentang** *about, concerning*

**betapa** *how; to what extent*
**kehidupan** *life*
**meneruskan** *to continue*
**katanya** *they say, it is said*
**mengakhiri** *to end, finish*
**masing-masing** *each, every*
**jasa** *service*

## Cultural note

Visiting graves (**berziarah**), is an important duty in Indonesian society, as it shows respect and care for loved ones. Cemeteries become very crowed before and after the fasting month, when many Muslims wish to ask forgiveness for their sins and start afresh. Typically, visitors will pour water and scatter flower petals on the grave, before tidying it up. Heroes' cemeteries are usually much neater and better maintained than public cemeteries, which are often overcrowded with headstones laid in a disorderly fashion.

### Exercise 5

Match the phrase or sentence with the appropriate picture. Write the Indonesian caption in the space below the correct picture.

1. **Bendera berkibar di atas tiang.**
2. **Pemimpin upacara memberikan hormat.**
3. **Polisi melakukan upacara bendera.**
4. **Seorang tentara memberikan pidato.**
5. **Taman Pahlawan**
6. **Warung-warung menjual bunga.**

A. _____

B. _____

C. _____

D. _____

E. _____

F. _____

## Grammar note: *Per-an* and *peN-an* nouns

**Per-an** and **peN-an** are prefix-suffix pairs that are used to turn base words into general nouns.

### *Per-an* nouns

**Per-an** nouns are related to **ber-** verbs, and are used to refer to general concepts. Here are some examples of **per-an** nouns that we have already learned, along with their **ber-** verb counterparts.

| | |
|---|---|
| **perjuangan** *struggle* | **berjuang** *to struggle* |
| **pertempuran** *fight, battle* | **bertempur** *to fight, battle* |
| **perlombaan** *contest* | **berlomba** *to contest* |
| **pertandingan** *competition* | **bertanding** *to compete* |
| **pertemuan** *meeting* | **bertemu** *to meet* |
| **perusahaan** *company, business* | **berusaha** *to try; to do business* |

### Exercise 6

Fill in the table with the nouns in their **per-an** forms, and give their meanings.

| *ber-* form and base meaning | *per-an* form | *per-an* meaning |
|---|---|---|
| **berbéda** *to be different* | **perbédaan** | *difference* |
| *to compete* | **perlombaan** | *competition* |
| **berusaha** *to try; to do business* | | *company, business* |
| *to camp* | **perkémahan** | *campsite* |
| **berkembang** *to develop* | | *development* |
| *to get together* | **perkumpulan** | *group, gather* |
| **bermain** *to play* | | *game* |
| **bersaudara** *to have siblings* | | *brotherhood* |
| **bertemu** *to meet* | | *meeting* |
| **berteman** *to be friends* | | *friendship* |

Not all **ber-** verbs have a **per-an** form, and not all **per-an** nouns come from a **ber-** verb. For example, we also have **per-an** nouns from base words, such as,

| | |
|---|---|
| **ingat** *to remember* | **peringatan** *warning* |

However, **ber-** verbs and **per-an** nouns are generally related in meaning and use.

### *PeN-an* nouns

**PeN-an** nouns are linked to **meN-** verbs. These nouns tend to describe processes that involve a second noun.

| | |
|---|---|
| **membagikan** *to divide something up* | **pembagian** *division (of something)* |
| **merayakan** *to celebrate something* | **perayaan** *celebration (of something)* |

**Exercise 7**

Fill in the table with the nouns in their **peN-an** forms, and give their meanings.

| *meN-* form and base meaning | *peN-an* form | *peN-an* meaning |
|---|---|---|
| **mendidik** *to educate* | **pendidikan** | |
| **menghargai** | **penghargaan** | *appreciation* |
| **melaksanakan** *to hold, conduct* | | *event, when something is being held* |
| **menutup** *to close* | | *closing (ceremony)* |
| **menghormati** *to respect* | | *show of respect* |
| **menerbangkan** *to fly (something)* | | *flight* |

# 11.5 **Peribahasa**  Sayings or proverbs

It is very common in Indonesia to install lots of banners across streets to promote various upcoming events, or to simply make public service announcements. Have a good look at some proverbs (**peribahasa**) written on banners you may find on the street during **Hari Pahlawan**.

**"Bersatu kita teguh, bercerai kita runtuh"**
*Together we are strong, divorced we fall*
*(United we stand, divided we fall)*

**"Berat sama dipikul, ringan sama dijinjing"**
*Carry the weight on your shoulder together, carry something light together by hand*
*(Many hands make light work)*

**"Sedia payung sebelum hujan"**
*Prepare an umbrella before it rains (Be prepared for a rainy day)*

**"Sedikit demi sedikit lama-lama menjadi bukit"**
*Bit by bit, slowly will become a hill (Building up, bit by bit)*

**"Di mana bumi dipijak, di situ langit dijunjung"**
*Where the earth is trodden, the sky is upheld (When in Rome, do as the Romans)*

## Exercise 8

Match the most suitable saying for each of the situations below.

1. Sutomo said that if we unite, we can be stronger.

   _____

2. As a foreigner living in Indonesia, Danny always remembers to eat with his right hand.

   _____

3. The mayor of Surabaya has created many new parts. As the years pass, Surabaya has become more and more attractive.

   _____

4. Everyone has to work together to make the city better. If one person smiles, everyone smiles. If one cries, then everyone cries.

   _____

5. Before making a speech, Sutomo always made notes to carry in his hand so that, if he forgot something, he could still read what needed to be said.

   _____

## Unit review

### Part 1

Choose the correct form of the word.

1. **Bunga-bunga itu dibagikan / pembagian / membagikan kepada pengunjung toko.**
2. **Danny dan Adi ikut serta / keikutsertaan / mengikutsertakan dalam lomba.**
3. **Berteman / Pertemanan Adi dan Danny semakin dekat.**
4. **Saya berkunjung / mengunjungi / pengunjung taman pahlawan.**

### Part 2

Translate the above sentences into English.

1. _____

2. _____

3. _____

4. _____

## Unit 11 End-of-unit vocabulary list

aktif *active*
arsitéktur *architecture*
baik ... maupun ... *both ... and ...*
bendéra *flag*
berharap *to hope*
berjuang *to struggle*
berkibar *to fly, flutter*
berkunjung *to (pay a) visit*
berolahraga *to do sport*
berpidato *to give a speech*
bersantai *to relax*
bertindak *to take action*
berziarah *to visit a grave*
betah *feel at home*
betapa *how, to what extent*
Bung *(elder) Brother*
bunga *flower*
dahsyat *powerful*
dalam negeri *local, domestic*
dingin *cold*
fasilitas *facilities*
gelar *title*
indah *beautiful (of an object, scene)*
inspiratif *inspirational*
institut téknologi *institute of technology*
jaga, menjaga *to take care of*
jasa *service*
kabar *news*
katanya *says, said*
keadaan *condition, situation*
kecéwa *disappointed*
kehidupan *life*
kejadian *incident, happening*
kepanduan *old name for Scouts*

kewartawanan *journalism*
kini, sekarang *now, present*
kuburan *grave; graveyard*
lalu *then*
laporan *report*
luar negeri *international*
maju *developed; move ahead*
mana-mana *everywhere*
marah *angry*
masa *time, period*
masing-masing *each, every*
masyarakat *society, community*
maupun *also (when listing a second element)*
memberikan *to give (something)*
membesarkan *to raise, bring up*
memelihara *to maintain, look after*
menaburkan *to sprinkle, strew*
menaikkan *to raise, put up*
menambah *to add*
mencintai *to love someone*
menengah *middle*
menertibkan *to regulate, control*
meneruskan *to continue something*
mengakhiri *to finish, end something*
mengatur *to arrange*
menghargai *to evaluate, appreciate*
mengibarkan *to fly, flutter, wag something*
menguburkan *to bury*
menjaga *to take care of*
menurunkan *to lower, bring down*

menyampaikan *to express, deliver*
merobék *to tear, rip*
mohon *to request*
pedagang kaki lima *street vendor (lit., "five foot seller")*
penerbangan *flight*
penghargaan *award, appreciation*
pengunjung *visitor*
peninggalan *heritage*
peribahasa *saying, proverb*
peringatan *commemoration; warning*
pertempuran *battle*
petugas *officer*
pidato *speech*
polisi *police*
pramuka *Scouts*
préstasi *achievement*
sarjana *bachelor's degree*
segera *immediately, at once*
semakin *increasingly*
semangat *spirit*
semoga *may; hopefully*
serta *as well as*
sukses *success, successful*
surat kabar *newspaper*
tambah, menambah *to add*
tampil *appear*
tentara *army, soldier*
tiang *pole*
tokoh *figure; character*
upacara *ceremony*
usaha *effort*
warganegara *citizen*
wartawan *journalist*

*This dialogue appears on pages 191 and 192.*

# UNIT
# 12

## Selamat Natal dan Tahun Baru /
### Merry Christmas and Happy New Year

In this unit, we will:

- Learn how to talk about Christmas, and how it is celebrated in Indonesia,
- Practice a simple telephone conversation,
- Learn how to use **bahwa** to create complex sentences,
- Understand how nicknames are used in Indonesia,
- Complete personal information in formats such as a profile and identity card,
- Discuss the issues of translation.

## 12.1 Kartu Natal   Christmas cards

 **Listening to a dialogue**

Danny is having a problem writing a greeting card to his friend. Adi is trying to help him by finding an example of a card. Listen to their conversation.

Untuk Yosef,
Selamat Natal dan Tahun
Baru! Apa kabar? Semoga
semua di Papua sehat.
Saya mau beritahu bahwa
saya mau pulang ke Perth
sebentar lagi.
Salam dari temanmu,
Danny

DANNY:   **Adi, saya mau minta tolong. Masih ingat Yosef, dari Papua? Saya mau kirim kartu Natal kepadanya.**

*Adi, I want to ask for help. Do you still remember Yosef, from Papua? I want to send a Christmas card to him.*

ADI:   **Iya ... sebentar lagi Natal, ya. Sudah beli kartu ucapan?**

*Yes ... it will be Christmas soon, won't it? Have you already bought a greetings card?*

DANNY:   **Sudah. Tapi saya bingung, mau tulis apa.** *Yes. But I'm confused, I don't know what to write.*

ADI:   **Kan sudah ada isinya. Danny tinggal menulis berita tambahan. Seperti "bagaimana kabarnya?" Lalu beritahu dia bahwa sebentar lagi, Danny mau pulang ke Australia.**

*Well, it's already got something written in it. You just have to write some extra news. Like "how are you?" Then tell him that soon, you're going home to Australia.*

DANNY:   **Baik, saya coba dulu ya. Nanti Adi yang perbaiki.**

*Fine, I'll try myself first, then. Later you can improve it.*

## New Words and Phrases

| | | |
|---|---|---|
| **ingat** *remember* | **kartu ucapan** *greetings card* | **beritahu, memberitahu** *to inform, let know* |
| **iya** *yes [emphatic]* | **'kan** *isn't/hasn't/doesn't* (short for **bukan**, *reinforcing something*) | **bahwa** *that (conjunction)* |
| **sebentar** *a moment* | | **perbaiki, memperbaiki** *to fix, correct, improve* |
| **sebentar lagi** *very soon, in a moment* | **berita kabar** *news* | |
| **Natal** *Christmas* | **tambahan** *additional, extra* | |

## Grammar note: *Bahwa*

**Bahwa** is a key conjunction, linking two clauses, and giving extra information about something. It translates as "that" or "which."

> **Lalu beritahu dia bahwa sebentar lagi, Danny mau pulang ke Australia.**
> *Then tell him that soon, you're going home to Australia.*

In shorter sentences, you can sometimes leave it out, but generally people would pause, or use a comma to separate the two parts of the sentence.

> **Saya tidak tahu bahwa dia bukan orang Indonesia.**
> **Saya tidak tahu, dia bukan orang Indonesia.**
> *I didn't know (that) she wasn't Indonesian.*

As it links two clauses, **bahwa** cannot start a sentence.

## Grammar note: *'kan*

You will hear this short word, which can act as a kind of filler, very often in spoken Indonesian. It comes from **bukan** ("no, not; isn't it?") and suggests that the speaker and listener are both already aware of something.

> **'Kan sudah ada isinya.**
> *Well, it's already got something written in it, hasn't it?*
> *(lit. it already has content)*

It is more common to hear **'kan** as a tag at the end of a sentence or phrase, but as the dialogue shows, it can also start a sentence, for added emphasis.

> **Sudah ada isinya, 'kan?**
> *It's got something in it, hasn't it?*

**'Kan** is a colloquial word which is spoken only, and not used in writing.

## Language note: Names as pronouns

You will see in the dialogue that instead of using familiar pronouns such as **kamu** or **engkau**, Adi and Danny instead use their own names to refer to "you."

> ADI: **Danny tinggal menulis berita tambahan.**
> ADI: *You just have to write some extra news.*

> DANNY: **Nanti Adi yang perbaiki.**
> DANNY: *Then you can improve it.*

However, when using the first person (to refer to themselves), they use **saya** or **aku**, not their own name.

### Exercise 1

Add **bahwa** to create a complex sentence.

1. **Danny tahu Yosef merayakan Natal.**
   *Danny knows Yosef celebrates Christmas.*

2. **Kartu tersebut akan beritahu Yosef, Danny akan pulang.**
   *The card will tell Yosef that Danny is going home.*

3. **Adi tahu Yosef tinggal di Papua.**
   *Adi knows Yosef lives in Papua.*

4. **Dia kirim berita, dia mau pindah.**
   *He sends news that he will move.*

## 12.2  Percakapan telepon  A telephone conversation

### Listening to a dialogue

Danny is planning to send a greeting card to his friend Yosef who lives in Papua, but he does not know the address, so he calls Yosef to find out where to send the card. Listen to their conversation.

DANNY: **Halo, Yosef! Apa kabar?** *Hello, Yosef! How are you?*

YOSEF: **Hai, Danny. Saya baik-baik saja.** *Hi, Danny. I'm just fine.*

DANNY: **Saya telepon kamu dari pagi, tapi kamu susah dihubungi, ya!**
*I have been ringing you all morning, but you are hard to contact!*

YOSEF: **Maaf, Danny. Mungkin saya sedang mengikuti misa di gereja. Jadi, saya tidak bisa terima telepon dari kamu. Ada yang bisa saya bantu?**
*Sorry, Danny. Perhaps I was at mass, at church. So I couldn't take your call. What can I do for you?*

DANNY: **Oh begitu. Saya mau kirim kamu kartu ucapan Selamat Natal. Tapi, saya tidak tahu alamat rumahmu. Boleh saya minta alamatnya?**
*Oh, really? I want to send you a Christmas card. But I don't know your address. May I ask for your address?*

YOSEF: **Aduh... Terima kasih. Kamu baik sekali. Ini alamatnya: Jalan Yos Sudarso No. 72, Sanggeng, Manokwari, Papua Barat 98312.**
*Oh ... thank you. You're very kind. Here is the address: Jalan Yos Sudarso No. 72, Sanggeng, Manokwari, West Papua 98312.*

DANNY: **Sip! Kamu tunggu kartunya, ya! Mungkin tiga hari lagi sampai.**
*Great! Watch out for the card, won't you? It might arrive in three days' time.*

YOSEF: **Terima kasih, teman! Saya tunggu, ya.** *Thanks, friend! I'll keep a lookout for it.*

## New Words and Phrases

**halo** *hello*
**dihubungi / menghubungi** *to be contacted / to contact (someone)*

**misa** *mass*
**terima, menerima** *to receive, accept*
**oh, begitu** *oh, is that so; oh really*

**alamat** *address*
**sip** *great, excellent*

### Exercise 2

Match up these expressions with their meanings.

1. **apa kabar**
2. **baik-baik saja**
3. **tidak bisa angkat telepon**
4. **oh begitu**
5. **alamat rumahmu**

a. *your address*
b. *I see*
c. *I'm fine*
d. *how are you*
e. *could not answer the phone*

## Indonesian and me

### Exercise 3

Role-play the conversation above with a partner using your own alternatives and information.

# 12.3 Yosef, gereja, dan Papua Yosef, the church and Papua

## Reading: Social Media

Yosef is a very religious, open-minded student from Papua. He has lots of friends from different walks of life. Look at what he wrote in his profile about himself on social media (**média sosial** or **médsos**).

Nama Lengkap:  Yosef Wempi Kaize
Nama Panggilan: Yosef
Umur:  17 tahun
Alamat:  Jalan Yos Sudarso No 72, Sanggeng
Manokwari, Papua Barat

| | |
|---|---|
| Sekolah: | SMA 1 Manokwari |
| Kegiatan: | • Ketua Remaja Gereja se-Manokwari (REGEMA) |
| | • Ketua Sekolah Minggu Gereja Sanggeng |
| | • Pramuka SMA 1 Manokwari |
| | • Anggota organisasi Persahabatan Antar Agama |
| Cita-cita: | Menjadi seorang pastor yang bijaksana untuk semua umat. |

## New Words and Phrases

**lengkap** *detailed, complete, full*
**nama panggilan** *nickname*
**ketua** *chair(person)*
**sekolah Minggu** *Sunday school*

**anggota** *member*
**persahabatan** *friendship*
**antar** *among*
**pastor** *(Catholic) priest*

**umat** *congregation; religious group*

## Exercise 4: Reading comprehension

Decide whether the following sentences are **Benar** (true) or **Salah** (false).

| | B (✓) | S (✗) |
|---|---|---|
| 1. Yosef lives in Jakarta. | _____ | _____ |
| 2. Yosef is very interested in religious activities. | _____ | _____ |
| 3. Yosef wants to be a minister. | _____ | _____ |
| 4. Yosef is not Muslim. | _____ | _____ |

## Cultural note: Nicknames

Nicknames are an important feature of Indonesian culture. All Indonesians are born with a formal name (**nama lengkap**). Some people have just one name, while others have long, often complicated names reflecting their ethnic or religious backgrounds, or specifically referencing when they were born, and to whom. Many Muslim names start with Muhammad or Siti, while F.X. (Francis Xavier) is common among Catholic males. However, nearly every Indonesian also has a shortened version of their name which people use to refer to them in daily life. The closest English equivalent would be a nickname.

Let's look at Adi as an example. His full name is Suriadi Wulandaru. He does not have a family name. Surnames are relatively new in Indonesia, although some ethnic groups use them (such as the **marga** or "clan" used in Batak culture). Adi is just his nickname, based upon the last two syllables of Suriadi. Note that unlike English nicknames, which tend to use the first part of the name (e.g., Danny for Daniel, or Chris for Christine), Indonesian nicknames tend to use the end of their formal name. Examples might include Li for Ramli, Yu for Ayu, or Man for Nyoman.

Another interesting feature of many Indonesian names is how they often refer to the month when the person was born. Here are some examples:

| Januar | Febriyanti | Aprilia | Meiny |
|---|---|---|---|
| Juniarso | Julianto | Agus | Agustina |
| Septian | Oktaviani | Novi | Desi |

If you meet someone called Febri, Juli or Novi as their everyday name, their formal name probably relates to the month when they were born.

How might you shorten your own name according to the Indonesian style, using the last or last two syllables (or the month of your birth) as a nickname?

# 12.4  **Kartu Tanda Penduduk**  Citizen identity card

## ▌ Reading

Names are an important part of Indonesian culture, as is true all over the world. For example, your name is very important as part of your official identity. For Indonesians over the age of 17, this will be your KTP (**Kartu Tanda Penduduk**), or citizen identity card. Below is a government notice explaining why Indonesians need to make one, and encouraging them to do so.

**Setiap orang Indonesia yang sudah berumur 17 tahun ke atas diwajibkan untuk mempunyai sebuah KTP (Kartu Tanda Penduduk) sebagai kartu identitas yang ada informasi tentang nama, alamat, agama, jenis kelamin, pekerjaan, dan informasi lain yang penting.**

*All Indonesians aged 17 and above are required to have an identity card (KTP) containing information about their name, address, religion, gender, work and other important information.*

**KTP sangat berguna untuk hal-hal berikut ini:**
1. **Identitas diri**
2. **Syarat utama untuk mendapatkan dokumen penting lainnya, seperti untuk mendapatkan kartu asuransi, SIM, dan lain-lain.**
3. **Jaminan untuk mendapatkan fasilitas lainnya seperti meminjam uang, atau mendapatkan kartu kredit.**
4. **Bukti identitas apabila terjadi kecelakaan**

*The identity card is very useful for the following:*
1. *One's own identity*
2. *The main requirement to obtain other important documents, such as insurance cards, driving licenses, and so on.*
3. *A guarantee to obtain other facilities such as borrowing money, or obtaining a credit card.*
4. *A source of identity in an accident.*

**Berikut adalah KTPnya Yosef:**
*Yosef's identity card is as follows:*

---

**PROVINSI PAPUA  BARAT**
**KOTA MANOKWARI**

N.I.K :   1234562803020001

| | |
|---|---|
| Nama | : Yosef Wempi Kaize |
| Tempat/Tgl Lahir | : Manokwari, 28/03/2001 |
| Jenis Kelamin | : Laki-laki |
| Alamat | : Jln Yos Sudarso No 72, Sanggeng, Manokwari, Papua Barat 98312 |
| RT/RW | : 01/01 |
| Kelurahan | : Sanggeng |
| Kecamatan | : Manokwari |
| Agama | : Katolik |
| Status Perkawinan | : Belum nikah |
| Pekerjaan | : Pelajar |
| Kewarganegaraan | : WNI |
| Berlaku Hingga | : 28/03/2023 |

## New Words and Phrases

**KTP (kartu tanda penduduk)** *identity card (lit., citizen identity card)*

**diwajibkan / mewajibkan** *to be obliged to or required; to make obligatory, required, compulsory*

**informasi** *information*

**jenis kelamin** *gender (lit., "sex type")*

**pekerjaan** *occupation, work*

**berguna** *useful*

**diri** *self, own*

**syarat** *condition, requirement*

**utama** *main*

**asuransi** *insurance*

**SIM (Surat Izin Mengemudi)** *driving license*

**jaminan** *guarantee*

**meminjam** *to borrow*

**krédit** *credit*

**kecelakaan** *accident*

**pemeluk** *believer*

**laki-laki** *male*

**kewarganegaraan** *nationality*

**WNI (Warga Negara Indonesia)** *Indonesian (citizen)*

**golongan darah** *blood type*

**tanda tangan** *signature*

### Exercise 5

Complete the following sentences by circling the correct word.

1. **Yosef orang laki-laki / perempuan.**
2. **Yosef adalah seorang pemeluk alamat / agama Katolik yang baik.**
3. **Danny ingin mengirim kartu Natal untuk Yosef, maka dia harus mempunyai agama / alamat Yosef dengan lengkap.**
4. **Yosef adalah orang Australia / Indonesia.**
5. **Yosef tinggal di Jawa / Papua.**

## Indonesian and me

### Exercise 6

Look at the blank KTP below. Imagine that it is yours. Fill it out using your own details.

PROVINSI _____

KOTA _____

N.I.K : 1234567891000001

| | |
|---|---|
| Nama | : |
| Tempat/Tgl Lahir | : |
| Jenis Kelamin | : |
| Alamat | : |
|     RT/RW | : |
|     Kelurahan | : |
|     Kecematan | : |
|     Agama | : |
| Status Perkawinan | : |
| Pekerjaan | : |
| Kewarganegaraan | : |
| Berlaku Hingga | : |

# 12.5 Natal di Indonesia bagian Timur
## Christmas in eastern Indonesia

Much of eastern Indonesia has been influenced by Christianity rather than Islam, the dominant religion in the west of the archipelago. In Flores, bamboo cannons explode throughout towns on Christmas Eve. Young people stay up all night on 24 December, setting off fireworks. In Ambon, the sounding of dozens of ships' horns and church bells signal the arrival of midnight. It is also a time for families to gather.

Another unique tradition is found in Papua, where traditional parties called **barapen** or hot stones (**bakar batu**) are used in a local culinary ritual to cook pork as a sign of Christmas joy. In addition, there are decorations showing the birth of Jesus, and you can hear Christmas carols around the clock.

## ▌ Basic Sentences

Below are a series of images showing Yosef's activities approaching and at Christmas.

1. **Yosef terima kartu Natal dari Danny. Dia sangat senang dengan kiriman tersebut.**
*Yosef receives a Christmas card from Danny. He is very happy to receive it.*

2. **Kartu Natal disimpan Yosef di dekat pohon Natal yang dihiasi dengan lampu berwarna-warni.**
*The Christmas card is placed by Yosef near the Christmas tree, decorated with colored lights.*

3. **Satu hari sebelum Natal, Yosef bersama teman-temannya mengikuti tradisi pesta barapen.**
*One day before Christmas, Yosef and his friends follow the tradition of having a **barapen** party.*

4. **Pesta Barapen adalah tradisi bakar batu untuk memasak daging babi sebagai ungkapan syukur.**
*A **barapen** party is a tradition where hot stones are used to cook pork as an expression of gratitude.*

5. **Daging babi tersebut akan dibagikan kepada semua masyarakat yang ada di daerah di mana pesta berlangsung.**

   *The pork will be divided up amongst the local community where the party is being held.*

6. **Sambil mendengarkan lagu-lagu Natal, Yosef berkumpul dengan semua anggota keluarga merayakan Natal.**

   *While listening to carols, Yosef and all his family members gather to celebrate Christmas.*

## ▌New Words and Phrases

| | | |
|---|---|---|
| **kiriman** *package, something sent* | **tradisi** *tradition* | **syukur** *gratitude* |
| **pohon** *tree* | **pésta** *party* | **berlangsung** *to happen, take place* |
| **dihiasi / menghiasi** *decorated with; to decorate something* | **bakar batu** *hot stones (method of cooking)* | **mendengarkan** *to listen to* |
| **berwarna-warni** *colorful* | **daging babi** *pork* | **lagu** *song* |
| | **ungkapan** *expression* | |

## Exercise 7

Fill in the missing words. All information is from the above text.

1. **Di rumah Yosef ada _____ Natal dan hiasan lainnya.**

   *At Yosef's house there is a Christmas _____ and other decorations.*

2. **Daging yang dibakar di atas batu dalam tradisi barapen adalah daging _____.**

   *The meat baked on top of stones in the **barapen** tradition is _____.*

3. **_____ dari barapen akan dimakan oleh masyarakat di dekat situ.**

   *The _____ from the **barapen** will be eaten by the local people nearby.*

4. **Yosef akan merayakan _____ bersama orang tua dan kakak adik.**

   *Yosef will celebrate _____ with his parents and siblings.*

# 12.6 Malam Kudus Silent Night

## Listening: Song

Find a recording of **Malam Kudus** on YouTube. Listen carefully to the Indonesian version of "Silent Night" while you read the lyrics below.

### *Malam Kudus* (Silent Night)

| | |
|---|---|
| **Malam kudus, sunyi senyap** | *Holy night, all is silent* |
| **BintangMu gemerlap** | *Your star shines bright* |
| **Juru selamat manusia** | *The savior of humanity* |
| **Ada datang di dunia** | *Has come to earth* |
| **Kristus Anak Daud,** | *Christ, the son of David,* |
| **Kristus Anak Daud.** | *Christ, the son of David,* |
| | |
| **Anak kecil, anak kudus,** | *Small child, holy child* |
| **Tuhanku Penebus** | *My God is the redeemer* |
| **Tentara surga menyanyi merdu** | *The soldiers of heaven sweetly sing* |
| **Bawa kabar kedatanganMu** | *bringing the news of Your arrival.* |
| **Kristus Anak Daud,** | *Christ, the son of David,* |
| **Kristus Anak Daud.** | *Christ, the son of David,* |
| | |
| **Malam kudus, sunyi senyap** | *Holy night, all is silent* |
| **BintangMu gemerlap** | *Your star shines bright* |
| **Aku datang ya Tuhanku,** | *I am coming, O my Lord* |
| **Bersembahyang di kandangMu** | *To pray in Your stable* |
| **Dan mengucap syukur.** | *And express gratitude* |
| **Dan mengucap syukur.** | *And express gratitude.* |

## New Words and Phrases

| | | |
|---|---|---|
| **kudus** *holy* | **manusia** *human, humanity* | **surga** *heaven, paradise* |
| **sunyi senyap** *completely silent* | **Kristus** *Christ* | **kandang** *stall, stable* |
| **bintang** *star* | **Daud** *David* | **merdu** *sweetly* |
| **gemerlap** *glittering* | **Tuhan** *Lord, God* | **mengucap** *to express* |
| **juru selamat** *savior* | **penebus** *redeemer* | |

## Language notes

As you can see, when translated literally into English, the Indonesian version has quite a different meaning from the well-known English version. This is because any form of literature, particularly poems or songs, are very difficult to translate word for word into another language. There are considerations of rhyme, number of syllables, concepts and much more.

The suffix -**Mu** (Your) is used as it is referring to God. The capital letter is used for respect, as in English.

## Exercise 8

1. Compare the version of "Silent Night" that you know, and the Indonesian one (use the translation if necessary). How are they different? Why do you think this is the case?

2. How would you translate the following Indonesian words/concepts into English? Give a reason for your answers.

   a. **pesta barapen**
   b. **nama panggilan**
   c. **Sumpah Pemuda**

## Course review

The time has come for Danny to pack his suitcases and say goodbye to Adi and his family. His year as an exchange student in Indonesia has come to an end, and he must return home.

As a final task for Pak Yusep back in Australia, Danny will write a review of his year in Indonesia, recalling everything that has happened throughout the year.

Pretend that you are Danny. In your notebooks, write a summary of the twelve months, using the information from the twelve units in sequence. The first month is done for you as an example.

> **Januari**
> **Rasanya belum lama sejak saya tiba di Jakarta naik penerbangan GA 700 dari Perth. Keluarga Adi begitu baik dan ramah menyambut saya! Waktu itu, saya belum begitu kenal mereka. Sekarang mereka sudah menjadi seperti saudara sendiri!**
>
> **Saya masih terkesan dengan perayaan Imlek. Tidak hanya Adi yang dapat hong pau dari ayahnya, tapi saya juga! Saya tidak pakai uangnya untuk belanja. Masih disimpan oleh saya, sebagai oleh-oleh yang istimewa.**

## Unit 12 End-of-unit vocabulary list

**alamat** *address*
**anggota** *member*
**angkat, mengangkat** *to pick up; to lift*
**antar-** *between, inter-*
**asuransi** *insurance*
**babi** *pig; pork*
**bahkan** *even*
**bakar, membakar** *to roast, grill, bake*
**bakar batu** *hot stones (method of cooking)*
**berguna** *useful*
**berita** *news*
**beritahu, memberitahu** *to inform, let know*
**berlangsung** *to happen, take place*
**berwarna-warni** *colorful*

**bintang** *star*
**bukti** *proof, evidence*
**darah** *blood*
**Daud** *David*
**diri** *self, own*
**gemerlap** *glittering*
**golongan** *group*
**halo** *hello*
**informasi** *information*
**ingat** *remember*
**iya** *yes (with emphasis)*
**jaminan** *guarantee*
**jenis** *type*
**juru selamat** *savior*
**kandang** *stall, stable*
**kecelakaan** *accident*
**kelamin** *sex*
**ketua** *chair(person)*

**kewarganegaraan** *nationality*
**kirim, mengirim** *to send*
**kiriman** *package, something sent*
**kredit** *credit*
**Kristus** *Christ*
**KTP** *identity card*
**kudus** *holy*
**lagu** *song*
**laki-laki** *male*
**lengkap** *detailed, complete*
**manusia** *human, humanity*
**média sosial, médsos** *social media*
**membakar** *to roast, grill, bake*
**memberitahu** *to inform, let know*
**meminjam** *to borrow*
**memperbaiki** *to fix, improve, correct*

**mendengarkan** *to listen to, hear*
**menerima** *to receive, accept*
**mengangkat** *to pick up; to lift*
**menghiasi** *to decorate something*
**menghubungi** *to contact someone*
**mengucap** *to express*
**menyimpan** *to put (aside), place*
**merdu** *sweet, sweetly*
**mewajibkan** *to make obligatory, compulsory*
**misa** *Mass*
**Natal** *Christmas*
**panggilan** *call*
**pastor** *(Catholic) priest*
**pekerjaan** *profession, work*

**pemeluk** *believer*
**penebus** *redeemer*
**persahabatan** *friendship*
**pésta** *party*
**pinjam, meminjam** *to borrow*
**pohon** *tree*
**sebentar** *in a moment*
**SIM (Surat Izin Mengemudi)** *driving license*
**sip** *great, excellent*
**sunyi senyap** *completely silent*
**surga** *heaven, paradise*
**syarat** *condition*
**syukur** *gratitude*
**tambahan** *extra, additional*

**tanda** *sign*
**tanda tangan** *signature*
**terima, menerima** *to receive, accept*
**tradisi** *tradition*
**Tuhan** *Lord, God*
**ucapan** *greeting*
**umat** *congregation; religious community*
**ungkapan** *expression*
**utama** *main*
**WNI (Warga Negara Indonesia)** *Indonesian*

**How to Download the Audio Recordings and Answer Key for this Book.**

1. Check your Internet connection.
2. Type the URL below into your web browser.

https://www.tuttlepublishing.com/Indonesian-for-Beginners

For support email us at info@tuttlepublishing.com

# Indonesian-English Glossary

## [A]

**acara** *program, event*
**ada** *(there) is/are; have, has*
**adalah** *is/are*
**adat** *tradition*
**aduh** *oh*
**adzan** *the call to prayer*
**agama** *religion*
**agar** *in order to, so*
**Agustus** *August*
**akad nikah** *Islamic marriage ceremony*
**akan** *will*
**akhir** *end, finish*
**akhirnya** *finally, in the end*
**aktif** *active*
**aku** *I, me (familiar)*
**Al-Quran** *the Koran*
**alamat** *address*
**Allah** *God*
**alun-alun** *town square*
**anak-anak** *children*
**anda** *you (singular, neutral)*
**anggota** *member*
**angkringan** *traditional Jogja roadside eatery*
**angkat, mengangkat** *to pick up; to lift*
**angkét** *survey*
**angkot (angkutan kota)** *public minibus*
**anjing** *dog*
**antar-** *between, inter-*
**antar, mengantar** *to deliver*
**apa kabar?** *how are you?*
**apa** *what*
**apabila** *if, when (future)*
**apakah, apa** *whether, if; makes a question*
**apalagi** *especially*
**api** *fire, flame*
**April** *April*
**arsiték** *architect*
**arsitéktur** *architecture*
**arti** *meaning*
**asal** *origin*
**asli** *original*
**assalamu'alaikum** *peace be upon you (Muslim greeting)*

**asyik** *fun*
**atas** *above, over*
**atau** *or*
**ayah** *father*
**ayam** *chicken, rooster*
**ayam pop** *skinless chicken*
**ayo** *come on, let's*

## [B]

**babi** *pig; pork*
**badan** *body*
**bagaimana** *how*
**bagi** *for, to (usually a person)*
**bagian** *part, share*
**bagus** *good*
**bahan** *ingredient, material*
**bahasa** *language*
**bahkan** *even*
**bahwa** *that*
**baik ... maupun ...** *both ... and ...*
**baik** *well, good; kind*
**baik-baik saja** *just fine*
**baju** *clothes; top*
**bakar batu** *hot stones (method of cooking)*
**bakar, membakar** *to roast, grill, bake*
**balai** *hall*
**bangga** *proud*
**bangsa** *people, nation*
**bangun** *wake up, get up*
**bantu, membantu** *to help*
**banyak** *many*
**barat** *west*
**baru** *just now; new, newly*
**batik** *traditional Indonesian wax-dyed cloth*
**bawah** *below, beneath*
**bayam** *spinach*
**bayar, membayar** *to pay*
**beberapa** *several*
**begini** *like this*
**begitu** *like that*
**bekerja** *to work*
**béla, membéla** *to defend*
**belajar** *to study, learn*
**belakang** *back, behind*

**Belanda** *Dutch, the Netherlands*
**belanja** *to shop, go shopping*
**belas** *-teen*
**belasan** *dozens; teens*
**bélok** *to turn*
**belum** *not yet*
**benar** *correct; true*
**bendéra** *flag*
**bepergian** *to go out (many people/places)*
**beragama** *religious, to have a religion*
**beraktifitas** *to do an activity, be busy*
**berambut** *to have hair*
**berangkat** *to depart, leave*
**berani** *brave*
**berapa** *how many*
**berarti** *to mean*
**berasal** *to come from*
**berbadan** *-bodied*
**berbagai** *various*
**berbahasa** *to speak a language*
**berbakat** *talented*
**berbangsa** *to have a nationality or nation*
**berbaris** *to stand, line up*
**berbéda** *different*
**berbéda-béda** *different (of many things)*
**bercanda** *to joke around*
**berdiri** *to stand*
**berdoa** *to pray*
**bergaul** *to mix with others, socialize*
**berguna** *useful*
**berharap** *to hope*
**berhasil** *to succeed*
**berikut** *following, to follow*
**beristirahat** *to rest*
**berita** *news*
**beritahu, memberitahu** *to inform, let know*
**berjuang** *to struggle*
**berjudul** *entitled, titled*
**berkawan** *to have a friend*

**berkémah** *to camp, go camping*
**berkembang** *to develop, blossom*
**berkibar** *to fly, flutter*
**berkulit** *-skinned*
**berkunjung** *to (pay a) visit*
**berkurban** *to make a sacrifice (of an animal)*
**berlangsung** *to happen, take place*
**bermain** *to play*
**bernama** *to be named*
**bernyanyi** *to sing*
**berobat** *to seek medical advice*
**berolahraga** *to do sport*
**berombak** *wavy*
**berpidato** *to give a speech*
**berpuasa** *to fast*
**bersalaman** *to shake hands with each other*
**bersama** *together*
**bersantai** *to relax*
**bersatu** *to unite*
**bersaudara** *to have siblings*
**bersemangat** *enthusiastic*
**bersembahyang** *to perform prayers*
**bersembahyang** *to pray*
**bersenang-senang** *to have fun*
**berseru** *to shout out*
**bersiap-siap** *to get ready*
**bersifat** *to have a nature or characteristic*
**bersih** *clean*
**berteman** *to have a friend*
**bertempat** *to take place*
**bertindak** *to take action*
**bertumpah** *to spill*
**berubah** *to change*
**berumur** *aged*
**berwarna** *colored*
**berwarna-warni** *colorful*
**berziarah** *to visit a grave*
**besar** *big, large*
**bésok** *tomorrow, the next day*
**betah** *feel at home*

**betapa** *how, to what extent*
**biasa** *usual, ordinary*
**biasanya** *usually*
**bidang** *field, area*
**bijaksana** *wise*
**biji** *seed*
**bila** *if, when (future)*
**bilang** *to say (informal)*
**bingung** *confused*
**bintang** *star*
**bioskop** *cinema*
**biru** *blue*
**bis** *bus*
**bisa** *can, be able to*
**bola basket** *basketball*
**bola voli** *volleyball*
**boléh** *may, permitted, allowed*
**botak** *bald*
**Bu, Ibu** *Mum, mother, you (to mother or older woman)*
**buah** *fruit; object (counter)*
**bubur** *porridge*
**bubur sumsum** *porridge made from fine rice flour*
**budaya** *culture*
**buka, membuka** *open*
**buka puasa** *break the fast*
**bukan** *no, not (noun)*
**bukti** *proof, evidence*
**buku** *book*
**bulan** *month*
**bulu tangkis** *badminton*
**bumbu** *sauce, spice*
**Bung** *(elder) Brother*
**bunga** *flower*
**bungsu** *youngest (in family)*
**burung** *bird*
**butir** *counter for eggs*

**[C]**
**candi** *(Buddhist/Hindu) temple*
**cantik** *beautiful*
**cara** *way; method*
**celana** *pants, trousers*
**cendol** *green, white and red drink*
**céngéng** *complaining*
**cepat** *fast, quick*
**cerah** *sunny*
**cerita** *story*
**cinta** *(romantic) love*
**cita-cita** *dreams, ambition*

**coba** *try*
**cokelat** *brown*
**cuaca** *weather*
**cukup** *quite, enough; satisfactory*
**curiga** *suspicious*

**[D]**
**daérah** *region, area*
**dagang** *trade*
**daging** *meat*
**dahsyat** *powerful*
**dalam** *in, inside*
**dalam negeri** *local, domestic*
**damai** *peaceful*
**dan** *and*
**dan lain-lain (dll)** *etc., et cetera*
**danau** *lake*
**dapat, bisa** *can; be able*
**darah** *blood*
**dari** *from*
**dari, daripada** *than*
**datang** *come*
**Daud** *David*
**daun singkong** *cassava leaves*
**dekat** *close, near*
**delapan** *eight*
**démokratis** *democratic*
**dengan** *with, by*
**depan** *front*
**désa** *village*
**Désémber** *December*
**di** *at, in*
**di luar** *out, outside*
**di mana** *where*
**di samping itu** *aside from that*
**dia** *he, she, it*
**dibandingkan** *compared with*
**dingin** *cold*
**diréktur** *director*
**diri** *self, own*
**diskon** *discount*
**ditunggu-tunggu** *long-awaited*
**dokter** *doctor*
**domba** *sheep*
**dua** *two*
**duduk** *sit*
**dulu** *before*
**dunia** *world*

**[E]**
**ékonom** *economist*
**ékonomi** *economics*
**ékor** *tail; counter for animals*
**empat** *four*
**énak** *nice, pleasant*
**enam** *six*
**engkau, kau** *you (familiar)*
**és** *ice*
**étnik** *ethnic*

**[F]**
**fasilitas** *facilities*
**Fébruari** *February*
**féri** *ferry*
**formulir** *form (to be completed)*
**foto** *photo*
**fotografi** *photography*
**futsal** *indoor soccer*

**[G]**
**gado-gado** *Indonesian salad with peanut sauce*
**gamelan** *traditional Javanese orchestra*
**ganjil** *odd*
**ganteng** *handsome*
**gelap** *dark*
**gelar** *title*
**gembira** *happy, excited*
**gemerlap** *glittering*
**gemuk** *fat*
**genap** *even*
**gerakan** *movement*
**geréja** *church*
**gol** *goal (score)*
**golongan** *group*
**goréng** *fried*
**gratis** *free (of charge)*
**gudeg** *cooked jackfruit*
**gula** *sugar*
**gula mérah** *brown sugar*
**gunung** *mountain, mount*
**guru** *teacher*

**[H]**
**habis** *finished*
**hadiah** *gift, prize*
**haji** *a man who has performed the pilgrimage to Mecca*
**hal** *matter, thing*
**halo** *hello*

**hampir** *almost, nearly*
**hanya** *only, just*
**harapan** *hope*
**harga** *price*
**hari** *day*
**hari ini** *today*
**hari raya** *festival, holiday*
**harum** *fragrant, smells good*
**harus** *must*
**hasil** *result*
**hébat** *great, wonderful*
**hiasan** *decoration*
**hidung** *nose*
**hidup** *to live*
**hijau** *green*
**Hindia Belanda** *Dutch East Indies*
**hitam** *black*
**hobi** *hobby*
**horé** *hooray, hurrah*
**hormat** *respect*
**hotel** *hotel*
**HP** *('handphone') mobile (phone), cellphone*
**hujan** *rain*
**HUT (hari ulang tahun)** *anniversary; birthday*

**[I]**
**ibu** *mother; woman*
**ibu rumah tangga** *housewife*
**ibukota** *capital city*
**ide** *idea*
**Idul Adha** *the Feast of the Sacrifice, held during the haj season*
**Idul Fitri** *Eid-ul-Fitr, end-of-fasting celebration*
**ikal** *wavy*
**ikan** *fish*
**ikat** *tie*
**ikut** *to join (in), follow*
**Imlék** *Chinese New Year*
**indah** *beautiful (of an object, scene)*
**informasi** *information*
**ingat** *remember*
**Inggris** *England, English*
**ingin** *to wish*
**ini** *this*
**insinyur** *engineer*
**inspiratif** *inspirational*

**institut téknologi** *institute of technology*
**Insya Allah** *God willing (from the Arabic)*
**IPA (Ilmu Pengetahuan Alam)** *Natural Sciences*
**IPS (Ilmu Pengetahuan Sosial)** *Social Sciences*
**isi, mengisi** *to fill*
**isteri** *wife*
**istiméwa** *special*
**istirahat** *rest*
**itu** *that*
**iya** *yes (with emphasis)*
**izin** *permission*

**[J]**
**jadi** *become*
**jaga, menjaga** *to take care of*
**jajahan** *colony*
**jakét** *jacket*
**jalan raya** *main road, highway*
**jalan** *street*
**jalan-jalan** *to go out*
**jam** *hour, o'clock*
**jaman** *era, time*
**jaminan** *guarantee*
**Januari** *January*
**jas** *jacket, coat*
**jasa** *service*
**jatuh** *fall; falls*
**jauh** *far*
**Jawa** *Java, Javanese*
**jaya** *victorious*
**jemput, menjemput** *to pick up, collect*
**jenis** *type*
**Jepang** *Japan, Japanese*
**jingga** *orange*
**jiwa** *soul*
**juara** *winner, champion*
**juga** *also, too*
**jujur** *honest*
**Juli** *July*
**Jumat** *Friday*
**jumlah** *number, total*
**Juni** *June*
**juru masak** *chef, cook*
**juru selamat** *savior*
**jus** *juice*
**juta** *million*

**[K]**
**kabar** *news*
**kacang** *bean, nut, legume*
**kacang panjang** *string beans*
**kadang-kadang** *sometimes*
**kain** *women's sarong*
**kain kebaya** *women's traditional dress, consisting of blouse and sarong*
**kakak** *older sibling*
**kakék** *grandfather*
**kaki** *foot, leg*
**kalah** *lose*
**kalau** *if; when (in future)*
**kali** *time*
**kalian** *you (plural)*
**kamar** *room*
**kambing** *goat*
**kami** *us (exclusive)*
**Kamis** *Thursday*
**kampung** *(urban) village*
**kamu** *you (singular, familiar)*
**kanan** *right*
**kandang** *stall, stable*
**kantor** *office*
**kapan** *when?*
**karena** *because*
**kartu** *card*
**karyawan, karyawati** *employee (m/f)*
**kasih** *love*
**kata** *word*
**katanya** *says, said*
**kau, engkau** *you (familiar)*
**kaum** *tribe, community*
**kaus** *(loose) top (clothing); covering*
**kaus kaki** *sock, socks*
**kawan** *friend*
**ke** *to (a place)*
**keadaan** *condition, situation*
**keagamaan** *religious*
**kebangsaan** *nationality*
**kebaya** *traditional blouse*
**kebun binatang** *zoo*
**kecelakaan** *accident*
**kecéwa** *disappointed*
**kecil** *small, little*
**kedinginan** *to feel cold*
**kedokteran** *medical, medicine*
**kedua** *both; second*
**kegiatan** *activity*

**kehidupan** *life*
**kejadian** *incident, happening*
**kelamin** *sex*
**kelas** *class*
**kelautan** *maritime*
**kelénténg** *Chinese temple*
**keliling** *around*
**kelinci** *rabbit*
**kelompok** *group*
**keluar** *to go out, exit*
**keluarga** *family*
**keluarga besar** *extended family*
**keluhan** *complaint*
**kelurahan** *sub-district*
**kemarau** *dry (season)*
**kemarin** *yesterday*
**kembali** *return, again, back*
**kembang api** *fireworks*
**kembar** *twin(s)*
**keméja** *shirt (with collar)*
**kemerdékaan** *independence*
**kemudian** *then*
**kentang** *potato*
**kepada** *to, for (a person)*
**kepala** *head*
**kepanduan** *old name for Scouts*
**kepulauan** *archipelago*
**kerajaan** *kingdom*
**keras kepala** *stubborn*
**keraton** *Javanese palace*
**kerbau** *buffalo*
**keréta api, KA** *train*
**keriting** *curly, curled*
**kesebelasan** *team*
**ketika** *when (in past)*
**ketua** *chair(person)*
**keturunan** *descent*
**keuangan** *finance, financial*
**kewarganegaraan** *nationality*
**kewartawanan** *journalism*
**khas** *special, typical*
**khusus** *special*
**kini, sekarang** *now, present*
**kiri** *left*
**kirim, mengirim** *to send*
**kiriman** *package, something sent*
**kita** *we (inclusive)*
**kol** *cabbage*
**kolak** *sweet traditional snack*

**kongrés** *congress*
**Koréa** *Korea*
**kota** *city, town*
**kotor** *dirty*
**kraton** *Javanese palace*
**kréatif** *creative*
**kredit** *credit*
**Kristus** *Christ*
**KTP** *identity card*
**kuburan** *grave; graveyard*
**kuda** *horse*
**kudus** *holy*
**kuil** *(Indian Hindu) temple*
**kuliah** *(university) lecture; to go to university, take lectures*
**kulit** *skin*
**kuning** *yellow*
**kuping** *ear, ears*
**kurang** *less, -er, fewer; to (the hour); unsatisfactory*
**kurban** *sacrifice (animal)*
**kurma** *date (fruit)*
**kurus** *thin*

**[L]**
**-lah** *(polite ending)*
**lagi** *again, more*
**lagu** *song*
**lahir** *born*
**lain** *other*
**laki-laki** *male*
**lalu** *then*
**lama** *long, far*
**lampu** *light*
**langsung** *direct(ly), straight*
**lapangan** *open space, field*
**lapar** *hungry*
**laporan** *report*
**laut** *sea*
**lawan** *opponent*
**layangan** *kite*
**Lebaran** *Idul Fitri*
**lebih** *more*
**lengkap** *detailed, complete*
**léwat** *past; via*
**liburan** *holiday*
**licin** *slippery*
**lihat, melihat** *to see*
**lihat-lihat** *have a look*
**lima** *five*
**lomba** *race, contest*
**lontong** *rice cake*
**luar** *outside*

**luar negeri** *international*
**lucu** *funny, cute*
**lukis** *painting, drawing*
**lurus** *straight*

**[M]**
**maaf** *sorry*
**macan** *tiger*
**mading (majalah dinding)** *wall newspaper*
**mahal** *expensive*
**mahasiswa** *university student*
**main** *play*
**maju** *developed; move ahead*
**maka** *therefore, thus*
**makam** *grave*
**makan** *eat*
**makanan** *food*
**makanya** *that's why*
**malam** *evening, night*
**malas** *lazy*
**mana** *which; where*
**mana-mana** *everywhere*
**mancanegara** *international*
**manis** *sweet*
**manusia** *human, humanity*
**marah** *angry*
**Maret** *March*
**mari** *let's, come on*
**masa** *time, period*
**masih** *still*
**masing-masing** *each, every*
**masuk** *to go in, enter*
**masukan** *suggestion, feedback*
**masyarakat** *society, community*
**mata** *eye, eyes*
**matahari** *sun*
**matang** *cooked, ripe*
**matematika** *mathematics*
**mau** *want; will*
**maupun** *also (when listing a second element)*
**mbak** *term of address, lit., older sister*
**média sosial, médsos** *social media*
**Mei** *May*
**méja** *table*
**melaksanakan** *to hold, conduct*

**melakukan** *to do, carry out*
**melamar** *to apply, propose*
**melawan** *to oppose, fight back*
**Melayu** *Malay*
**meliburkan** *to give a holiday to someone*
**memaafkan** *to forgive*
**memakai** *to wear; to use*
**memakan** *to eat*
**memancing** *to fish, go fishing*
**memandu** *to guide*
**memanggil** *to call*
**memasak** *to cook*
**membagi** *to hand out, share, divide up*
**membahayakan** *dangerous, to put in danger*
**membakar** *to roast, grill, bake*
**membandingkan** *to compare*
**membangun** *to build, create*
**membantu** *to help*
**membayar** *to pay*
**membébaskan** *to free something*
**membeli** *to buy*
**membentuk** *to form, shape*
**memberi** *to give*
**memberikan** *to give (something)*
**memberitahu** *to inform, let know*
**membersihkan** *to clean*
**membesarkan** *to raise, bring up*
**membuang** *to throw away*
**membuat** *to make*
**mendirikan** *to establish, set up*
**memégang, pégang** *to hold*
**memelihara** *to maintain, look after*
**memenjara** *to jail, imprison*
**memesan** *to order*
**memilih** *to choose, elect*
**meminjam** *to borrow*
**meminta, minta** *to ask, request*
**memperbaiki** *to fix, improve, correct*
**memperhatikan** *to watch closely, take notice of*

**memperingati** *to commemorate*
**mempersatukan, menyatukan** *to unite*
**memproklamasikan** *to proclaim*
**mempunyai** *to have, own, possess*
**memukuli** *to hit repeatedly, batter*
**menaburkan** *to sprinkle, strew*
**menaiki** *to climb*
**menaiki** *to travel by, climb onto*
**menaikkan** *to raise, put up*
**menambah** *to add*
**menang** *win*
**menanjat** *to climb*
**menarik** *attractive*
**mencapai** *to reach*
**mencari** *to look for, find*
**mencintai** *to love someone*
**mencoba, coba** *to try*
**mendaki** *to climb (a mountain, tree)*
**mendapat, mendapatkan** *to get, obtain*
**mendengarkan** *to listen to, hear*
**mendirikan** *to establish, found, set up*
**mendung** *cloudy*
**menengah** *middle*
**menerima** *to receive, accept*
**menertibkan** *to regulate, control*
**meneruskan** *to continue something*
**mengadakan** *to hold, run*
**mengajak** *to invite, ask along*
**mengaji** *to recite from the Koran*
**mengakhiri** *to finish, end something*
**mengaku, mengakui** *to declare, claim*
**menganggap** *to consider*
**mengangkat** *to pick up; to lift*
**mengantar** *to sweep*
**mengapa** *why*
**mengatur** *to arrange*
**mengékspor** *to export*

**mengenal** *to know, recognize*
**menggunakan** *to use*
**menghabiskan** *to finish off, finish up*
**menghargai** *to evaluate, appreciate*
**menghias** *to decorate*
**menghiasi** *to decorate something*
**menghubungi** *to contact someone*
**mengibarkan** *to fly, flutter, wag something*
**mengikuti** *to follow, attend, go to*
**menginap** *to stay overnight*
**mengirim** *to send*
**mengisi** *to fill (in)*
**mengobrol** *to chat*
**mengolési** *to smear, grease, oil*
**mengubah** *to change something*
**menguburkan** *to bury*
**mengucap, mengucapkan** *to express*
**mengumumkan** *to announce, make public*
**mengunjungi** *to visit*
**menikah, nikah** *to marry*
**meninggal dunia** *to die*
**menit, saat** *minute*
**menjadi** *to become*
**menjaga** *to take care of*
**menjelang** *to approach, approaching*
**menjemput** *to pick up, collect*
**menjual** *to sell*
**menjunjung** *to hold in high esteem*
**menonton** *to watch (a film, TV)*
**menteri** *minister*
**menuang** *to pour (out)*
**menuju** *to head for, approach*
**menuju** *to move towards*
**menulis** *to write*
**menunggu** *to wait*
**menurunkan** *to lower, bring down*
**menurut** *according to*
**menyajikan** *to serve up*

**menyalakan** *to light, switch on*
**menyambut** *to welcome*
**menyampaikan** *to express, deliver*
**menyanyi** *to sing*
**menyarankan** *to recommend*
**menyayangi** *to love (someone)*
**menyenangkan** *pleasant*
**menyiapkan** *to prepare, get ready*
**menyimpan** *to put (aside), place*
**menyusun** *to arrange, pile up*
**mérah** *red*
**merasa** *to feel*
**merata** *evenly*
**merayakan** *to celebrate*
**merdéka** *free, independent*
**merdu** *sweet, sweetly*
**meréka** *they, them, their*
**merobék** *to tear, rip*
**mesjid** *mosque*
**meskipun** *although*
**mewajibkan** *to make obligatory, compulsory*
**Minggu** *Sunday*
**minggu** *week*
**minta, meminta** *to ask, request*
**minuman** *drink*
**minyak** *oil*
**misa** *Mass*
**miskin** *poor*
**mobil** *car*
**modérn** *modern*
**mohon** *to request*
**monyét** *monkey*
**muda** *young*
**mudah** *easy*
**mudah-mudahan** *hopefully*
**mulai** *start, begin*
**mulia** *lofty; pure*
**mulut** *mouth*
**muncul** *appear*
**mungkin** *maybe, perhaps*
**murah** *cheap, inexpensive*
**murid** *pupil, student*
**mushola** *small prayer room*
**musim** *season*

**musim gugur** *fall, autumn*
**musim semi** *spring (season)*
**Muslim** *Muslim, Moslem*

## [N]

**naga** *dragon*
**naik kelas** *graduate or be promoted to the next grade*
**naik, menaiki** *to ride, travel on*
**nakal** *naughty*
**nama** *name*
**nanti** *later*
**nasi padang** *Padang-style food with rice*
**nasional** *national*
**Natal** *Christmas*
**negara** *country, state*
**negeri** *country, nation*
**nénék** *grandmother*
**ngabuburit** *kill time before breaking the fast*
**nikah, menikah** *to marry*
**nilai** *score, points*
**nomor** *number, no. (in a list)*
**nonton, menonton** *to watch (a film, TV)*
**Novémber** *November*
**nusa** *island, archipelago*
**Nusantara** *another name for Indonesia ("the islands between")*
**-nya** *possessive; the*
**nyalé** *sea-worm (Lombok)*
**nyanyi** *sing*

## [O]

**Oktober** *October*
**olahraga** *sport*
**oléh** *by*
**oléh-oléh** *souvenirs*
**ongkos** *fee, charge (for a service)*
**orang** *(counter for) person; person*
**organisasi** *(social) organization*

## [P]

**pacar** *boyfriend/girlfriend*
**pada** *on, at, in (time)*
**pagi** *morning*
**pagi-pagi** *early in the morning*

**pahlawan** *hero, heroine*
**Pak RW (Rukun Warga)** *local neighborhood head*
**pakai, memakai** *wear; use*
**pakaian** *clothing*
**pakét** *package, packet*
**paling** *most, -est*
**panas** *hot*
**pancaroba** *changeover (season)*
**pandai** *clever*
**pandu** *guide*
**pangéran** *prince*
**panggilan** *call*
**panitia** *committee*
**panjang** *long*
**panjat pinang** *greasy pole climb*
**pantai** *beach*
**para** *(more than one)*
**parah** *severe, grave*
**pariwisata** *tourism*
**pasar** *market*
**pasti** *must, definitely*
**pastor** *(Catholic) priest*
**payung** *umbrella*
**péci** *men's velvet cap*
**pedagang kaki lima** *street vendor (lit., "five foot seller")*
**pégang, memégang** *to hold*
**pegawai negeri** *civil servant*
**pekerjaan** *profession, work*
**pelajar** *student, learner*
**pelajaran** *lesson, subject*
**pelaksanaan** *event, when something is held*
**pelukis** *painter, artist*
**pemain** *player*
**pemandu** *guide*
**pemarah** *angry person; bad-tempered*
**pembantu** *maid, helper*
**pemeluk** *believer*
**pemerintah** *government*
**pemimpin** *leader*
**pemotongan** *slaughtering*
**pemuda** *youth*
**penasaran** *curious*
**péndék** *short*
**pendékar** *fighter*
**pendidikan** *education*
**penduduk** *inhabitant, resident*
**penebus** *redeemer*

**penerbangan** *flight*
**penerjemah** *translator, interpreter*
**pengacara** *lawyer*
**pengajar** *teacher*
**pengalaman** *experience*
**péngén** *really want to (informal)*
**penggemar** *fan, supporter*
**penghargaan** *award, appreciation*
**pengumuman** *announcement, notice*
**pengunjung** *visitor*
**pengusaha** *entrepreneur*
**peninggalan** *heritage*
**penjaga** *guard, night watchman*
**penjual** *seller, vendor*
**penonton** *viewer, audience, crowd*
**pénsil** *pencil*
**penting** *important*
**penuh** *full*
**penumpang** *passenger*
**penutupan** *closing*
**penyayang** *loving*
**perahu** *boat*
**peran** *role*
**perancang** *designer*
**perawat** *nurse*
**perayaan** *celebration*
**perempuan** *woman, female*
**pergi** *to go*
**peribahasa** *saying, proverb*
**perikanan** *fisheries*
**peringatan** *commemoration; warning*
**peringkat** *rank*
**perjuangan** *struggle*
**perlombaan** *competition*
**perlu** *need*
**pernah** *once, ever*
**persahabatan** *friendship*
**persatuan** *unity*
**perséntase** *percentage*
**pertama** *first*
**pertandingan** *match, competition*
**pertanyaan** *question*
**pertempuran** *battle*
**pertemuan** *meeting*
**perusahaan** *company, business*

pesan *message*

pesan, memesan *to order*

pesawat (terbang) *airplane, aircraft*

peserta *participant*

pésta *party*

peta *map*

petani *farmer*

petugas *officer*

pidato *speech*

pilih, memilih *to choose*

pindah *to move*

pinggir *side, edge*

pinjam, meminjam *to borrow*

pintar pandai *smart, clever*

pintu *door, gate*

pirang *blond(e)*

piring *plate, dish*

pisang *banana*

piyama *pajamas*

pohon pinang *areca palm*

pohon *tree*

polisi *police*

Porseni *Sports and Art Week*

pos *post*

potong *slice; to cut*

potong, memotong *to cut*

potongan *slice*

PPKn (Pendidikan Pancasila dan Kewarganegaraan) *Civics & Pancasila*

pramuka *Scouts*

Présidén *President*

préstasi *achievement*

pria *male*

proklamasi *proclamation*

provinsi *province*

puasa *to fast*

pukul *o'clock, :00*

pulang *go home*

pulang kampung *to go back to the village*

pulau *island*

puluh *multiple of ten*

puluhan *tens, dozens*

pun *also, even*

punya, mempunyai *have, own, possess*

pura *(Hindu) temple*

pusaka *heirloom, something of great value*

putih *white*

putra *son; child*

putri *daughter; princess*

**[R]**

Rabu *Wednesday*

rajin *diligent*

rakyat *people, public*

ramah *friendly*

ramai *noisy, eventful*

rambut *hair*

ranking *rank*

rapi *neat*

rapot *(school) report*

rasa *think, feel, taste*

rata-rata *average*

ratus *hundred*

raya *great, greater*

rebus *boil*

remaja *teenager, youth, young adult*

rendang *special Padang meat dish*

républik *republic*

resép *recipe; prescription*

resépsi *reception*

ribu *thousand*

romantis *romantic*

rombongan *group*

ruang *room*

ruangan *room, indoor space*

rumah *house*

**[S]**

saat *moment, time*

sabar *patient*

Sabtu *Saturday*

sahur *pre-dawn meal*

saja *just, only*

sajikan, menyajikan *to serve, present*

sakit *ill, sick*

salah *wrong; false*

salah seorang *one of (person)*

salam *greetings, regards*

saling *each other*

salju *snow*

sama *same*

sambil *while, -ing*

sampah *rubbish, trash*

sampai *until, to*

samping *side*

samudera *ocean*

sana *over there, yonder*

sandiwara *play*

sangat *very*

santan *coconut milk*

sapi *cow*

sarapan *breakfast*

sarjana *bachelor's degree*

sarung *sarong*

saté *satay*

satu *one*

saudara *relation, family (member)*

saya *I, me, my*

sayang *love, tender feeling*

sayuran *vegetables*

SD (Sekolah Dasar) *Primary School*

sebagai *as*

sebaiknya *it's best*

sebelah *beside, next to*

sebelas *eleven*

sebelum *before (time)*

sebelumnya *previous(ly)*

sebentar *in a moment*

sebuah *a, one (general counter)*

secara *in a ... way*

sedang *medium (of size, length)*

sedih *sad*

sedikit *a little*

segera *immediately, at once*

seharian *all day*

séhat *healthy*

seikat *a bunch*

sejak *since, from*

sejarah *history*

sejati *real, true*

sejuk *cool*

sekali *once*

sekali *very (after word)*

sekalian *all (at once)*

sekarang *now*

sekolah *school*

selada *lettuce; salad*

selain *apart from*

selalu *always*

selama *during, while*

selama ini *until now*

selama-lamanya *forever*

selamat *good, happy, safe; congratulations*

Selasa *Tuesday*

selat *strait*

selatan *south*

seléndang *shawl, sash*

selesai *finished, over*

seluruh *all, entire*

semakin *increasingly*

semangat *spirit*

sembako (sembilan bahan pokok) *(one of nine) staple foods*

sembilan *nine*

sementara *while, meanwhile*

seméster *term, semester*

semoga *may; hopefully*

semua *all*

senang *happy*

sendal *sandal*

sendal jepit *plastic sandals, thongs, flipflops*

sendiri *self, oneself*

senggang *free, spare*

seni *art*

Senin *Monday*

sénsitif *sensitive*

seorang *a (person)*

sépak bola *soccer, football*

sepatu *shoes*

sepatu selop *slip-on shoes*

sepéda *bicycle*

seperempat *quarter*

seperti *like*

sepertinya *it seems*

sepotong *a slice*

Séptémber *September*

sepuluh *ten*

seragam *uniform*

seratus *one hundred*

seri *draw*

sering *often*

serta *as well as*

seru *fun, exciting*

sesudah *after (time)*

setahun *a year*

setasiun *station*

setelah, sesudah *after*

setengah *half*

setia *faithful*

setiap *each, every*

seumur *the same age*

shio *Chinese zodiac*

sholat *one of the five daily prayers*

sholat tarawéh *voluntary evening prayers during Ramadhan*

**siang** *middle of the day*
**siap** *ready*
**siapa** *who*
**siapa saja** *whoever*
**SIM (Surat Izin Mengemudi)** *driving license*
**sini** *here*
**siomay** *a kind of dim sum*
**sip** *great, excellent*
**siswa** *(school) student, pupil*
**situ** *there*
**SMA (Sekolah Menengah Atas)** *Senior High School*
**SMP (Sekolah Menengah Pertama)** *Junior High School*
**soré** *(late) afternoon*
**sore hari ini** *this afternoon*
**soto** *clear meat soup*
**spanduk** *poster, banner*
**stadion** *stadium*
**suasana** *atmosphere*
**subuh** *pre-dawn prayer (Islamic)*
**sudah** *already*
**suka** *like; tend to*
**suka** *often, tend to (colloquial)*
**sukses** *success, successful*
**sulit** *difficult, hard*
**sulung** *eldest (in family)*
**sumbangan** *donation*
**Sumatera** *Sumatra*
**sumpah** *oath, pledge; swear*
**sungguh** *truly*
**sunyi senyap** *completely silent*
**supaya** *so that*
**supir** *driver, chauffeur*
**surat kabar** *newspaper*
**surga** *heaven, paradise*
**susah** *difficult, hard*
**susun, menyusun** *to arrange, pile up*
**syarat** *condition*
**syukur** *gratitude*
**syukuran** *thanksgiving ceremony*

**[T]**

**tadi** *just now, last ...*
**tahu** *tofu*
**tahun** *year*
**takut** *scared*
**taman** *garden, park*

**taman kanak-kanak (TK)** *kindergarten*
**taman** *park, garden*
**tamansari** *water gardens*
**tamat** *graduate*
**tambah, menambah** *to add*
**tambahan** *extra, additional*
**tampil** *appear*
**tamu** *guest*
**tanah air** *homeland (lit., earth and water)*
**tanda** *sign*
**tanda tangan** *signature*
**tangan** *hand, arm*
**tanggal** *date*
**tanya** *ask*
**taogé** *bean sprouts*
**tapi, tetapi** *but*
**tari** *(traditional) dance*
**tas** *bag*
**tata tertib** *rules*
**téh** *tea*
**télepon, menélepon** *to ring, telephone*
**telinga** *ear, ears*
**telur** *egg*
**teman, kawan** *friend*
**tempat** *place*
**tempat duduk** *seat*
**tempat pénsil** *pencil case*
**témpé** *tempeh (unprocessed soybean cake)*
**tengah** *central, middle*
**tentang** *about, concerning*
**tentara** *army, soldier*
**tepat** *correct*
**terang** *light; bright*
**terbang** *(to) fly*
**terbentuk** *formed, created, shaped*
**terbit** *rise; be published*
**tercinta** *beloved*
**terdekat** *nearest, closest*
**terdiri** *consisting*
**terganggu** *disturbed*
**tergantung** *hanging; to depend*
**terhormat** *respected*
**terima, menerima** *to receive, accept*
**terima kasih** *thank you*
**terjadi** *to happen, occur*
**terkenal** *famous*
**terlalu** *too (much, many)*

**terletak** *to be located, lie*
**termasuk** *including*
**terima** *get, accept*
**terpilih** *elected, chosen*
**tersayang** *dear, beloved*
**tersebut** *that (one), the (aforementioned)*
**tertarik** *interested*
**tertawa** *to laugh*
**tertawa-tawa** *to laugh a lot*
**tertulis** *written, inscribed*
**terus** *straight; then, so*
**terutama** *especially, particularly*
**tetapi, tapi** *but*
**tiang** *pole*
**tiba** *to arrive*
**tidak** *no; not (for adjectives)*
**tidur** *sleep*
**tiga** *three*
**tikét** *ticket*
**tikus** *rat*
**tim** *team*
**timun** *cucumber*
**timur** *east*
**tinggal** *to live; to remain*
**tinggi** *tall; high*
**Tionghoa** *Chinese*
**tipis** *thin, narrow*
**toko** *shop, store*
**tokoh** *figure*
**tolong** *help; please*
**tonggak** *moment, milestone*
**topi** *hat, cap*
**tradisi** *tradition*
**tradisional** *traditional*
**tua** *dark (of color); old*
**tuang** *pour*
**tugu** *monument*
**Tuhan** *Lord, God*
**tujuan** *aim, destination*
**tujuh** *seven*
**tulis, menulis** *to write*
**tumpah** *to spill, fall*
**tumpeng** *ceremonial rice-cone*
**tunggal** *only, single, sole*
**tunggu, menunggu** *to wait*
**turun** *fall; go down*

**[U]**

**uang** *money*
**ubah, mengubah** *to change something*

**ubi** *sweet potato*
**ucapan** *greeting*
**Uda Minang** *term for older brother*
**ujian** *exam, test*
**ujung** *end, point*
**ular** *snake*
**umat** *congregation; religious community*
**umum** *general, public*
**umur** *age*
**ungkapan** *expression*
**univérsitas** *university*
**untuk** *for, to*
**upacara** *ceremony*
**usaha** *effort*
**utama** *main*
**utara** *north*

**[W]**

**wah!** *wow! (exclamation)*
**wahai** *O! Oh!*
**wakil** *deputy, vice*
**waktu** *time; (informal) when*
**walaupun** *although*
**walikota** *mayor*
**wanita** *woman, female*
**warga** *local, resident*
**warganegara** *citizen*
**warna** *color*
**wartawan** *journalist*
**warung** *roadside stall*
**wisata** *tourist, tourism*
**wisatawan** *tourist*
**WNI (Warga Negara Indonesia)** *Indonesian*

**[Y]**

**ya** *yes*
**yaitu** *that is, i.e.*
**yang** *which, that*

**[Z]**

**zakat** *(Islamic) alms*

## "Books to Span the East and West"

**Tuttle Publishing** was founded in 1832 in the small New England town of Rutland, Vermont [USA]. Our core values remain as strong today as they were then—to publish best-in-class books which bring people together one page at a time. In 1948, we established a publishing outpost in Japan—and Tuttle is now a leader in publishing English-language books about the arts, languages and cultures of Asia. The world has become a much smaller place today and Asia's economic and cultural influence has grown. Yet the need for meaningful dialogue and information about this diverse region has never been greater. Over the past seven decades, Tuttle has published thousands of books on subjects ranging from martial arts and paper crafts to language learning and literature—and our talented authors, illustrators, designers and photographers have won many prestigious awards. We welcome you to explore the wealth of information available on Asia at **www.tuttlepublishing.com**.

Published by Tuttle Publishing, an imprint of Periplus Editions (HK) Ltd.

**www.tuttlepublishing.com**

Copyright © 2019 by Periplus Editions (HK) Ltd.

Library of Congress Control Number: 2019931654

ISBN 978-0-8048-4918-0

Distributed by

**North America,**
**Latin America & Europe**
Tuttle Publishing
364 Innovation Drive
North Clarendon,
VT 05759-9436 U.S.A.
Tel: 1 (802) 773-8930
Fax: 1 (802) 773-6993
info@tuttlepublishing.com
www.tuttlepublishing.com

**Indonesia**
PT Java Books Indonesia
Jl. Rawa Gelam IV No. 9,
Kawasan Industri Pulogadung,
Jakarta 13930, Indonesia
Tel: 62 (21) 4682 1088
Fax: 62 (21) 461 0206
crm@periplus.co.id
www.periplus.com

**Asia Pacific**
Berkeley Books Pte. Ltd.
3 Kallang Sector #04-01
Singapore 349278
Tel: (65) 6741-2178
Fax: (65) 6741-2179
inquiries@periplus.com.sg
www.tuttlepublishing.com

First edition
26 25 24 23        6 5 4 3        2312VP
Printed in Malaysia

TUTTLE PUBLISHING® is a registered trademark of Tuttle Publishing, a division of Periplus Editions (HK) Ltd.